**Reading**
BOROUGH COUNCIL

ROYAL
MURDERS

DULCIE M. ASHDOWN

First published 1998
This edition published 2009

The History Press
The Mill, Brimscombe Port
Stroud, Gloucestershire, GL5 2QG
www.thehistorypress.co.uk

British Library Cataloguing in Publication Data.
A catalogue record for this book is available from the British Library.

ISBN 978 0 7524 4937 1

Typesetting and origination by The History Press
Printed in Malta

CONTENTS

By the same author

Queen Victoria's Mother

Queen Victoria's Family

Ladies-in-Waiting

Royal Paramours

Princess of Wales

Royal Children

Royal Weddings

Victoria and the Coburgs

Tudor Cousins

Over the Teacups (anthology)

Christmas Past (anthology)

... let us sit upon the ground
And tell sad stories of the death of kings –
How some have been depos'd, some slain in war,
Some haunted by the ghosts they have depos'd,
Some poison'd by their wives, some sleeping kill'd,
All murder'd – for within the hollow crown
That rounds the mortal temples of a king
Keeps Death his court ...

Shakespeare, *King Richard II*: III, ii

A Note on Names

It would be impossible to style all the foreign names consistently. I started off determined to use the indigenous styles, because in seeking books on foreign subjects I suffered from inconsistencies such as Joanna, Joan, Jane, Jeanne and Giovanna for one woman, a queen of Naples. It was not too difficult until I reached the chapter on Russia, when it occurred to me to ask: surely it was ridiculous to write about Piotr the Great, Ekaterina II and Nikolai II? At that point I thought of changing every name already written, to put it into a familiar English form: Knud to Canute, Henri to Henry etc. Then I thought of King Umberto of Italy and King Ludwig II of Bavaria: Kings Humbert and Lewis?

So the names in this book are a compromise: foreign where possible (Ivan – not John – the Terrible) but the English form where that seemed sensible (William – not Willem – the Silent).

ACKNOWLEDGEMENTS

Thanks are due, as ever, to the staff of the British Library, the British Library's Colindale Newspaper Library and above all the London Library; also to Jon Henley of the *Guardian*, who has kindly supplied me with information on Sweden, for the last chapter, and finally to my mother, who has typed some hundred thousand words.

INTRODUCTION

In March 1982, I attended a party at which her Majesty the Queen was the guest of honour. While the Queen circled the room, occasionally pausing to speak to one of the guests, I stood chatting (with some awe) to a famous naturalist. He was well known to members of the royal family and had a piece of news for the Queen about some recent phenomenon of British bird life. When the Queen approached, he stepped forward, and as he did so, three men suddenly appeared at our left and right and from behind the Queen. With a slight wave of her hand, the Queen halted them, and she and the naturalist conversed for a few minutes before she moved on.

For the first time, I appreciated the vigilance of the Queen's bodyguards. It seemed to me that royal security was admirable. I was mistaken. Despite the fact that, the previous year, there had been two IRA plots to kill the Queen, and a man had fired at her as she rode to the ceremony of Trooping the Colour, royal security was still lax. In June 1982 a man was able to enter Buckingham Palace unobserved *on two occasions* and even to invade the Queen's bedroom. He was not an armed assassin but he might have been.

Royal security has tightened considerably since then, but Elizabeth II still lives with the knowledge that at any moment, at home or abroad, she may be killed by a 'madman' – or by a terrorist. So far, there have been only threats and false alarms but the Queen can never be entirely certain of her safety. Today or tomorrow she may again become the target of bomb or bullet. And her fears for herself are compounded by those for her children and grandchildren.

Although the British queen is by no means the only head of state to need protection from would-be assassins, in recent years the threat to monarchs and members of their families has in fact diminished as power has been transferred to elected representatives of the people.

Between 1898 and 1913 four European kings, a queen and an empress were assassinated, and there were attempts on the lives of several monarchs and members of their families; in 1914 the heir to the Austro-Hungarian Empire was assassinated; in 1918 the Russian Tsar, his wife and his children were murdered. Since then, only one European king has been assassinated (in 1934). However, attempts on and threats to the life of Spain's King Juan Carlos, by ETA, the Basque terrorists in the 1990s show that the danger remains.

Royal murder is older than recorded history, for legend told of it long before reliably factual history was recorded. The Bible has instances, and so do the records of several pre-Christian era cultures. However, this chronicle of Europe's royal murders begins in the Middle Ages, as it seems wise to avoid the uncertainties of ancient history. There is one important omission: the Byzantine Empire. So numerous were the murders of (and by) Byzantine emperors and of (and by) members of their families that recounting them might double the length of this book. In fact, the eighteenth-century historian Edward Gibbon filled several volumes with *The History of the Decline and Fall of the Roman Empire*, which traces in detail the lives of Byzantium's rulers to their fifteenth-century demise.

Not all royal murders have been assassinations. The term 'assassination' means the killing of a public figure for a matter of principle. 'Murder', on the other hand, encompasses a range of personal motives: anger, hatred, revenge, jealousy, greed etc.

The royal murders perpetrated before the sixteenth century were largely committed by people with personal motives – usually the usurpation of a monarch's power; only a few can be called 'tyrannicide', the killing of a tyrant, which does qualify for the term 'assassination'.

In the sixteenth century, the killing of prominent figures – monarchs, statesmen, noblemen – had a new motive: religion. After the European Reformation, it was widely regarded as heroism to kill a Protestant or a Catholic monarch, depending on one's own religious convictions. Inventive theology blended with the medieval philosophy of tyrannicide to justify acts that were generally the work of fanatics.

Tyrannicide resurfaced in England in the seventeenth century, in France in the eighteenth, with Kings Charles I and Louis XVI brought to trial, convicted and executed. While their judges justified the kings' deaths as punishment for crimes, those deaths have also been called 'judicial murder' – a debatable point.

'Death to the tyrant' was also a slogan of the nineteenth-century revolutionaries, but their aspirations sometimes included the ending of the monarchical system as well as the killing of individual monarchs. Political murders – assassinations – proliferated in the late nineteenth century, during the last years in which European monarchs wielded real power in government.

However, the term 'royal murder' has two faces: not just the murder *of* monarchs but murder *by* monarchs and members of royal families. Often the two overlap, when one king is murdered by – or by order of – the man who takes his place: in England, for example, in the fifteenth century, with the murders of two (arguably three) kings by their successors. But there are also monarchs who have been accredited with murder on a large scale, and none more famously than Ivan 'the Terrible', Tsar of Russia, who was responsible for the death of thousands of men, women and children, many of them personally supervised by the man who delighted in the most hideous forms of torture ever devised.

For centuries, the extent of a monarch's power was so great that it is no wonder that claimants fought for crowns, usurpers killed for them. And it is no wonder that, over the past couple of centuries, it has been thought unreasonable that one person, a monarch, should wield power that is denied to millions of people. Monarchs have clutched so fiercely at their cherished power that in many countries it has had to be prised from them by violent means. Even those who are today 'constitutional monarchs', some mere figureheads, have been threatened by those who resent their personifying the power of government and of an 'establishment' that jealously hoards its privileges, refusing to share them with those not born among the elite. As long as there is such inequality of power and wealth – and it is impossible to envisage its ending – there will be people who regard monarchs as personal enemies or as 'enemies of the people'. It seems unlikely that the last royal murder has been committed.

'I love a good murder,' say the readers of detective fiction, and the inventive genius of the crime writer is untiring. But in factual history there are stories that rival any fiction ever written. Some are whodunits, some why-dunits; some have a twist of motive or means or the murderer's temperament that adds a thrill of surprise or horror. And when these historical murders are those of monarchs – of men and women whose lives have the glamour of power, wealth and fame – they may affect the life and well-being of a nation. In the context of royal murder, mere names in history books, associated with wars and laws, ceremonial and pageantry, are transformed into people with recognisable personalities, as victims of murder or themselves murderers.

These stories, reflecting changes of motive and means as the centuries pass, may be viewed as relating the development of monarchical government and of the opposition to it, but they also present a compendium of the human emotions and aspirations that have caused men and women to challenge 'the dread and fear of kings'.

CHAPTER ONE

SWORD AND ARROW

To anyone who lived a thousand years ago (and for several centuries afterwards and certainly in all the centuries before), modern Britain would seem like a heaven of peace, inhabited by angels.

For centuries, life was held cheaply: murder was committed frequently and not only in the course of a robbery or rape but deliberately, for the avenging of a wrong or to hasten an inheritance, and heedlessly, in a rage of anger. As to punishment for crime, beheading was the least to fear, a quick and thus merciful end reserved for the elite. Hanging might be supplemented by the drawing of entrails before death, the dreadful plunging of the hand into flesh to extract the heart; then the body was quartered, each limb tied to a different horse and the four driven apart; those quarters would be sent to various parts of a city, county or even country, depending on the magnitude of the crime or the fame of the criminal, to serve as a warning to others. On river bridges and city gates, severed heads were set on poles, to meet the gaze of passersby; birds pecked out the eyes, and the flesh rotted to reveal the skull. Public executions and punishments were popular forms of entertainment.

There were many royal murders in the Dark Ages and Middle Ages,* usually the work of a claimant to a throne. A ruler's combination of power and wealth was a temptation irresistible to those who had – or believed they had – a claim to the throne. The main danger was the transfer of power at the death of a ruler, when rival claimants might dispute – and fight. A disputed succession divided a kingdom's loyalty, raised civil war and left the kingdom a prey to outside enemies. The succession of father to son thus

---

* Generally accepted as AD 410–800 and 800–1492 respectively.

emerged in the Middle Ages as being the safest way of ensuring a crown's peaceful transition. Monarchs (notably Henry VIII, King of England) went to extraordinary lengths to ensure a father-son transfer of power.

Revenge was also frequently a motive: one murder might beget another. King Radomir of Bulgaria was murdered by his cousin Jan Vladislav in 1015: Jan Vladislav had a claim to the throne, but he was also the son of a man whom Radomir had had murdered. As king, Jan Vladislav had Radomir's immediate family killed too; that was a way of ensuring that there would be no one to seek revenge in the future.

Some monarchs did not need an excuse for murder, only the power to avoid retribution. Clovis, King of the Franks, has generally been accounted a great king, from the evidence of his conquests and the admiring words of Gregory of Tours, his chronicler, but even Gregory had to admit that Clovis had consolidated his kingdom by killing off relatives and appropriating their lands. Clovis extended his borders by guile as well as conquest. In the first decade of the sixth century he persuaded Chlodoric, son of Sigebert 'the Lame', King of the Rhineland Franks, to kill his father. When Chlodoric had done so, he went through his father's treasure chest to find a reward for his friend Clovis, but as he bent over the chest, one of Clovis's men came up behind him and split his skull with an axe. Clovis informed the Rhineland Franks that Chlodoric had killed Sigebert and had himself been killed, and he offered himself for the kingship. Needless to say, he was accepted.

Meagre as Gregory's history of Clovis's reign may be, it is more than can be found for the majority of monarchs of the period. Many of the stories of kings, saints and warriors that have come down to us are mere legend – and they were the only people of interest to storytellers. It was only very gradually that 'real history' emerged from fictionalised accounts of a nation's heroes, and the transition is too blurred for the two to be distinguished.

The Danes were fond of stories. Their sagas may stretch back hundreds of years beyond the identifiable points of their early history. One such story is that of Prince Amled – and it may sound familiar.

Once upon a time there were two brothers, Horvendel and Fenge, who were co-rulers of Jutland. Fenge killed Horvendel, in order to rule alone, and he married Horvendel's widow, Geruth. Horvendel's only son, Prince Amled, was afraid that Fenge would kill him too, to prevent his challenging for the crown, so he pretended to be mad – and thus harmless. But Fenge still suspected Amled and sent him off to England, with two companions, to deliver a letter to the King of England. Amled was wary: he killed the two men sent to watch him and opened the letter. It requested the King of England to kill Amled. So he destroyed the letter and, still journeying on to England, stayed there for a year. On his return to Jutland, Amled was welcomed with apparent pleasure by King Fenge. After the celebration banquet, when the King's warriors were lying around drunk, Amled covered them all with carpets and set light to them. Then he went into Fenge's chamber and ran him through with his sword. At a gathering of the people the next day, Amled was proclaimed king.

This story was, of course, the basis of Shakespeare's *Hamlet, Prince of Denmark*, the archetypal tragedy in which 'the stage is littered with bodies'.

In fact, Scandinavia produced more medieval regicides than any other country. In the Dark Ages, it was the rule rather than the exception for a king's reign to end in his violent death, and as the Middle Ages opened, with the Vikings' incursions into western Europe and the British Isles, little changed.

For example, there was the killing in the mid-ninth century of the Viking warrior Ragnar Lodbrok, condemned by Ælla, King of Northumbria, to die in a snakepit, after he had been taken prisoner in the aftermath of battle. In 867, Ælla was himself defeated by Ivar, son of Ragnar, and he was sentenced to the most painful of ritual deaths: the outline of an eagle was carved in the flesh of his back, the skin turned over to reveal his bones, and salt rubbed into the wounds. Ivar was also responsible for the murder, in 869, of St Edmund, King of East Anglia, who was tied to a tree and shot full of arrows. In pagan defiance of Christianity's insistence on burial, Ivar had Edmund's corpse beheaded and the head cast away in the woods. According to legend, when Edmund's men went out searching for it, the head called out to them until they found it and took it for burial.

After some two centuries of armed incursions into England, in 1016 Knud (Cnut or Canute), King of Denmark, became King of England. He left his Norwegian brother-in-law Ulf to govern Denmark while he was in England. During one of the King's visits to Denmark, he and Ulf had a disagreement over a game of chess, and rather than admit defeat, Ulf got up and left the game unfinished. Knud called him a coward; Ulf retorted that it was Knud and his Danes who were the cowards, in their recent war with the Swedes, reminding Knud that a Norwegian fleet had rescued the Danes from a sea battle. Knud brooded on the insult and the next morning sent a man to kill Ulf as he knelt at the altar rail in St Lucius' church. Later the King repented what he had done, and he paid his widowed sister Estrid the 'bloodfine' due from a murderer to the victim's family.

A century later, Ulf's grandson Nils was king of Denmark and, as was usual, he employed various members of his family to rule the provinces that made up his kingdom. His nephew Knud Lavard governed the province of Slesvig – and governed it so well that Nils' son Magnus was jealous, certain that Knud Lavard would be chosen as the next king, as there was still no automatic father-son succession to the Danish throne. In January 1131, Knud Lavard was on his way home from spending Christmas with the King when Magnus caught up with him, resting in a wood, and murdered him. Three years later, Knud Lavard's death was avenged when his half-brother Erik Emune killed Magnus in a battle at Fotevig. King Nils fled, but he made the mistake of seeking shelter in Slesvig, where Knud Lavard had been popular. As the King had the gates of the castle bolted behind him, he heard bells peeling out from the nearby town. They were the bells of the Guild of St Knud, of which Knud Lavard had been master and whose members were all sworn to avenge the death of a murdered brother. They took the castle and killed King Nils.

In the thirteenth century, four Danish kings in succession were murdered, three of them within a decade of each other. The first was King Erik 'Ploughpenny' (named from his taxation of peasants by the number of ploughs they owned), who ruled between 1241 and 1250. He was allegedly killed at the orders of his brother Abel, who had festering grievances against Erik. Abel's knights beheaded Erik and threw his body into the River Sli, loaded with chains so that it would sink the more easily. Abel not only swore to his people that he had not killed Erik but had twenty-four knights support him on oath; but apparently no one believed the perjurers. Nevertheless, when Abel was killed two years later, it was not in revenge for his brother's death but for the wrongs he had done a wheelwright, Hans of Pelvorm, who accosted him on the road and killed him with a sledgehammer.

Erik and Abel's brother Christoffer was the next king, reigning between 1251 and 1259. He resented the wealth accumulated by the Danish Church and the privileges that his predecessors had granted to the clergy; in his attacks on the Church, he went so far as to imprison the Archbishop of Copenhagen, bringing down a sentence of excommunication on himself and his council. Some of the Danish clergy continued to administer the Eucharist to the King, however, in defiance of the Church but probably in fear of their lives. When Christoffer died suddenly, on 29 May 1259, it was widely believed that he had been given a poisoned wafer at Mass by Abbot Arnfast – who significantly became a bishop on the Archbishop's release.

Christoffer's ten-year-old son Erik, who succeeded him, had scarcely any peace in his kingdom throughout his entire reign. The Church continued to challenge royal power; so did the King's cousins, with their claims to independent power in their provinces. At last, in 1286, even Erik's own retainers turned against him. Resting in a barn on the night of 22 November, after a hunt, the King was set on by men who left fifty-six stab wounds in his body.

In most of these Scandinavian murders, the murderer – or the man who ordered the murder – came to power through his crime. Not so in the case of King Erik. His son, another Erik (aged eleven), succeeded him, and his murderers were proclaimed outlaws and were forced to flee. They took refuge in strongholds along the Danish coast and became virtual pirates by their preying on shipping. It was many years before Denmark was free of them, some dying of natural causes, others captured and brought to justice.

In view of the high proportion of Scandinavian royal murders that were family affairs, it is a wonder that any man could trust his brother, but apparently the princes Erik and Valdemar of Sweden had no suspicions when, in 1317, their brother King Birger invited them to spend the Christmas holiday with him at Nyköping. He said that his castle there was too small to accommodate their servants – the well-armed retinue without which no nobleman travelled. So Erik and Valdemar were left unprotected when Birger had the gates of his castle locked and the drawbridges raised. When the princes' friends heard that they had been imprisoned, and began to gather an army to demand their release, Birger neither panicked nor prepared to make a stand against them. He simply abandoned the castle, throwing the keys into the water of the moat. Erik and Valdemar were left to starve before their friends arrived. And Birger's motive for killing his brothers? Some years earlier, they had forced him to sign over to them a great measure of independence for the provinces they governed under him. Although Birger regained power there through his brothers' deaths, they resulted in a national uprising. Birger's (innocent) son was executed in revenge, and he died in exile.

The stories of Scandinavian royal murders show how common was murder within royal families there. Almost every European royal dynasty can also offer an example of murder by a brother, a cousin or even a wife. Thus it is not surprising that the murder of England's King William II in the year 1100 has been attributed to his brother, who became King Henry I, despite the ostensible 'facts of the case' presented by the chroniclers.

William II, King of England, who reigned between 1087 and 1100, was, according to the chronicler William of Malmesbury, a 'well set' man, '. . . his complexion florid, his hair yellow; of open countenance; different coloured eyes, varying with certain glittering specks; of astonishing strength, though not very tall, and his belly rather projecting; of no eloquence but remarkable for a hesitation of speech, especially when angry'. Another chronicler, Gaimar, wrote: '. . . he was always happy and creating mirth. He had a red beard and blond hair, on which account and for which reason he had the surname of "the red king"' – or William 'Rufus'.

Gaimar's account of William is full of praise for the justice he meted out and the peace he established in England: 'This noble king, through great courage, held his kingdom with honour.' Another chronicler, Ordericus Vitalis, disagreed: 'He was liberal to his military men and foreigners, but the poor natives of his realm were severely oppressed and he exacted from them what he so prodigally bestowed on foreigners.' William of Malmesbury was in two minds:

> Greatness of soul was pre-eminent in the King, which, in process of time, he obscured by excessive severity; vices, indeed, in place of virtues, so insensibly crept into his bosom that he could not distinguish them. . . . At last, however, in his latter years, the desire after good grew cold, and the crop of evil increased to ripeness; his liberality became prodigality, his magnanimity pride, his austerity cruelty. He was . . . of supercilious look, darting his threatening eye on the bystander and, with assumed severity and ferocious voice, assailing such as conversed with him.

From a much greater distance in time and with the benefit of scholars' analysis of plentiful evidence, William II appears to have been an extremely competent king, who exercised masterful control over his kingdom; stood no nonsense from the Church, whose higher clergy were always on the lookout for means of extending their power; bought off the elder brother who might have made trouble; and made his mark on the Continent, where he conquered the French county of Maine.

The elder brother was Robert, Duke of Normandy. He had been passed over, for the crown of England, in the will of their father, William I, but since the principle of primogeniture – the transition of property from father to eldest son – was not in force in the English royal succession, William II had no fear that Robert would oust him on a point of law. As long as William kept control of England and its nobles, he was safe from any pretension of Robert's. In fact, after a bout of arms, the brothers had come to an agreement: Robert mortgaged Normandy to William in return for the money that would outfit his army for a crusade in the Holy Land.

Had the third brother, Henry, not been ten years younger than William and only twenty when their father died, he might have put forward his own claim to the throne, for he was the only one of

William the Conqueror's sons to have been born after the Norman duke seized the English throne. Thus Henry could claim the throne by 'porphyrogeniture': he was 'born to the purple', the son of a king. Still, as William II was unmarried, Henry had only to wait for him to die and he would inherit the throne. Or would Robert challenge for the throne should William die? In the summer of the year 1100, it was known that Robert was on his way back to England; he had just married; would he one day claim England for himself and his heirs, as a rival to Henry?

So if anyone had a motive to kill William II in 1100, it was his brother Henry, anxious to establish himself on the throne before Robert of Normandy came home.

Tradition records that it was one Walter Tirel who was said to have fired the fatal arrow, though it is not easy to establish a motive for him to have done so. In fact, the chroniclers of the period generally agreed that Tirel killed the King accidentally, when William was struck by an arrow that Tirel had fired at a deer. However, according to Suger, Abbot of St Denis in France, 'I have often heard him [Tirel] assert on his solemn oath, at a time when he had nothing either to fear or hope, that on that day he was neither in the part of the forest where the King was hunting nor saw him at all while he was in the wood.'

Walter Tirel was lord of Poix in Ponthieu and was one of the foreigners whom Ordericus Vitalis noted were so attractive to William, though in fact all England's nobles were foreigners after the Norman Conquest, when William I had divided up his new kingdom between his relations, allies and vassals. Tirel was the brother-in-law of Roger and Gilbert de Clare, both of whom were in the hunting party in the New Forest on Thursday 2 August 1100, when William II was killed. So was the King's brother Henry.

It has been suggested that the Clare brothers were employed by Henry to engineer the death of the King. It seems unlikely that Tirel was their confederate. More likely, they used him as a scapegoat, perhaps ensuring his safe escape from England but not defending him from the charge that Tirel obviously knew to be untrue – that he had fired the arrow that killed the King. And was it the Clares who saw to it that the story of Tirel's loosing the arrow became established as 'fact' by such frequent repetition that the chroniclers came to record it, even though Tirel himself denied it? Who did fire that arrow must remain a matter for conjecture.

Some quarter-century after the death of William II, William of Malmesbury wrote of that afternoon of 2 August 1100:

> The sun was now declining when the King, drawing his bow and letting fly an arrow, slightly wounded a stag which passed before him and, keenly gazing, followed it, still running, a long time with his eyes, holding up his hand to keep off the power of the sun's rays. At this instant, Walter, conceiving a noble exploit, which was while the King's attention was otherwise occupied to transfix another stag which by chance came near him, unknowingly and without power to prevent it, oh gracious God!, pierced his breast with a fatal arrow.

Gaimar wrote:

> The King was in the thick part of the forest near a marsh. An inclination seized him to shoot at a stag which he saw go into a herd; he dismounted near a tree; he himself had his bow bent. The barons dismounted in every direction and beckoned the others who were near. Walter Tirel also dismounted; he was very near the King; close by an elder tree, he leaned his back against an aspen. As the herd passed by and the great stag came in the midst of it, he drew the bow which he held in his hand; by an unhappy fate he drew a barbed arrow. It happened that it missed the stag. It pierced as far as the heart of the King. An arrow went to his heart but they knew not who bent the bow; but the other archers said that the arrow came from the bow of Walter. There was an appearance of this, for he fled immediately . . . .

Ordericus Vitalis wrote: '. . . a stag suddenly running between them, the King quitted his station and Walter shot an arrow. It grazed the beast's grizzly back but, glancing from it, mortally wounded the King, who stood within its range. He immediately fell on the ground and, alas, suddenly expired.'

Whatever Tirel did or did not do, the hue and cry was raised against him. Even as he was riding hell for leather to the coast, Henry was taking possession of his brother's treasury, in nearby Winchester, and then making for Westminster, where he had himself proclaimed king. Everything went so smoothly that it is easy to believe that Henry had made his plans before his brother's death.

However, there is another version of the story of the death of King William II, one that does show Walter Tirel as the murderer but which also has William as a willing victim. This is the version that was offered by the anthropologist Margaret Murray in her book *The God of the Witches*, published in 1933. She propounded the theory that William II was a pagan, a member of that Old Religion that survived in England long after the coming of Christianity (see pp. 73–4). As king, William was also high priest, and he was the sacrifice to the Nature gods whose death would bring his people good fortune: his blood, falling on the earth, would fertilise it to bring rich harvests. Margaret Murray supported her theory with 'proof' chosen from the chroniclers' stories, notably an incident in which William gave Walter Tirel his arrows, remarking that '. . . the sharpest arrows should be given to him who knows best how to inflict mortal wounds with them' (Ordericus Vitalis). The chroniclers disagree about what happened after the arrow struck the King. According to Ordericus Vitalis, he '. . . fell to the ground and . . . suddenly expired', but Gaimar has a devoutly Christian William calling out to be given the Holy Sacrament – calling out four times, in fact, but without hope, for the hunters were too far from any church; one of them gave him 'herbs with all their flowers' instead (which may have some pagan significance). But William of Malmesbury, the first of the chroniclers to record the death of William II, has his own story: 'On receiving the wound, the King uttered not a word but, breaking off the shaft of the weapon where it projected from his body, fell upon the wound, by which it accelerated his death.' He may have done so to spare himself the pain of a long-drawn-out dying or it may have been part of the ritual of sacrifice.

The fact that the death of William II is still being treated as a 'whodunit' nine centuries later either speaks well of the efficiency of his murderers or testifies to a general unwillingness to treat any sudden death as an accident.

It would be tempting to characterise all medieval European monarchs as brutal, vicious, merciless, but there were degrees of evil even in their natures. The Angevin dynasty, for example, was renowned for its members' hasty tempers and spur-of-the-moment violence, where others might be more coolly and deliberately cruel.

Legend has it that the counts of Anjou, whose offspring sat on the thrones of England and Jerusalem, were descended from a man who brought home from his travels a beautiful wife, whose origins no one knew. Soon people began to notice that she never stayed in church throughout the Mass but withdrew at the last moment before the consecration of the host. One day, a knight deliberately trod on the hem of the Countess's gown, and she was detained long enough to witness the elevation of the consecrated host – whereupon, with a terrible shriek, she flew out of the window, never to be seen again. She was the Devil's daughter, Melusine, and her descendants were renowned for their fiendish tempers.

King Henry II, half Angevin by birth, had the Angevin temper. It was demonstrated in his dealings with his own family: he kept his wife, Eleanor of Aquitaine, imprisoned for years (see p. 27), and when he died, he was in the midst of a war against his sons. But Henry's chief infamy was the murder of his Archbishop of Canterbury, Thomas Becket, which was done for his benefit if not at his command.

Becket was a remarkable man on many counts. In an age in which the highest offices of state and the highest ranks in the Church were almost entirely the prerogative of the nobly born, Becket, the son of a merchant, became both Chancellor and Archbishop of Canterbury. He became Chancellor in 1155, just a year after Henry II's accession to the throne, when the King was gathering able men for his government, and he used his position as a powerbase, to gain access to the whole spectrum of power: he even rode to war with the King and mounted military campaigns on his own account, though he had spent the first twenty-odd years of adult life as a priest, scholar and lawyer.

When, in 1162, Henry appointed him archbishop of Canterbury, Becket prophesied that it would be the end of their friendship, for the interests of Church and State were certain to clash. Not only did he change in externals (wearing a hairshirt, becoming a vegetarian, spending hours in prayer) but he began to place loyalty to the Church's interests above loyalty to the King. He insisted on the Church's full rights: Church land confiscated by the King must be restored; men convicted by Church courts must not be sentenced in lay courts; taxes from which the Church had been granted remission should not now be demanded. The mounting tension between the King and the Archbishop ended with Becket's being named a traitor, in 1164, and fleeing to France. In retaliation, Becket excommunicated his enemies – notably those bishops who had resented his leapfrogging them to become primate of England. Eventually papal envoys managed to patch up the quarrel, and on 1 December 1170 Becket returned to England.

King Henry was in France that month, and news began to come in that in England the newly returned Archbishop of Canterbury was excommunicating everyone who had ever opposed him – even that he was gathering an army. These reports came largely from the Archbishop of York and the Bishops of Salisbury and London, who had themselves been excommunicated and were making a last-ditch attempt to unseat Becket before he managed to regain control of the English Church. The reports were untrue, but Henry II believed them. With a show of the notorious Plantagenet temper, he roared 'Will no one rid me of this turbulent priest?'

Among those who heard Henry were four knights, Reginald FitzUrse, William de Tracy, Hugo de Morville and Richard le Brito. They entered Canterbury on the morning of 29 December and went, unarmed, to confront the Archbishop at home. After high words, they left. In the darkness of the midwinter afternoon, they entered the cathedral; now they were in full armour, and they carried swords. The Archbishop stood at the altar of the chapel of Our Lady. Words were exchanged but soon enough the swords were at work: Becket was struck down, his skull cleft by a heavy blow.

When the news reached King Henry, he shut himself away for three days; when he emerged, he was wearing sackcloth, the marks of ashes on his head. Later he sent word to the Pope that he had played no *direct* part in the murder, but he was willing – almost eager – to accept the penance that Alexander III imposed: to finance 200 crusading knights, to acknowledge the ancient rights of the Church and restore its property, and in future always to recognise the rights of the English Church and Papacy.

The murder of Thomas Becket, apparently at his command, obviously frightened Henry II at the time, but it did not make a saint of him. Becket, on the other hand, was canonised as St Thomas of Canterbury in 1173.

John, King of England, the youngest son of Henry II, succeeded his brother Richard on the throne in 1199 and reigned until 1216. Traditionalist history books have always vilified John, because the chroniclers of his time were all against him: the chroniclers were churchmen, and John was excommunicated by the Pope in 1208 and England laid under an interdict for six years. Admittedly King John did much to earn his bad reputation, but there have been worse kings whose reputations have been enhanced rather than blackened by the historians of their reigns. John is remembered as the 'wicked prince' of the Robin Hood stories and as having rebelled against his father; then there was the challenge to his rule posed by his barons, and his capitulation to them in granting Magna Carta; and finally, John is remembered for having had his own nephew murdered. This incident, immortalised in Shakespeare's eponymous play, is King John's ultimate condemnation.

When King Richard died, his heir might have been his nephew Arthur, Duke of Brittany, son of the late Duke Geoffrey, who was senior to John. However, the strict laws of inheritance were not yet in force in England, and the mature John was obviously a more desirable king than Arthur, who was only thirteen years old. Besides, had the crown been offered to Arthur, John would have been sure to challenge for it. Inevitably, Arthur grew up resenting the loss of his 'rights'; in 1202 he did homage to the King of France, Philippe Augustus, for French counties that in fact belonged to his grandmother, Eleanor of Aquitaine, showing his uncle John that he would know no peace in his French domains while France was Arthur's ally.

When the octogenarian Queen Eleanor heard that her grandson Arthur and his small army were heading towards her, she left the abbey of Fontevrault, where she had expected to live out her last years in peace, and headed for the fortifiable town of Poitiers. But Arthur was close; Eleanor had to seek refuge in the castle of Mirebeau and, when Arthur took the town that surrounded it, she became a virtual prisoner. However, before his arrival, she had managed to send a message to her son John, and now he arrived with his army to relieve her. Eleanor was released, Arthur captured. That was in August 1202; for the next nine months, Arthur was held a prisoner in Rouen. The King ordered his captor, Hubert de Burgh, to blind and castrate the Duke, but he refused.

On Maundy Thursday, 3 April 1203, King John was staying in Rouen. That night he got drunk and, whether because of his state or needing it to give him courage, he killed his sixteen-year-old nephew with his own hands. He and another man went out in a boat on the River Seine and, having tied a heavy stone to the body, to make it sink, threw it into the river.

The veracity of the story can scarcely be doubted. John's companion that night was William de Braose, and the chronicle in which the story first appeared was written in a monastery in Margam, in Glamorgan, of which William was a patron. Further, when William de Braose fell from royal favour, some five years later, and the King demanded that he send his young sons to be hostages, William's wife Matilda refused, saying that she would not entrust them to him because he had murdered his nephew.

Of course, it was suspected that the King was responsible for Arthur's death, but there was no proof. The body had risen to the surface of the Seine when it became caught in a fisherman's net, and had been taken away for secret burial, but only someone with inside information could have been as certain as Matilda de Braose seems to have been. She, her husband and their children fled to Ireland, but in 1210 they fell into the King's hands. John allowed William to go to his French estates to try to raise money for a ransom, but before he could return, Matilda and their eldest son died in prison. Report had it that they had been deliberately starved.

Many other deaths were credited to John. In May 1194 he had had 300 captives beheaded at Evreux, after a rebellion. In 1212 he hanged twenty-eight Welsh boys whom their fathers had given as hostages for their obedience to the Crown. Nevertheless, repulsive as such acts may be today, such things happened in every European country in the early Middle Ages – and in some places long after. It was not these incidents but the interdict imposed by the Papacy on the English Church between 1208 and 1214 that really shocked the monk-chroniclers and ill-disposed them to King John. They told, with relish, not only the story of how the King forced a Jew of Bristol to reveal the hiding-place of his treasures, by having one of his teeth knocked out each day until he spoke, but also such tales as that of the loaf illicitly baked on a Sunday (the holy day and holiday) which ran with blood when a knife cut it. The more colourful details of many a medieval royal murder may also owe something to a monk's imagination.

On the night of 9 September 1238, a man gained access to the palace at Woodstock in Oxfordshire by climbing through the window of the King's bedroom. He was carrying a knife and was intent on killing Henry III, King of England. Fortunately, the King was not in his own bed but in that of his wife, in another room. Also, one of the Queen's ladies was still awake: Margaret Bisset, 'a holy maid', was singing psalms by the light of a candle. When she heard the man moving about – and actually 'asking in a terrible voice where the King was' – she raised the alarm by screaming. The King's attendants came running and broke open the door to the Queen's room, which the man had just bolted.

The King and his attendants recognised the man immediately. He had presented himself at Court only the previous day and had been thought to be mad, because he had said to the King, 'Resign to me the kingdom which you have unjustly usurped and so long detained from me.' There was, in fact, no doubt about Henry's right to the throne, and he had been ruling more than twenty years already, so he could afford to be merciful: he prevented his men from inflicting any violence on the madman. After the murder attempt, however, the man had to be taken more seriously. He confessed that he had not come to kill the King on his own account but had been sent by one William Marsh.

Now the King understood the motive. William Marsh was the son of Geoffrey Marsh, who had been in the royal service until April 1234, when he had been suspected of and executed for killing Richard de

Burgh, the Earl Marshal – or at least he had been made the scapegoat for the killing. William Marsh had sworn vengeance on the King for his father's execution and had taken to piracy, based on Lundy island, off the Devon coast. Although Marsh's hired assassin was, of course, immediately executed, he himself was not brought to justice until 1242, when he was hanged, even though he claimed not to have been guilty of the attempt on the King's life.

One interesting point about this story, as retailed by the contemporary chronicler Matthew Paris, is the sentence, 'He . . . confessed that he had been sent there to kill the King, after the manner of the Assassins . . . .' This term was not a generalisation but referred to a Middle Eastern sect that specialised in the murder of specific victims, named by their leader and selected either for the sect's own benefit or because someone had paid them to 'do the deed'.

There has been some controversy over the origin of the word 'assassin'. On the surface, it seems to derive from 'hashish', alias marijuana, thought to have been used by the sect. More likely, the name derived from the Arabic '*assasseem*', 'guardians', for members of the sect claimed to be guardians of the secrets of Paradise.

The story told by European travellers – including the famous Marco Polo – was as follows. The sect controlled the mountainous region south of the Caspian Sea. Its leader, called 'The Old Man of the Mountains', had young men brought to his castle, drugged into unconsciousness and carried through a secret passage to a garden in a beautiful valley, in which they were treated to a brief experience of a sensuous paradise. Emerging from the dream, back in the Old Man's palace, initiates were told that they could earn eternity in Paradise by obeying him implicitly: they were to be trained to kill, at his command, and if it so happened that they were themselves killed, they would go immediately to the Paradise for which they now craved.

Whatever the incentive offered by the Old Man, his followers were certainly highly motivated and well trained: they were taught not only skill in the use of all sorts of weapons but foreign languages, the art of disguise and the background knowledge of foreign lifestyles and beliefs that would help them pass unnoticed when they travelled abroad. This was doubtless a late development in the Assassins' system, for at first they were a purely local force. They were, it is said, founded in 1090 as a 'hit squad' for the Shi'ite sect of Islam, against the Sunni Muslims. However, they moved onto a broader stage with the coming of the Christian Crusaders, in the twelfth and thirteenth centuries, striking at them from a new base in Syria.

The first Crusader 'assassinated' was Raimond, Count of Tripoli, in 1129. The most important was Conrad of Montferrat, murdered in Tyre in 1192. The story goes that Conrad, who in 1190 had married Isabelle I, Queen of Jerusalem, was preparing for his coronation as King of Jerusalem in his own right. When granted this honour, he had fallen on his knees and begged God to take the crown from him if he was not worthy of it. Before he could be crowned, on 28 April 1192, Conrad was murdered in Tyre by a band of Assassins disguised as monks.

Two years later, the Old Man himself died, and his successor (who took the same title) sent a fulsome apology for Conrad's murder to Henri of Champagne, who had married the widowed Isabelle and become King of Jerusalem. The new Old Man entertained Henri in his citadel and gave him a demonstration of the Assassins' obedience: on his orders, one man after another killed himself, until Henri begged the Old Man to cease. When he left, the King was loaded with gifts and carried with him the assurance (unasked-for) that the Old Man would have the Assassins kill anyone he cared to name.

In 1232 the Assassins sent warnings into the West that the Mongols were coming. The terrifying Oriental Horde was flooding westward, conquering everything in its path. In 1238 the chronicler Matthew Paris reported that the Assassins were actually soliciting Anglo-French aid against the Mongols, who were threatening their strongholds. When Louis VIII, King of France, went on crusade in 1250, he and the Old Man exchanged gifts, and subsequently they formed an alliance against the Sunni Muslims; but they could not hold back the Horde. The end came when the Mongols and the Mameluke Sultan of Egypt joined forces. By the 1270s Assassin castles in Syria were in Egyptian hands. The sect broke up and within a few years was heard of no more in the West.

Before that, however, a couple of attempts left a last and lasting impression on Europe. The first was successful: in 1270, Philippe de Montfort, Lord of Tyre and Toron, was murdered while at prayer. The second failed, but its story has come down in English history because of the picturesque part in it played by a Spanish princess. In 1272 an English Crusader prince, the future King Edward I, was in Tyre. When an attempt was made on his life by an Assassin who penetrated the royal apartments and stabbed Edward, it was fortunate that his wife, Eleanor of Castile, was with him: she immediately sucked the wound, lest the knife had been poisoned. Perhaps it had, for Edward was ill for months afterwards; but he survived.

Civil wars and foreign invasions were implicit in an unsettled succession to a throne. Such disorder afforded noblemen a welcome opportunity to rule their lands unfettered by royal authority; to the peasantry, it was a curse, their farms plundered by foreign armies, their sons taken away from ploughing and harvest to serve as soldiers.

However, even before a succession struggle began in Hungary in 1290, such anarchy was not new. King László IV was unable to control his nobles, who took advantage of the breakdown of central authority to increase their own power. At the same time, the Cumans (Kuns), semi-nomadic people who had been absorbed into Hungary over the past century, felt free to plunder where they would, safe under the King's patronage, for his mother was a Cuman. But in 1290, for nothing more than a personal quarrel, some young Cumans turned on László and murdered him.

The King had no son to succeed him, and the throne passed to his cousin Endre – King Endre III. But there were other claimants to the throne, chief among them the Angevin dynasty who ruled in Naples. In 1301 Endre was preparing to do battle with the Neapolitans when he suddenly died. It was said that he had been poisoned by a cook secretly in the employ of the Neapolitans. If that was so, they had no benefit from the murder, for now the Hungarian nobles took the initiative and offered the crown not to any of the Angevins but to the thirteen-year-old Prince Václav of Bohemia. The boy was sent to Hungary and crowned there, and a council of Hungarian and Bohemian nobles attempted to rule on his behalf, but they had to contend with the Neapolitan challenge and with a revolt of the Cumans. In 1305 the King of Bohemia recalled his son, and in 1308 the Neapolitan claimant took the throne, becoming King Robert Karolyí.

Soon after his return home, the redundant Václav inherited from his father both Bohemia and Poland.[*] But he did not live long enough to make anything of his inheritance: on 4 August 1306, at the age of eighteen, he was murdered.

Back in Hungary, there was a lull in the kingdom's troubles while two generations of Angevins ruled – Robert Karolyí and Lajos 'the Great'. But as Lajos's reign drew to a close, he could foresee a renewal of war and civil war, for he had no son to succeed him. Time and again, throughout Europe, such a situation was the ruin of a kingdom's well-being. One solution for a king who lacked a son was to marry his daughter to the cousin most likely to challenge for the throne, or he might marry her to a man who (or whose family) had sufficient military might to uphold his wife's claim against all-comers. Without such male support, ensured by marriage, a queen regnant was easy prey to predators.

In the last years of his life, when he realised that his wife would not give him a son, Lajos, King of Hungary, betrothed his daughter Mária to Sigismund of Luxembourg, son of the Holy Roman Emperor Karl IV, who was also King of Bohemia. Then Lajos strengthened Mária's position by having her cousin Carlo of Durazzo, King of Naples, take an oath that he could recognise her as heir to Hungary (see family tree, p. 33). To the medieval mind, such an oath was a weighty matter, but Lajos was king not only of Hungary but also of Poland, and it was altogether too tempting an inheritance for Carlo to renounce. Thus, when King Lajos died in September 1382, and his daughter Mária was crowned Queen of Hungary and Poland, she did not wear the crowns for long.

First the Poles rebelled, mainly as a protest against having Mária's husband Sigismund of Luxembourg as their ruler. The Queen Mother, Erzsébet of Bosnia, offered them a compromise: her second daughter, Jadwiga, would come to them as queen, and she would marry Wladisław Jagiello, Duke of Lithuania, their own choice as king.

[*] Poland derived from his father's marriage to the daughter of the late King Przemysław II of Poland, who had been murdered in 1296.

Then, in 1385, Carlo III, King of Naples, marched on Hungary. Sigismund's armies came too late to prevent his seizure of the kingdom and its young queen. She and her mother were forced to attend his coronation, which they thoroughly spoiled with their noisy weeping.

That was in December 1385. In February 1386, while Carlo – in Hungary, King Karolyí – was engaged in putting down Hungarian rebellions, the Queen Mother invited him to meet her, to discuss a truce. Seated, his attention held by Erzsébet's words, the King was suddenly struck from behind and then carried away, unconscious, to the fortress of Viŝegrad, where he was strangled.

Croatia, where the insurrection on behalf of Carlo of Naples had begun, was the first region to oppose the government set up by the Queen Mother on behalf of her daughter. Unwisely, the two Queens followed the army sent against the rebels: they were captured and imprisoned. When Hungarian forces came up to lay siege to their fortress prison, in an attempt to rescue them, Erzsébet of Bosnia was murdered – strangled in the presence of her daughter.

Queen Mária survived her imprisonment and in March 1387 saw her husband crowned King of Hungary and Bohemia. With the power of those kingdoms behind him, Sigismund was elected King of the Romans and, in 1411, Holy Roman Emperor. It was for power of that magnitude that medieval monarchs fought, killed and sometimes violently died.

Although it was generally kinship that encouraged claimants to fight to gain a throne, it meant very little in personal terms: the royal murders that caused a crown to pass from victim to killer were usually family affairs. But even when a crown was not at stake, and even when a murderer could not hope to profit by his crime, the tensions of life under a monarch who was also a relative might provoke an outburst of violence.

This was the case with the murder of Albrecht, Duke of Austria and King of the Romans, in 1308.

On 1 May 1308 King Albrecht crossed the Swiss River Reuss, on his way to join his army at Rheinfelden. His escort watched the King's eighteen-year-old nephew Johannes cross the river first, with his own entourage, then the King, with a single attendant. While the rest of the party embarked, those who had crossed first rode on. The late-comers included Albrecht's son Leopold. Later that day he caught up with his father, whom he found on the point of death, obviously the victim of an attack by swordsmen.

By then, Johannes of Habsburg was in fast flight southwards, his three fellow-murderers with him. The Swiss refused to shelter them, so Johannes rode on into Italy. There he threw himself on the mercy of Pope Clement V, confessing that he had killed his uncle because Albrecht had withheld his inheritance. Absolved from his sin, he retired to a monastery, but in 1312 a new King of the Romans, Heinrich VII, imprisoned him; in 1313 he died. How could he ever have expected to get away with his crime? It must have been committed in the heat of a quarrel with his uncle.

Albrecht's sons executed the only one of Johannes' fellow-murderers who was captured; the other two evaded justice, so the Austrians took vengeance on the families and retainers of the guilty men. A thousand people were said to have paid the price of the murder of Albrecht of Austria.

CHAPTER TWO

A WOMAN'S WEAPONS

Very few women have committed – or are alleged to have committed – royal murders. For one thing, in the centuries in which the main motive for murder was a transfer of power, few women sought it for themselves: when power was at stake, a woman might murder to have her son the beneficiary, rarely herself. Of course, the motives of hatred, revenge and jealousy also feature in the chronicle of murders by – or instigated by – women, but such motives must have been intense to have outweighed the natural fear of the risks involved.

Lacking a man's physical strength or expertise in weaponry, a woman contemplating murder had either to employ a man to commit the crime on her behalf or resort to 'the woman's weapon': poison. In the context of a man's powers, poison has been called 'the coward's weapon', but understandably it has been the first resort of the woman who must rely on her own resources.

The scorn in which poisoning was held is shown in a story from central Europe.

The Hungarian king Mátyas Hunyádi, who reigned between 1458 and 1490, went to war with Jiri of Poděbrady, King of Bohemia. Unable to defeat him by force of arms, Mátyas was willing to listen to a man who offered to attack Jiri personally, engaging him in armed combat. But the man found that Jiri was always surrounded by bodyguards; any attack on the King must be by stealth. When the would-be killer returned to King Mátyas to admit defeat, he suggested that he might try poisoning the Bohemian king. Mátyas was shocked. 'We fight with arms,' he said, 'not with poison.' At once he sent a message to Jiri warning him to beware: to have all his food and drink tested before he consumed it. Obviously, it was 'not good form' for a man devoted to the ideals of chivalry to resort to underhand means to kill an enemy.

Perhaps murder by poison has been associated with women

because for so long women were held to lack that code of honour by which 'gentlemen' lived. For honour's sake, a man must face his intended victim and give him a chance to defend himself – at least, that was the ideal. The fact that men, as murderers, were rarely so honourable and that there have been male as well as female poisoners dispels that myth.

In the year 567, Alboin, King of the Lombards (a people whose lands lay in what is now Slovakia), defeated and killed Cunimund, King of the Gepids (who lived further south, their territory stretching through parts of modern Romania and Hungary). Among Alboin's spoils of war was Cunimund's daughter Rosamund, whom he married. Perhaps to save her life, she never let him know how much she hated him.

Another of Alboin's trophies was the skull of Cunimund, which he caused to be set in metal as a cup. One night in 573, when he was roaring drunk, he called for the cup, filled it, drank and then refilled it and passed it to Rosamund. She raised it to her lips and pretended to drink from it but in her mind she was cursing her husband.

Rosamund blackmailed a man into agreeing to kill Alboin. When her husband lay in a drunken sleep, she unbolted the door of their chamber and admitted him. Alboin awoke and reached for his sword, but Rosamund had already fastened it to its scabbard. The King picked up a stool and tried to fend off his assailant but fell beneath his spear.

Rosamund failed to persuade the Lombard army to accept her lover, Helmichis, as their King, and together they were forced to flee. At Ravenna they were given shelter by the governor of the city, Longinus, another man dazzled by Rosamund's beauty. Needing Helmichis no longer and anxious to take advantage of Longinus' interest, Rosamund procured a draught of poison, which she presented to Helmichis disguised in a drink. However, its taste alerted him to the danger, and although he had already drunk enough to kill him, Helmichis used the last moments of his life to ensure that Rosamund did not go unpunished. His dagger at her throat, he forced her to drain the cup, so that she too died.

That story, from the border-time of legend and history, is one of a very few stories about women that have survived from the centuries of the Dark Ages, beyond those of the Eastern and Western European empresses who were at the pinnacle of society. Even the wives of kings had only a ceremonial role in public life, unless, as widows and the mothers of young sons, they were accepted as regents. This was the case with the Frankish queens Brunhilda and Fredegunde, who were so remarkably evil that in France their story has been told with horror – and a little relish – ever since.

The tale begins with the death of King Chlothar I in 561, when his kingdom was divided between his four sons. One of them, Sigebert, married Brunhilda, daughter of the Visigoth king of Spain; his half-brother Chilperic separated from his wife Fredegunde in order to marry Brunhilda's sister, Galswintha. Relations between the brothers were not ideal even before the sudden death of Galswintha, found strangled in her bed. When Chilperic took Fredegunde back, soon afterwards, Brunhilda was not the only person to suspect her of Galswintha's murder. However, it was not this but a territorial dispute that sent Chilperic and Sigebert to war against each other, though Fredegunde was again blamed when King Sigebert was axed to death on his way to do battle with Chilperic in 575.

The murder of King Chilperic, in 584, was followed by a power struggle between Brunhilda and Fredegunde and a series of family wars of immense complexity, overflowing into the next generation. Both queens employed killers to rid them of all who opposed them. Fredegunde (who died of natural causes in 597) murdered a stepson, thus ensuring that her own son would become king: Chlothar II. Pursuing the old feud, in 613 he made Brunhilda his prisoner. For three days the elderly queen was tortured, then she was led through the ranks of the Frankish army on a camel, before being tied by her hair and one arm and leg to the tail of an unbroken horse, which was turned loose to trample her to death.

English history can boast no story to rival France's of Fredegunde and Brunhilda. However, it does repeat the archetypal tale of a stepmother resorting to the murder of her stepson in order to put her own son on the throne.

When King Edgar 'the Peaceful' died in 975, his heir was the thirteen-year-old Edward, son of his first wife, and he was accepted as king, even though his stepmother, Elfrida, tried to persuade the Witan (Parliament) to choose her son Ethelred. Disappointed, Elfrida retired to Corfe Castle in Dorset.

One version of Edward's murder has him visit Elfrida to reprove her for some misdeed of which the local people had complained. Having heard him out, presumably with some resentment, she stabbed him to death. Another version has Edward hunting in the neighbourhood and, 'gasping with thirst', riding to Corfe Castle, 'unattended and unsuspecting, as he judged of others by his own feelings'. Elfrida came to meet him in the courtyard and gave him a 'stirrup cup', before he had dismounted. While he was drinking, one of her people stabbed him. Though dreadfully wounded, the King escaped, riding off to seek his friends, but he could not stay in the saddle and, with one foot caught in a stirrup, was dragged by his horse along forest paths. His corpse was found by the huntsmen.

The result of this murder was, as Queen Elfrida intended, the accession to the throne of her ten-year-old son, Ethelred. He was the wrong king for the time, coming to earn the name Ethelred 'the Unready' or 'Redeless', meaning that he lacked resources within himself to deal with the problems of his reign. The main problem was the repeated invasions of England launched by the Danes, who in 1013 caused Ethelred to flee the kingdom. He was recalled to reign in 1014 but had failed to regain a grip on government by the time of his death in 1016.

Given the magnitude of the problem, could Edward, had he lived, have done better?

Medieval chroniclers, especially those who afforded the most colourful stories, were not always careful to check their facts, and once one of them had recorded a false story, others, using the earlier chronicle when compiling their own, would repeat that story until it came to have the force of truth. So, through the centuries, someone may be left with the reputation of having been a murderer until a modern historian uses other sources to check the facts and finds that the alleged murder could not possibly have happened. This is the case with the story of Eleanor of Aquitaine, wife of England's King Henry II, and 'the fair Rosamund', Henry's mistress.

Eleanor was duchess of Aquitaine in her own right, and she had been queen of France for some fifteen years, as wife of Louis VII, before the couple divorced and she married the future King Henry II of England (reigned 1154–89). Despite these dignities, it would have been unreasonable for Eleanor to have expected fidelity from her second husband: fidelity was rare in medieval royal marriages, and Henry II was not one of the few royal saints. However, the open parading of a woman as the King's 'companion' was another matter.

Henry II's affaire with Rosamund Clifford apparently began in about 1166, the year in which Queen Eleanor gave birth to her last child. After that, she and Henry were rarely together; generally the Queen was to be found in southern France, administering her own lands.

'The fair Rosamund' was remembered in legend long after her death, in 1176, and the most persistent of the stories concerned its cause. It was said that Queen Eleanor had gone to the palace of Woodstock, where Rosamund was living in Henry's absence; the Queen had found her way through a labyrinth or garden maze, at whose centre Rosamund had gone to shelter when she heard of Eleanor's arrival. It seems that Henry had the maze erected for Rosamund's protection against this very eventuality; after all, no royal servant would dare refuse to lead the Queen to Rosamund if her whereabouts were known, so the secret place had been planned to shelter her. Yet somehow Eleanor found the way through the maze. One story has it that Rosamund had a reel of thread in her hand when the news of Eleanor's arrival was brought to her, and that as she ran through the maze she left a trail of it behind her, which the Queen followed. At the centre of the maze the Queen confronted Rosamund, offering her a choice of poison or a dagger as a means of death. Rosamund chose the poison.

In fact, Rosamund died at a convent at Godstow, near Woodstock, apparently of natural causes. And Eleanor had long since found a much more satisfying way of avenging herself on her husband. In

1173 she had encouraged her eldest son to raise a rebellion against his father, over in Normandy, in alliance with the King of France. But when, in the autumn of 1174, a treaty was arranged to end the family war, Eleanor was not present to bargain for terms: for the past year she had been her husband's prisoner – and a prisoner she was to remain for the next fifteen years, until Henry II's death. So she could not have hounded 'the fair Rosamund' to her death in 1176.

The hatred that Isabelle of France felt for her husband, Edward II, King of England, resulted in his murder in 1327.

In 1308, aged sixteen, Isabelle had married the 23-year-old King, who had only recently come to his throne. The couple lived together in apparent amity for more than a dozen years, and they had four children. However, in the early years there was a person whose presence in the inmost circle of the Court must have infuriated Isabelle. This was Piers Gaveston, companion of King Edward from their earliest childhood, now chamberlain of his household and also his homosexual partner. In the reign of the King's father, Edward I,* Gaveston had briefly been exiled from England, presumably to break up their intimacy. When Edward II came to the throne, Gaveston was immediately called home and created Earl of Cornwall. Though he was loathed by Edward's nobles, who were on the worst possible terms with the King over long periods, Queen Isabelle was apparently complaisant. Then, in 1312, Gaveston was captured by a coalition of noblemen and murdered.

King Edward's second 'favourite' is thought not to have had any sexual relationship with him, but the King was certainly as dependent on Hugh Despenser as he had ever been on Gaveston, and as generous to him. By 1322, Queen Isabelle had become alienated from her husband; in September 1324 much of her property was confiscated, ostensibly because she was a Frenchwoman and there was the prospect of war with France – perhaps reasonable enough,

---

*   English kings are numbered from the Norman Conquest of 1066; thus Edward I reigned in 1272–1307, though there had been two Anglo-Saxon kings named Edward before the Conquest.

but it was Hugh Despenser and his equally hated father who had suggested it; to cap it all, Despenser's wife was placed in Isabelle's household, to act as her husband's spy. The Queen remained calm. Her husband still trusted her sufficiently to allow her to go to France, in March 1325, on a peace mission to her brother, King Charles IV.

In France, Queen Isabelle found a coterie of Englishmen thoroughly disaffected from the Despenser-dominated regime. Among them was Roger Mortimer of Wigmore, who had escaped from the Tower of London in 1323. He became her lover.

Isabelle's diplomacy – or an outline of her secret long-term strategy – induced the French king to agree to return Edward II's French territories, but on condition that he render homage for them. Charles – and Isabelle, of course – must have known that Edward would not leave England in its then parlous state to do homage in person; it was a plausible and effective ploy to persuade the King to send his heir, another Edward, to do homage in his place.

It was about this time that Walter Stapledon, Bishop of Exeter, who had accompanied the Prince to Paris, took note of the relationship between Isabelle and Mortimer. Hastening home, he reported to the King. But when Edward summoned Isabelle back to England, she refused to go: she said that she dare not, for she knew that Despenser had designs on her life.

Isabelle had her son as a hostage and pawn, but she was disappointed if she had expected to return to England at the head of a French army. Denied aid by her brother, she and Mortimer and their new partisans found a more generous ally in the Count of Hainault, largely by betrothing her son to his daughter. Using a substantial down-payment on the girl's dowry, Isabelle bought herself an army and on 24 September landed in England, near Harwich.

As the Queen's army moved westward, Edward and Despenser fled before it. There was no need for Isabelle to threaten London with her forces: Londoners made clear their opposition to the King. In mid-November Edward and Despenser were captured. Despenser was executed at Hereford.

On 15 January 1327, a week after Parliament had opened, the Archbishop of Canterbury announced that Edward II had been deposed. Before the month was out, his son, the fourteen-year-old Edward III, had been crowned.

The 'Articles of Deposition' that summarised Edward II's misdeeds were brief and succinct: he had shown himself incapable of personal rule and had refused all good counsel: he had lost power over Scotland (of which his father had been acknowledged overlord) and control of parts of Gascony and Ireland; he had attacked churchmen and noblemen, killing some, imprisoning others; he had sold justice for his own profit; he had ruined the realm and shown himself incorrigible, beyond any hope of reformation.

It was, of course, too much to hope that Edward II would be allowed to live out a natural lifespan in anything like comfort and freedom, now that he had been removed entirely from government. On 21 September 1327 it was announced that the King had died of natural causes in his prison in Berkeley Castle in Gloucestershire. Soon afterwards, it was being said that he had been murdered.

Unfortunately, the best of the stories cannot be believed. This was the one that said that Adam Orleton, Bishop of Hereford, had sent a message to Berkeley saying, '*Edwardum occidere nolite timere bonum est*', which could be read in two ways, depending on the presence and placing of a comma before or after '*timere*', which would give alternative translations: 'Do not kill Edward; it is a good thing to fear' or 'Do not fear to kill Edward; it is a good thing.' In fact, Orleton was in France at the time of the murder and can have known nothing of it until it was accomplished. Several chronicles tell how the former King's gaolers killed him: by inserting a red-hot rod in the anus and thence through his body, so that there should be no mark on him to show that he had been murdered.

The order for the King's death must surely have come from the Queen. On who else's authority would Lord Berkeley and his men have acted? Yet Queen Isabelle joined her son at her husband's funeral, in St Peter's Abbey, Gloucester.

Together Isabelle and Mortimer were now in control of both king and kingdom. They were scarcely a success: war with Scotland threatened again, but rather than face the armies crossing the border, the Queen and her lover conceded everything the Scots demanded. At the time, none of the English nobles opposed the Anglo-Scots Treaty of Northampton, but it was a major factor in their disaffection from Isabelle, along with hatred of the Queen's lover, resenting his unprecedented power.

At some time in 1330, the young King's cousin Henry, Earl of Lancaster, made contact with him, and together they planned Mortimer's downfall.

In October the Court was at Nottingham for a meeting of the royal Council. Isabelle and Mortimer had somehow been alerted to the probability of revolt, and they locked the castle gates and set guards everywhere. However, the constable of the castle was in connivance with the conspirators, and he showed them an underground passage that led right inside the castle. The King himself joined them as they entered. Bursting in on Mortimer, they had him in their power when the Queen came in, begging her son to have mercy on 'gentle Mortimer', to no avail.

A few weeks later, Parliament declared Mortimer a notorious traitor and he was sentenced to be hanged, drawn and quartered. He died on 29 November 1330.

Queen Isabelle was not even imprisoned. The considerable income she had claimed in recent years was much reduced, but her allowance was still generous and no restraint was placed on her freedom; nor was she ostracised by the royal family. She died in 1358, wearing the habit of a Poor Clare nun, and was buried in the Newgate church of the Poor Clares' brother Franciscans in London. Perhaps she had repented.

Poison has always been associated with late-medieval Italy – and especially with Italian women. The very name Lucrezia Borgia conjures up lurid stories of sudden death by poison. For centuries, that daughter of Pope Alexander VI has been reviled.

In England, the legend of Italy's sophisticated methods of murder must have begun to circulate when Lionel, Duke of Clarence, second son of King Edward III, died in Italy, where he had married Violante Visconti, daughter of the Lord of Milan. The wedding took place in June 1368: four months later Lionel died – of a fever, it was said; of poison, it was rumoured: most likely it was food contamination that killed him. Why his English attendants should have blamed the Viscontis is unclear: after all, the family had been proud of the match with English royalty. Nevertheless, so certain were Lionel's English attendants that the Duke had been murdered that they attempted to raise an army from the numerous English mercenaries employed in the Italian states. Milan was subjected to the rioting and looting of some 2,000 Englishmen before the more organised force of the Viscontis drove them out of the city.

Violante Visconti's brother, Giangaleazzo, Lord and later Duke of Milan, gained a reputation as an arch-poisoner, based initially on his reputed murder of his uncle Bernabo, co-ruler of Milan. In 1385, Giangaleazzo mounted a *coup*, defeated Bernabo, imprisoned him and allegedly had him poisoned. (Bernabo was then aged seventy-six; perhaps the defeat and captivity were themselves enough to kill him.)

In 1387 Giangaleazzo Visconti's daughter Valentina was sent into France to marry Louis, Duke of Orleans, brother of King Charles VI. It was unfortunate for her that Charles's wife was her cousin Isabeau of Bavaria, granddaughter of Bernabo. The French King was prone to bouts of madness; Isabeau looked to her brother-in-law for support in government and took him as her lover. In 1396 the Queen put out the story that Valentina was a witch, using her black arts to poison the King (which explained his madness, said Isabeau), in order to gain the throne for Louis of Orleans. The Queen's propaganda inflamed the volatile Parisian mob, and Valentina was forced to depart from Court, leaving Isabeau and Louis to enjoy each other (see pp. 40–41).

Borgia, Visconti, Sforza, Gonzaga, Farnese, Orsini, d'Este, de' Medici: scarcely one of the great ruling families of Italy lacked some story of a murderer or victim in the fourteenth and fifteenth centuries. Poison and the dagger were the preferred weapons, and the motives, as ever, were power and revenge. The word 'vendetta' is, after all, Italian.

Caterina Sforza, illegitimate daughter of Galeazzo Maria Sforza, Duke of Milan, was the wife of Girolamo Riario, Duke of Forlí. When Girolamo was murdered in 1488, Caterina escaped but had to leave her children behind, prisoners of the murderers. When she fortified the city of Forlí against them, they threatened to kill the children if she did not submit. Caterina mounted the battlements and, in full view of the enemy camped around the city, lifted her skirts high: she was unmistakably pregnant.

'Fools!' she cried. 'Look! I can make more children!'

It was said that Caterina Sforza was a witch, for she was so beautiful that only witchcraft could account for it. She was also a ruthless killer: when her lover was murdered, she had not only his murderers killed but also their entire families – some forty men, women and children.

Of all the Italian women who reputedly combined beauty and evil, Giovanna I, Queen of Naples, ranked highest. She reigned between 1343 and 1380.

Giovanna's grandfather, King Roberto 'the Wise', proclaimed her his heir in 1330, when she was about six years old, and in 1333 he betrothed her to her cousin Endre of Hungary, in an attempt to end the Hungarian royal family's claims to the throne of Naples. Unfortunately, not only did Giovanna and Endre grow up to hate each other but Giovanna showed so little interest in governing Naples that her husband's Hungarian staff gained control.

On the night of 18/19 November 1345, the royal couple were staying at Aversa but preparing to leave for Naples the next day. It was on that night that Endre was found hanging from the balustrade of a balcony, a silk cord round his neck, a glove stuffed in his mouth to stifle his cries.

Giovanna, six months pregnant, denied any part in the murder and appealed to the Pope for help; he sent a bishop and cardinal to govern in her name. Apparently the Pope believed the Queen innocent of the crime, but many others did not. Not that she could have killed Endre herself, of course, but she had friends who had been his enemies. There was Giovanna's former governess and present confidante, Filippa da Catania, and her family; there was Giovanna's great-aunt-by-marriage, Caterina, Princess of Taranto, who wanted the crown to devolve on her branch of the family – it was rumoured that she was sheltering the probable killers, Giovanna's chamberlain and his son, neither of whom was seen again after the murder; then there was Carlo, Duke of Durazzo, husband of Giovanna's sister Maria but also another of their first cousins, with a claim to the throne rivalling that of the Tarantos. In fact, Carlo forestalled accusations by himself accusing Giovanna of having instigated the murder. He had Filippa and her family arrested

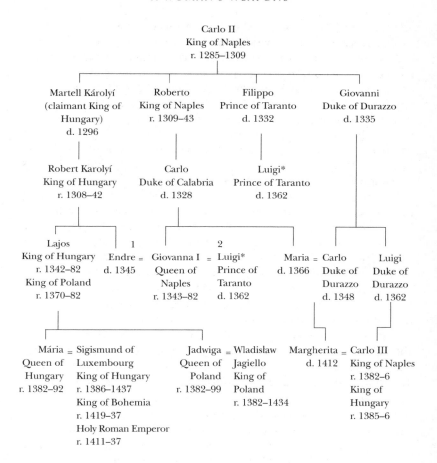

Carlo II
King of Naples
r. 1285–1309

Martell Károlyí
(claimant King of
Hungary)
d. 1296

Roberto
King of Naples
r. 1309–43

Filippo
Prince of Taranto
d. 1332

Giovanni
Duke of Durazzo
d. 1335

Robert Karolyí
King of Hungary
r. 1308–42

Carlo
Duke of Calabria
d. 1328

Luigi*
Prince of Taranto
d. 1362

Lajos
King of Hungary
r. 1342–82
King of Poland
r. 1370–82

Endre =
d. 1345

1

Giovanna I =
Queen of
Naples
r. 1343–82

2

Luigi*
Prince of
Taranto
d. 1362

Maria =
d. 1366

Carlo
Duke of
Durazzo
d. 1348

Luigi
Duke of
Durazzo
d. 1362

Mária =
Queen of
Hungary
r. 1382–92

Sigismund of
Luxembourg
King of Hungary
r. 1386–1437
King of Bohemia
r. 1419–37
Holy Roman Emperor
r. 1411–37

Jadwiga =
Queen of
Poland
r. 1382–99

Wladisław
Jagiello
King of
Poland
r. 1382–1434

Margherita =
d. 1412

Carlo III
King of Naples
r. 1382–6
King of
Hungary
r. 1385–6

T   HOUSE OF ANJOU IN NAPLES,
     HUNGARY AND POLAND
     SEE PAGES 19–20 AND 32–5.

and tortured. The old lady died before her execution; some members of the family were hanged, others burned alive.

A further factor in the complex power-struggle was Hungary – the cousins who had agreed to Giovanna's keeping the crown if she married Endre of Hungary. Now Endre's brother, King Lajos of Hungary, became another of Giovanna's accusers, and he backed his words by sending an army against her. In August 1347 Giovanna married her cousin Luigi, Caterina's son, and he stood by her, but his brothers went over to the Hungarian side, as did Carlo of Durazzo. With the Hungarian army surging into Naples, in January 1348 Giovanna was forced to leave her kingdom.

However, Lajos, King of Hungary, who now arrived in Naples, placed little faith in the Italian cousins who apparently welcomed him. At Aversa, he made Carlo of Durazzo show him the place where his (Lajos's) brother Endre had been murdered. He accused Carlo of having taken part in the murder and, though Carlo denied it, stood by while a Hungarian hacked him down with a sword.

In March 1348 Giovanna had reached Avignon, which, though in France, was part of her patrimony. At that time the Pope was living there, and before his court and in the presence of Hungarian envoys, the Queen conducted her own defence and was acquitted. In June, she agreed to sell Avignon to the Papacy and with the gold from that transaction bought an army which she dispatched to invade Naples. Victorious, on Whit Sunday 1351 Giovanna and Luigi were crowned there together.

That was by no means the end of the Queen's trials. She married twice more, she saw plague – the Black Death – leave thousands of Neapolitans dead in its wake as it surged through Europe, and there was intermittent rebellion throughout the kingdom. In 1380 Giovanna was excommunicated by Pope Urban VI for having supported the 'anti-Pope' Clement VII at Avignon, and so her throne was declared forfeit. With Urban VI's support, one of the Durazzo family, a younger Carlo, was made king.* In March 1382 Giovanna became his prisoner in the castle of Muro, and there, on 22 May, while she was praying in the chapel, she was strangled to death.

* He subsequently became King of Hungary too; see p. 20.

Since she had been excommunicated, there was no funeral; the whereabouts of her grave is unknown.

Ines de Castro was the mistress of Pedro, heir to the throne of Portugal, and bore him three children before their secret wedding on 1 January 1355. Since Pedro's father, Affonso IV, King of Portugal, was at that time hoping to marry his son to a foreign princess, Pedro's refusal to comply alerted his father to the marriage to Ines, whom Affonso mistrusted as a Spaniard and whose kinsmen were known to exert a strong influence on the Prince. In fact, King Affonso had good reason for his concern: it was not unlikely that, when Pedro came to the throne, he would set aside his legal heir, son of his former wife, in favour of Ines's eldest son, thus setting the scene for a civil war between the half-brothers for possession of the crown of Portugal. Such civil wars, fought between brothers or cousins, were the bane of medieval Europe.

So it was that King Affonso sent three armed men to kill Ines de Castro at the Villa of Tears, as her house was later known.

Affonso had not reckoned with the rage that accompanied Pedro's grief. The Prince gathered his followers and prepared for war against his father, so frightening Affonso that he agreed to banish the murderers. However, at Affonso's death in 1357, Pedro drove a bargain with the King of Castile by which he returned Castilian prisoners in exchange for two of the murderers who had found shelter in Castile (the third had escaped to Italy). Inevitably they too were killed, but not until the King had enjoyed the torments they suffered in various tortures.

Another expression of King Pedro I's grief was the honour paid to his late wife. Her body was taken from its grave, robed in scarlet and ermine and carried to Coimbra Cathedral, where the corpse was solemnly crowned Queen of Portugal. Members of the Court filed past it, kissing the fleshless hand. Then, at night, with flaming torches lighting the way, the Queen's body was carried to the monastery of Santa Maria in Alcobaça, to be laid in a tomb still to be seen today, on which the effigy of Ines de Castro lies as if asleep, opposite that of her husband, Pedro I, King of Portugal.

To return briefly to the reign of Affonso IV: in 1328 his daughter, Pedro's sister Maria, married Alfonso XI, King of Castile. Theirs was one of the least successful of the arranged marriages decreed by affairs of state. The King of Castile was devoted to his mistress, Leonor de Guzman, who travelled everywhere with him and presented him with several children, while Maria was left neglected in a provincial castle, the mother of just one son.

In March 1350 Alfonso of Castile died, a victim of the plague called the Black Death that was then devastating Europe. His heir was Maria's son, Pedro I, still in his early teens. Immediately, Queen Maria had Leonor de Guzman imprisoned in the castle of Talavera; she was subsequently strangled. Certainly Maria must be blamed for the murder; whether the young King Pedro shared the responsibility is not certain.

Enmity and friendship were fickle commodities in medieval Spain, and it was not long before Pedro I was faced with a rebellion whose leaders included not only his half-brothers but his mother. For four years he was in the power of those unlikely allies before he managed to escape. When Pedro laid siege to the town of Toro in 1355, his mother was there, and she summoned the help of Leonor de Guzman's sons, but it was her own son who won the day. When Maria went out to meet Pedro and submit to him, she was accompanied by the noblemen who had supported her, among them her lover, Don Martín de Tello. As they approached the King, Martín and three others were struck down by men armed with maces.

In 1356 Maria was allowed to leave Castile for her father's Court in Portugal. When she died, in 1357, it was said that she had been killed by the order of her father, who was disgusted by her 'licentious passions'. Since Affonso IV, King of Portugal, was known to have killed his daughter-in-law, Ines de Castro, why not his own daughter too?

'Good Queen Bess': the English monarch whose face is more familiar than any other's and whose fame is remembered when school history lessons are long forgotten. In her 'finest hour', when the Spanish Armada threatened England in 1588, Elizabeth Tudor had reigned thirty years and was secure in her people's loyalty. In September 1560 she was less than two years into her reign, and only twenty-seven years old, when she was implicated in a suspected murder that threatened to ruin and depose her.

On 9 September 1560 Elizabeth's courtiers and councillors learned of the death of Lady Robert Dudley at her house at Cumnor in Berkshire. Even before details could be added, there was avid speculation that she had been murdered. Lord Robert Dudley cared nothing for his wife; he cared very deeply for the consort's crown he would gain when, as a widower, he married Queen Elizabeth. His wife's death was convenient.

Too convenient. Everyone recognised Dudley's ambition and the Queen's love for him. They had known each other since childhood; when Elizabeth's half-sister Mary was on the throne, both had been prisoners in the Tower, Elizabeth suspected of treason, Robert Dudley convicted of that crime after his father had persuaded Jane Grey to usurp Mary's throne. Perhaps it was a common fear of the block and axe that had drawn them together. Dudley was already married then, but after Queen Mary's death, when Elizabeth came to the throne, Lady Robert Dudley – better known by her maiden name, Amy Robsart – never went to Court. Dudley was known to be the Queen's 'favourite', suspected of being her lover; it was everywhere whispered that only the existence of his wife prevented their marrying.

The news of Amy's death created a furore of scandalous gossip and rumour. Of course, it could not be said that Dudley himself had killed his wife. In modern terms it would be called 'a contract killing'. But with so strong a motive for ridding himself of his wife, he would find the man to do it for him. Rumours such as that caused Dudley to retire from Court, though only to his house at Kew. His enemies, resentful of his influence and fearful of his potential power, did not wait to hear the coroner's jury's verdict before condemning him. It was inevitable that the Queen was suspected of having been a party to the murder; or at least, hearing of it, had she suspected Dudley, challenged him, heard his confession and sought to protect him?

In fact, it had been known for a fair while that Amy had a 'malady', which was probably cancer, in one breast. Had she died after weeks of pain, surrounded by doctors, clergy and servants, the rumours of murder would have evaporated. But she had been found lying at the foot of a staircase, her neck broken.

One solution to the mystery was not overlooked: that of suicide. If Amy knew she was suffering from cancer and could not face the agony that must end her life, she might well have killed herself. The fact that she had sent her servants out that day, to a local fair, suggests such a plan. Her own maid insisted that Lady Robert Dudley would never do such a thing, but she had spoken of overhearing her mistress praying that God would 'deliver her from her desperation'. Was it the cancer or her husband's neglect that drove her to despair? Did the despair cause her to commit suicide?

Inevitably the coroner's jury returned a verdict of accidental death. There was no evidence of murder, after all. But that did not prevent the dangerous gossip and speculation which not only spread through the kingdom but became the substance of foreign ambassadors' reports to their masters. At the scandal's peak, rumour had it that the Queen's suspected part in the murder would cause her to be deposed. Would she and Dudley end their lives under the axe after all?

Queen Elizabeth survived. Dudley survived, returning to Court, still high in the Queen's favour, apparently still the man most likely to become her husband. But of course Elizabeth could never marry him now: if she did, suspicions of their complicity in murder would revive, with possibly fatal consequences. In 1562 the Queen contracted smallpox and was for a while on the brink of death; her first act, on recovery, was to nominate Dudley to be 'Protector' of the kingdom in the event of her death, until her successor could take the throne. Two years later, the Queen created him Earl of Leicester, apparently with an eye to sending him to Scotland to marry the Scots queen Mary. Whether Elizabeth really intended to sacrifice her closest friend – or lover – to the cause of Anglo-Scottish peace was never tested, for Mary married another man, without Elizabeth's approval. And in 1578 Leicester married – also without royal approval – the Queen's cousin Lettice Knollys, the widowed Countess of Essex. His disgrace did not last long and when he died, in Armada year, Elizabeth was devastated. When she died, in 1603, and a little casket by her bed was opened, it was found to contain a parchment marked 'His last letter'.

Leicester was long credited with the murder of his first wife – and of others who stood in his way over the years, and as long as he was suspected, Queen Elizabeth was viewed as a possible party to the crime. However, it is now known that breast cancer causes the spine to become so brittle that even the slightest jar can cause the neck to break. Was that what killed Amy Robsart?

CHAPTER THREE

A FAMILY AFFAIR

England's Henry I may have killed his brother William II. King John probably killed his nephew Arthur. Certainly some of the Scandinavian royal murders of the Middle Ages were a family affair. Crowns – or rather the power they represented – were such a prize that, when a king died without a direct heir or when there was some doubt as to a monarch's legitimate birth or when he showed himself unusually inept, there were always men eager to use that pretext to press their own claims. In the late Middle Ages, most of the royal murders that occurred were committed by – or by order of – a claimant to a crown or by the ambitious cousin of a king.

Brothers, cousins, uncles, nephews: who could be trusted when a crown was at stake?

In the second half of the fourteenth century, Enrique, Count of Trastámara, disputed the throne of his half-brother, Pedro I, King of Castile. However, there was a personal element in their war too: in 1351 Pedro's mother had had Enrique's strangled, she having been their father's mistress (see p. 36); then in 1358, Pedro had Enrique's twin brother Fadrique murdered too. 'Pedro the Cruel' he was called, and several other murders were attributed to him – that of his mother's lover, for example, those of his aunt Leonor, dowager queen of Aragon, in 1359, and her son and daughter-in-law, and possibly that of his wife, Blanche of Bourbon, though he had had her imprisoned for a long time and she might have died of natural causes. At the time, no one gave him the benefit of the doubt.

The whole of Pedro's reign was taken up with war and civil war and the putting-down of rebellions, and there seemed no prospect of peace, for Pedro had no indisputably legitimate son to succeed him, only two daughters, and they were the offspring of a woman whom he *said* he had married but . . . It was inevitable that his half-brother Enrique would only redouble his efforts to gain the throne after Pedro's death.

In March 1369, Pedro was withstanding a siege at Montiel. The situation seemed hopeless. Then Bertrand du Guesclin, commander of Enrique's French mercenaries, offered Pedro a means of escape. Suspecting nothing, for mercenaries were notoriously fickle when a bribe was offered, on the night of 23 March Pedro made his way into the enemy encampment – only to be confronted by Enrique himself. The half-brothers began to fight, Pedro unarmed but superior in strength, Enrique armed with a dagger. One version of the story has Enrique stabbing Pedro, then leaving him for others to finish off; another has du Guesclin plunging a dagger into Pedro's back as he grappled with Enrique on the ground.

Pedro the Cruel had hoped to have his daughter Costanza succeed him on the Castilian throne and had married her to an English prince, John of Gaunt, Duke of Lancaster, who brought an English army to his aid. After Pedro's death the English remained in Castile, and the civil war continued until Enrique of Trastámara was at last acknowledged the victor and recognised as King Enrique II. Under the terms of the Anglo-Castilian peace, Pedro the Cruel's granddaughter, Katherine of Lancaster, was given in marriage to Enrique's grandson, the future King Enrique III.

Second only to civil war, the rivalry of noblemen was the prime cause of a medieval kingdom's weakness. This was the situation in France in the reign of Charles VI (1380–1422). In 1392 the French King was suddenly seized with an urge for violence, taking up an axe and killing four men-at-arms. The madness returned periodically for the rest of his life. Initially Charles's brother, Louis, Duke of Orleans, and their uncle Philippe, Duke of Burgundy, disputed the leadership of the royal council that governed during the King's lapses; after Philippe's death in 1404, his son Jean was Louis's rival. One chronicler claimed that there were personal reasons for the cousins' enmity too. Louis of Orleans was a notorious womaniser, and it was said that he kept a picture gallery to remind him of all the women who had slept with him. One day he showed Jean of Burgundy his collection, gleefully displaying the portrait of Burgundy's wife.

As Louis of Orleans rode home through Paris on the night of Wednesday 23 November 1407, a band of men set on his party, scattering the armed escort. So firmly did the Duke hold on to his horse's reins that one of his assailants hacked off the hand that held them, to force the Duke out of the saddle. Then Orleans was stabbed and clubbed to death, his body left in the gutter.

At the inquest, next day, there was only one witness to the murder. Madame Griffart, a shoemaker's wife, had gone to her upstairs window to see if her husband was coming home and to pull in the pole on which some washing was drying. Looking up the street, she saw a nobleman on horseback, with five or six more mounted men and three or four men on foot, the whole party lit up by the flaming torches they were carrying. The nobleman was singing. For a moment Madame Griffart watched, then she turned away to put her child to bed. Cries of 'Kill him! Kill him!' brought her back to the window, the child in her arms. The nobleman was on his knees in the street, fending off the attack of seven or eight masked men armed with swords and axes. Madame Griffart screamed 'Murder!' and one man looked up. 'Be quiet, you damned woman!' he shouted. 'Be quiet!' At that moment another man – a big man in a red hood that hid his face – came out of the house 'at the sign of Our Lady'; he called, 'Put out the light! Let's go! He's dead.' The men turned and ran, leaving a torch burning on the ground. By its light Madame Griffart could see that there was a second man lying there; he raised his head and called something, which Madame Griffart thought was 'My lord!' By then she was shouting 'Murder!' again, and now so was a neighbour who had appeared in the street. Other people gathered, and someone identified the Duke of Orleans.

Also at the inquest were local water-carriers – men always about the streets, who might have seen something. The one who had delivered water at the house 'at the sign of Our Lady' was found to be a resident in the Duke of Burgundy's palace in Paris – not unusual in itself, for 'below stairs' in the city palaces were innumerable small rooms in which servants, their dependents and various hangers-on nested where they could; but everyone knew of the Dukes' enmity, so it was worth investigation.

A messenger was sent to the Duke of Burgundy. He was in council with other noblemen. When he heard that he was wanted for questioning, his face betrayed him; the Duke of Anjou read his look and asked if he had anything to do with the murder. Briefly Jean of Burgundy confessed. Then he left the council chamber and hurried downstairs. He passed the Duke of Bourbon and told him he was just on his way to the lavatory, but he made straight for his horse and, with an armed escort, fled north-east, to Flanders.

The Duchess of Orleans demanded that the Duke of Burgundy be brought to trial for her husband's murder, but no one would support her, even though Burgundy made no attempt to deny that he had instigated the crime. Nor would he ask for a royal pardon. In fact, he traded on the late Duke of Orleans' unpopularity and in February 1408 returned to Paris to find himself almost a hero for what he had done.

On 8 March the Duke of Burgundy stood trial before his peers and offered a justification for the murder of the Duke of Orleans. Louis had been a tyrant, he claimed, and a traitor. He declared that Louis had tried to bring about the King's death by witchcraft – not a sudden death but a slow one, to avert suspicion; he had had a sword, a dagger and a ring consecrated by two devils and rubbed on the flesh of corpses fresh from the gallows. Burgundy also brought up an old story, reminding the court of the night in January 1393 on which Charles VI had attended a fancy-dress ball and was watching the antics of some men dressed as animals when their shaggy costumes caught fire; the King himself had narrowly escaped death when a spark had set his clothing alight. Now Burgundy said that Orleans had been to blame, attempting to kill the King. There was talk of poison too, and the name of Louis's father-in-law, Giangaleazzo Visconti, was brought in, since 'everyone knew' that he used poison for political ends (see p. 31). Burgundy went on to say that Orleans had plotted with the Pope to seize the throne, that he was in control of key garrisons of troops and that he had used for his own purposes the taxes that had been imposed to finance the war against England.

That same day, Charles VI issued a formal pardon for Burgundy's crime.

However, the fortunes of politicians, medieval as well as modern, princes as well as commoners, fluctuate with circumstances. In 1412, Jean, Duke of Burgundy, was at the height of his power; by the end of 1413, he had been thoroughly excluded from government. The rivalry of the French noblemen was now complicated by the entry of a new force into French politics: in 1415 Henry V, King of England, mounted an invasion, won the Battle of Agincourt and occupied Normandy; later he claimed the French throne itself. Then fortune began to veer Burgundy's way again: by the summer of 1418 he had control of Charles VI – and of Paris, where the King's government was centred and his financial nucleus. Now Burgundy had another new enemy to face: the Dauphin Charles, albeit only fifteen years old, was beginning to rally support; it was inevitable that the future king should be more popular than the Duke, who must lose power when his pawn, the ageing, mad Charles VI, at last died. In July 1419 Duke and Dauphin came to terms.

Two months later, the two men planned to meet, apparently to cement their pact. Their rendezvous was to be on a bridge over the River Yonne, at Montereau, nearly fifty miles south-east of Paris. Each was to take with him only ten men, as a token that there was to be no battle.

A fenced enclosure had been built on the bridge, and the Dauphin and his party were already in it when the Duke and his men rode up to meet them; they too entered the enclosure, and the gate was closed behind them. After that, what happened? There are conflicting stories. The Dauphin's men asserted that there was a sudden scuffle and that the Duke of Burgundy was killed inadvertently; later the Dauphin amended this to say that Burgundy had drawn his sword and had been set on before he could harm him. Burgundy's supporters said that the Dauphin gave a signal to his men to kill the Duke; some said that he himself struck the first blow.

Whatever happened, the Dauphin had rid himself of a rival and an enemy. But it was to be more than thirty years before he found himself effectively King of France. When Charles VI died, in 1422, his throne was seized by the English on behalf of the infant King Henry VI, and it was many battles later, long after the death of

France's heroine Jeanne of Arc, who led the nation's armies against the English, before the Dauphin was securely seated on the throne as King Charles VII.

The circumstances that had caused civil war in Castile, under Pedro the Cruel, and the noblemen's vying for power in France in the reign of Charles VI, were present in England in the fifteenth century: a disputed royal succession, giving rise to civil war, and the rivalry of ambitious noblemen, which destabilised government even in times of peace. Three English kings were murdered during that century, and though the civil wars – the Wars of the Roses – were only intermittent, with parts of the country totally unaffected by the fighting, it was an era whose instability marred the lives of thousands of people and left a deep impression on the national consciousness.

The outbreak and development of the Wars of the Roses have been attributed to several factors, political and social. Among them was the personal deficiency of King Richard II: he was a 'bad' king, and so he was deposed; and he was childless, so that the man who deposed him, his cousin Henry, Duke of Lancaster, took the crown himself, becoming King Henry IV. In its turn, this usurpation sparked off the challenge to the House of Lancaster by the House of York – and the civil wars that followed.

Richard II came to the throne in 1377, while still a child, and his long minority saw the interplay of the ambitions of his uncles, the Dukes of Lancaster, York and Gloucester. So inept were Richard's own first attempts at governing, however, that in 1387 Gloucester pushed the young King back into a state of subservience to a ruling council. Two years later, Richard did break free, but it was not until 1397 that he had garnered sufficient power to strike back: Gloucester and his friends were arrested, and before the Duke could be brought to trial, it was announced that he was dead. No one doubted that his death had not been due to any natural causes.

Dissatisfaction with King Richard's rule was not confined to the nobility, who had been ousted from power, or to Parliament, which had been brazenly manipulated by the King; throughout the country there was outrage at Richard's subversion of justice, his flouting of Common Law, and everyone was affected by the taxes he imposed to pay for his army – not an army raised to fight a war abroad but a 'standing' army, kept at home to repress the people. However, it was not a popular revolution but a challenge from within his own family that deposed Richard II in 1399.

The challenge came from Richard's cousin Henry, Duke of Lancaster, whom the King had exiled and deprived of his inheritance. Taking advantage of Richard's absence in Ireland, in July 1399 Henry returned to England, now leading an army, and within days of Richard's landing in Wales, he had been taken prisoner and sent to the Tower of London.

It was put out that Richard II had abdicated 'with cheerful countenance' and that he had acknowledged Henry of Lancaster as his successor, even though Henry had less right to the throne than their cousin Edmund Mortimer. But whether voluntarily or by force, Richard II did abdicate, and the men assembled for the next Parliament heard the declaration of his abdication and confirmed it; they also listened to a statement of thirty-three reasons for the deposition of Richard II.

That was in September 1399; on 28 October Richard was taken from the Tower and moved to Leeds Castle in Kent; later he was sent to Pontefract Castle in Yorkshire.

Since Henry of Lancaster could not show an indisputable right to the throne by lineage, he declared that his victory over Richard proved that God sanctioned his taking the crown, and he pointed out the dangers of having a child as king, in order to eliminate Edmund Mortimer, aged eight, the cousin with the senior claim to the throne. At the time, not a voice was lifted in protest against the new King Henry IV.

Nevertheless, protest there was. It came to light early in the new year. One chronicle has it that Henry's cousin Edward of York betrayed his fellow-conspirators; another tells the story of a prostitute who heard of the plot from a client and passed it on to another client, one of Henry's servants. The plot involved the great tournament that Henry IV was planning to hold at Windsor on Twelfth Night (6 January) 1400: men were to be smuggled into the castle in wagons supposedly containing equipment for

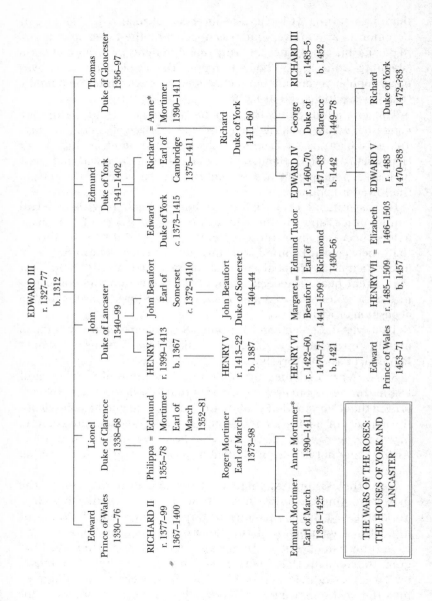

THE WARS OF THE ROSES:
THE HOUSES OF YORK AND
LANCASTER

the tournament; once inside, they were to find the King and his four sons (aged between nine and twelve) and kill them all. This done, they were to ride immediately to Pontefract, to release Richard II, but in the dangerous meantime they had a man who was his double, to impersonate him.

Henry had no army stationed at Windsor and, after the revelations, no time to raise one before the plot would be set in train. All he could do was hurry back to London, taking his sons with him. It may have been ignominious but it saved their lives, for only hours later the conspirators reached Windsor. Finding the King gone, they occupied the castle. In the days that followed, they attempted to raise an army from nearby towns and villages, but in London Henry had done the same, and with more success. The rebel leaders were arrested and either killed by local people or taken to London for execution; lesser men were treated more leniently.

The rebellion may have caused the killing of Richard II. The date of his death is unknown, but in February 1400 his corpse was brought ceremonially to Westminster Abbey and displayed there. It was rumoured that in his 'melancholy' he had refused to eat and had come to his senses too late to prevent his death. More likely he was smothered or strangled. Richard II's body was shown in several places before its burial at King's Langley in Hertfordshire,* largely to prove that he *was* dead. Even so, a belief persisted that he was still alive and had escaped from custody.

Henry IV lived until 1413. His was not a glorious reign but he did rule with sufficient firmness to ensure a peaceful accession for his son, Henry V. Although Henry V was only twenty-five years old when he came to the throne, he obviously had the makings of a 'good' king (one able to rule with convincing strength and not given to capricious taxation). It was proof of his self-assurance that he felt able to leave England in 1413 to make war in France, in an attempt to recover the lost duchy of Normandy. However, virtually on the eve of his departure for France, when Henry and his army were at Southampton, preparing to cross the Channel, the King received news of a plot against his throne – and ostensibly against his life.

---

* It was later moved to Westminster Abbey.

On Sunday 31 July 1415 Edmund Mortimer, Earl of March, came to his cousin the King and confessed to having been a party to a plot hatched by another cousin, Richard of York, Earl of Cambridge. Modern analysis of the evidence suggests that Cambridge wanted March to desert Henry V's expeditionary force and to make for Wales, where the cousins would raise a rebellion as soon as the King was safely abroad. At the time, however, it was alleged that Cambridge had intended to have the King, his three brothers and unnamed others killed, in order to put March on the throne. (As a child, Edmund Mortimer, Earl of March, had been Richard II's heir presumptive.) In law, this allegation was needed to ensure that Cambridge and his two main confederates could be tried for treason, under the terms of the 1352 Statute of Treasons. It was not enough to show that Cambridge and his friends had intended to rebel; it had to be shown that they had planned the undeniably treasonous act of regicide (see p. 76). All three were speedily arrested and brought to trial, with the inevitable result of conviction and execution.

The Southampton plot did not deter Henry V from crossing to France. On 25 October 1415 his army was victorious at the Battle of Agincourt and subsequently went on to occupy Normandy. But Henry had a greater goal: he laid claim to the crown of France itself, contending that he had a better right to it than Charles VI, then reigning. By arms and by diplomacy, Henry enforced his case, and on 21 May 1420 he was recognised as heir to the French throne. Of course, he had to go on fighting: Charles VI's son, the Dauphin Charles, would not accept his deposition; but Henry might have prevailed had he lived to lead more armies.

Henry V died, aged thirty-five, in May 1422. That October, Charles VI died too. So it came about that Henry's son – Charles's grandson through his daughter – became ruler of both kingdoms before he was a year old. Initially the heavy burden of Henry VI's realms was borne by his uncles, the Dukes of Bedford and Gloucester, but Bedford died in 1437, and in 1441 Gloucester's enemies attacked him through his wife (see pp. 74–5), so that his power began to wane. Thus, when Henry VI was declared of age in 1442, it might seem that he had a clear path to personal power: in fact, he had not the force of character that could dominate his nobles.

When, in 1447, Gloucester was finally eliminated, his fall was laid to the charge of William de la Pole, Earl (later Duke) of Suffolk. Gloucester was accused of plotting a rebellion and – a familiar story – died before he could be brought to trial. In the short term, Suffolk gained, becoming unchallenged leader in government, but in 1450 he was charged with having conspired with the French in their war to regain their country's independence and to place Charles VI's son on the throne. Suffolk too was murdered: on his way into exile, his ship was waylaid and he was taken off it; aboard a rowing-boat the Duke was beheaded – at whose orders is unknown; he had many enemies.

After Suffolk's death, the power vacuum in the King's council was filled by his cousins John Beaufort, Duke of Somerset, and Richard, Duke of York. Their rivalry came to a head in August 1453, when Henry VI lapsed into insanity (in modern terms, he is held to have suffered from schizophrenia). Somerset had the confidence of Henry's queen, Margaret of Anjou. It was said that the Duke was her lover; but York was created protector of the realm and president of the council. When Henry recovered his wits, Somerset was restored to power, but York regained control by defeating the King's army in battle at St Albans in May 1435, during which Somerset was killed.

The Battle of St Albans is generally reckoned the first battle of the Wars of the Roses, so called from the symbols adopted by the two parties, the red rose by Lancaster, the white by York. However, it was not until October 1460 that Richard of York pressed his claim to the throne, as senior descendant of King Edward III, through his mother, Anne Mortimer (see p. 46). On 30 December 1460 he was killed in battle at Wakefield, defeated by an army led by Henry Beaufort, Duke of Somerset, son of his old enemy.

Richard of York's claim to the throne was inherited by his son Edward, who marched on London, had himself proclaimed king there – as Edward IV – on 4 March 1461 and then soundly defeated the Lancastrians at Towton in Yorkshire on the 29th. For the time being, Henry VI was still at liberty, still the figurehead of the Lancastrian army, but in July 1463 he was captured by the Yorkists and brought ceremonially into London, to the Tower.

To those who had heard of the fate of Edward II and Richard II, it must have seemed inevitable that Henry VI would soon die in the Tower

– strangled, smothered or poisoned – but he did not. Even though his continued existence gave his supporters hope of his restoration, to the Yorkists it was better to have a live Henry (who could be paraded through London to prove that he still lived) than a dead Henry, replaced by his son, who was still free.

However, in 1469, Edward IV faced a challenge on a new front. His own brother, George, Duke of Clarence, joined forces with Richard Neville, Earl of Warwick, who had always been Edward's chief ally, to remove Edward from the throne. George's claim was that Edward was the son of their mother but not of their father, and so could have no right to be king. On 26 July Edward was defeated in battle at Edgecote in Oxfordshire and made a prisoner – but only for a few weeks: by mid-September he was free, apparently reconciled with his brother and with Warwick and restored to his throne. Then, the relationship deteriorated again, and in the spring Clarence and Warwick were forced to flee the country, denounced as traitors.

In France lived Henry VI's queen, Margaret of Anjou, and her son Edward, and now they found unlikely allies in Clarence and Warwick. In September 1470, all returned to England, bringing with them the nucleus of an army that was rapidly joined by Lancastrian sympathisers. It was now Edward IV's turn to leave the country, and Henry VI was brought out of his prison.

In the spring of 1471 the wheel of fate turned again. Edward IV reappeared, leading an army, and 'false, fleeting, perjur'd Clarence' defected from his enemies and was forgiven. On Easter Sunday, 14 April 1471, Edward defeated the army led by the Earl of Warwick, who died in the battle; on 4 May he inflicted a final, decisive defeat on the Lancastrians at Tewkesbury.

Chronicles written soon after the event say that Henry VI's heir, Edward of Lancaster, was killed during the Battle of Tewkesbury or in flight from the field. It is only the chronicles written much later, after the final fall of the Yorkist dynasty, that allege that the seventeen-year-old Prince was murdered: that he survived the battle to fall, as a prisoner, to the daggers of the Dukes of Clarence and Gloucester, Edward IV's brothers.

Henry VI was apparently still alive when Edward IV made his ceremonial entry into the City of London on 21 May, but on the evening of the 22nd his dead body was carried from the Tower to St Paul's Cathedral, to lie in state, the face exposed so that he might be identified.

It was given out at the time that the former King had died 'of pure displeasure and melancholy'. It seems more likely that Edward IV had decided that there was nothing to gain by keeping Henry alive any longer, and a danger that his continued existence would encourage Lancastrians not to accept their defeat. When Henry's bones were examined in 1910, it was found that his skull had been smashed in and that the remaining hair was matted with blood.

It had been a mistake to forgive Clarence his treachery, but Edward IV did not find that out until 1477. Since December 1476, when his wife died, Clarence had been pressing Edward to make diplomatic moves for him to marry the heiress of the huge and immensely wealthy duchy of Burgundy. This Edward refused to do, for it would not only revive the enmity of France, which had only recently been mollified after its 'war of independence', but afford Clarence the means of buying an army with which to press his claims to the English throne. The Duke was already repeating his allegation that the King was not the son of Richard, Duke of York, but was born of his duchess's adultery; further, he was having his servants spread the word that his brother Edward practised the 'black art' (witchcraft) and was using his esoteric knowledge to poison his enemies.

In April 1477 the Duke of Clarence ordered the arrest of a woman named Ankarette Twynho, a former servant of his late wife, and had her charged with having poisoned the Duchess. The jury that heard the case was terrorised into finding her guilty, and she was hanged, along with a man found guilty of having poisoned the Clarences' baby son. It seems obvious that the Duke meant people to read into the supposed murders the background malice of the King – or of the Woodvilles, the Queen's family (see p. 75). Elizabeth Woodville was known to blame Clarence for the execution of her father and brother John, as his prisoners, back in 1469.

Whether or not Clarence's suspicions about the prevalence of witchcraft in the royal family were true, he himself was apparently not guiltless. In May 1477 his servant Thomas Burdett was charged with having used necromancy to predict the King's imminent death – and of working to fulfil the prophecy. Burdett was hanged. He had not implicated the Duke of Clarence in his crime, but . . .

Clarence was arrested in late June 1477, but he was not tried until Parliament assembled, the following January. The King brought a bill of attainder against his brother and himself outlined the Duke's past crimes, his own leniency and Clarence's 'incorrigibility'. On 7 February 1478 Clarence was found guilty of treason and sentenced to death.

The Duke was executed privately in the Tower, Englishmen were told a few days later, but the story went round that Clarence had died by drowning in a butt of malmsey wine. It was said that he had once joked with the King about dying in this way, and that, when it came to the point, he had asked if that strange means of execution could be used.

Throughout Clarence's years of disloyalty and chicanery, King Edward could always rely on his other brother, Richard, Duke of Gloucester. Richard might not care for the Woodville element at Court (nor they for him) and he rarely appeared there, but his absence was apparently not seen as a disparagement. As 'Lord of the North' he was successful in imposing order on a formerly lawless region and reconciling it to the government of the Yorkist dynasty.

It was only when Edward IV died, on 9 April 1483, after a brief illness, that Richard's intentions became clear.

The heir of Edward IV was a boy twelve years old, Edward V. When his father died, he was at Ludlow Castle, on the border of Wales, and it was nearly a week before news came of his accession. It took even longer for messengers to ride to Middleham Castle in Yorkshire, where Richard, Duke of Gloucester, lived. In fact, his first informant was not a royal official but a man sent by a friend at Court, who also told him that he had been named regent for his nephew.

In Westminster, the boy King's Woodville uncles and his half-brothers, the Greys, had hoped to withhold the news from his uncle Richard, while they were deliberating how best to deal with him and keep their own power. They decided to confirm that the Duke was indeed 'Protector' of the King and kingdom but only as head of a regency council, not as sole ruler. They wrote at last to Richard, inviting him to meet up with Edward V at Northampton, on his route to London.

When Richard arrived at Northampton, on 29 April, he found that the King had not yet arrived. That evening he was joined by Anthony Woodville, Lord Rivers, who told him that Edward V had bypassed the town and was to spend the night at Stony Stratford. Rivers must have regretted that he did not ride away and do the same, for the next morning he woke up to find himself a prisoner. That day Richard of Gloucester also took possession of his nephew.

The news went ahead of them to the capital. Elizabeth Woodville, the Queen Mother, gathered her other children and, with her brother the Bishop of Salisbury and her elder son by her first marriage, the Marquess of Dorset, sought sanctuary in the precincts of Westminster Abbey.

Arriving in Westminster, Richard gave orders for preparations for the coronation and for the assembling of a new Parliament, but he also sent the Archbishop of Canterbury to persuade the Queen to give up her younger son, another Richard, the Duke of York. The nine-year-old was sent to join his brother the King in the Tower. Not that they were imprisoned there: it was customary then, and long after, for a monarch to spend the days before his coronation in residence in the Tower.

However, the Queen and her family were left in no doubt as to Richard's malice towards them when, on 23 June, her brother, Lord Rivers, and her younger Grey son were executed.

The day before was a Sunday, and as usual the citizens of London supplemented their church-attendance by flocking to listen to open-air sermons. To their surprise, the subject of some of them – by carefully primed preachers – was the assertion that Edward V, his brother and his sisters were not the legitimate children of the late King: Edward IV had been 'pre-contracted' to another woman when he married Elizabeth Woodville, so that their marriage was illegal and their children were ineligible for the crown. Similarly the Duke of Clarence's children could not inherit it, since their late father was a convicted traitor. So Richard of Gloucester was king of England – King Richard III. The same arguments were put to members of Parliament on 23 June. On 6 July Richard was crowned.

During the next few weeks, Edward V and his brother Richard were seen playing in the gardens of the Tower. Then, no more. At home and abroad, rumours began to circulate that 'the Princes in the Tower' were dead.

Of course, Richard III is the prime suspect for their murder. It could scarcely be otherwise. For centuries it was taken for granted. It is only in the past century that historians have claimed to be dissatisfied with the evidence against him and have looked elsewhere for the murderer.

The traditional story is that Richard III commissioned Sir James Tyrell to kill his nephews. Tyrell was given a letter addressed to the governor of the Tower of London, ordering him to surrender the keys to Tyrell, for one night. Thus he had the run of the large complex of fortified buildings that made up the Tower of London. At dead of night, he and two other men, Miles Forrest and John Dighton, went unchallenged to the room in which the boys were sleeping. Tyrell himself stayed outside; Forrest and Dighton entered and smothered the boys in their bed.

That was the story recounted by Sir Thomas More in *The History of King Richard the Third*, which he wrote in the teens of the sixteenth century. More was a lawyer, used to dealing with fragmentary evidence and marshalling it into a persuasive case; he was also accustomed to assessing the truth of the stories told to him, and in this instance he took those that came from 'them that knew much and had little cause to lie'. More was also a man of the highest integrity: in 1535 he was executed for putting loyalty to the Church above obedience to the King. Whatever he wrote about the death of 'the Princes in the Tower', he believed. There is also evidence from Richard III's own brief reign, in chronicles and letters, to show that his subjects believed that he had killed his nephews.

In August 1485 Richard III was defeated and killed in battle by Henry Tudor, a member of the House of Lancaster, who became King Henry VII. Thereafter the stories of Richard's crime increased – and it was also said that he had killed Edward of Lancaster and been present at the murder of King Henry VI and the highly unusual execution of George, Duke of Clarence; and it was even alleged that he was responsible for the death of his own wife, though in fact she had been ill for several months before she died. Taken together, this shows just how deliberate was the blackening of Richard III's character in the years following his death, in order to justify his deposition.

It is this that has led some modern historians to publish elaborate and persuasive vindications of Richard III. They base their case primarily on Richard's 'good character' up to the moment of his deposition of Edward V; indeed, they also attempt to show that he was justified in dethroning his nephew. Then there is analysis of the sources of the story of the Tyrell murder, allegedly instigated by Richard, which certainly does show that the bulk of the material comes from the reign of Henry VII and so was certainly coloured by antipathy to the House of York, and especially to Henry's predecessor, which was understandable under the new regime. Some have, in fact, made out a case against Henry himself: that he found Edward V and Richard of York still alive, in the Tower, when he became king, and that he had them killed lest they become future leaders of the Yorkist cause. The Yorkists had been placated by Henry's marriage to the eldest sister and heiress of Edward V, but Henry's reign was still troubled by their rebellions: one on behalf of Richard of York, the other for Clarence's son – or rather, for impostors posing as those princes.

There are points in the case that exonerates Richard which do bear serious consideration; it is impossible to dismiss the modern interpretation of evidence and analysis of sources that would clear Richard's name and his labelling as the archetypal 'wicked uncle'. In fact, a trial of Richard III, on television in 1984, did just that. But the trial was conducted under the English system of law, which demands a 'guilty' or 'not guilty' verdict. It would surely be more realistic to bring in the verdict permissible in Scottish law: 'not proven'.

It was not unknown, in the Middle Ages, for a king to be at variance with his heir: in the twelfth century, for example, the three elder sons of Henry II, King of England, mounted rebellions against their father. Nor was every king satisfied with the worthiness of his heir apparent to succeed him: Shakespeare effectively dramatised the tension between England's King Henry IV and his son the future King Henry V, in the fifteenth century. However, medieval history holds no example of a king having his son killed, to prevent his succeeding to the throne. That was a crime first attributed to Philip II, King of Spain between 1556 and 1598, who was alleged to have had his son Carlos murdered. (See also p. 130 for a Russian example of the crime, in the eighteenth century.)

Don Carlos was born in 1545, Philip II's son by his first wife, Maria of Portugal. Philip and Maria were not only first cousins but the children of first cousins, so that the family trait of insanity was strong in their heredity. From childhood Carlos was prone to sudden, violent tempers; after a fall in 1562, when he was found unconscious after hitting his head, his eccentricities became detrimental to his dignity – and occasionally dangerous. For example, one story had it that when the Prince took a dislike to a new pair of boots, he had them cut up, stewed and fed forcibly to the unfortunate cobbler.

In 1567 Carlos became president of Spain's Council of State, which suggests that his father put some trust in his heir. At the same time, however, Philip suspected that his son was in touch with the Dutch rebels and that he was preparing to leave Spain to join them.

On Christmas Day 1567, Don Carlos made his confession to the Prior of Atocha, asking absolution for the sin – the crime – that he was planning to commit. When the Prior heard that the Prince was intending to kill a man, he refused him absolution and with keen questioning discovered that the intended victim was the Prince's own father. Immediately he sent a message to the King.

On the night of 18/19 January 1568, Philip II entered his son's bedroom, accompanied by a dozen guards.

First the Prince's weapons and papers were removed, then the room was entirely stripped, except for the bed and mattress. When Don Carlos tried to throw himself on the fire, he was restrained until it could be put out. Bars were placed on the windows and guards left at the door. Don Carlos was not seen again.

On 24 July it was announced that the heir to the throne of Spain had died. The King informed the Courts of Europe that his son had long been trying to kill himself, first by starvation, then by over-eating, by lying naked among blocks of ice, by trying to set fire to his bed . . . Eventually, Philip said, Carlos had died of a fever, brought on by those excesses. At the last the King had visited the Prince but had found him unconscious; he had given his son his blessing before he died.

The truth of the matter is impossible to determine. Possibly Don Carlos was planning treason and was imprisoned and killed at his father's orders, the rumours of his madness being a cover for the murder. More likely, Don Carlos would today be diagnosed schizophrenic, did have treasonous plans (even his father's murder) and was given free rein to kill himself in his own inefficient way.

CHAPTER FOUR

SCOTLAND

There is something in human nature that makes a murder story appealing to all sorts of people. That was as true in past centuries as it is in the present. When Shakespeare was writing his plays, he made shrewd use of violence, often engaging his audience's emotions in sympathy not only with the victim but also with the murderer. The psychological insights he brought to his subjects invested them with enduring power.

Shakespeare also knew how to tailor a play to a specific audience, and he could turn the 'bare bones' of history into a masterpiece of tragic drama. That is what he did when he was commissioned to write a play to be performed at the palace of Hampton Court on 7 August 1606 in the presence of James I, King of England, who was also James VI, King of Scotland, and had come south only some three years earlier, to inspect his new realm.

In writing *Macbeth*, Shakespeare not only chose as his plot a theme from Scottish history but found one that featured witchcraft, in which the King was keenly interested. In Shakespeare's play, three witches prophesy that the Scottish nobleman Macbeth will become king of Scotland; to do so, he murders King Duncan, but then he is himself overthrown and killed.

The history of Macbeth's reign (1040–57) was not recorded in detail until some four or five centuries after his death. Chroniclers built (and elaborated) on early, fragmentary works. Legends were incorporated into the chronicles along with known facts, and with the chroniclers' interpretation of events adding colour to them. Shakespeare may have read the story of Macbeth in the chronicle of Raphael Holinshed, from which he derived his plays on English history. Holinshed's work did refer to the Scottish witches – a 'find' for the playwright seeking to cater for the King's interests.

Macbeth was only one of several early Scottish monarchs who killed a king, seized the throne and then met with a violent death, murdered or killed in battle against a rival. In 997 King Constantine III was killed by the man who became his successor, Kenneth III; in 1005 Kenneth III was killed by Malcolm II; in 1040 Malcolm II's grandson Duncan I was killed by Macbeth; and after ruling for seventeen years, Macbeth was killed by Duncan I's son Malcolm, who also killed Macbeth's stepson, King Lulach, in 1058, and became king as Malcolm III. (Malcolm III was himself murdered in an ambush in 1093, but not by a rival for the crown.)

What gave rise to these murders was the fact that the principle of primogeniture was not yet established in Scotland – that is to say, a king was not automatically succeeded by his eldest son. When a king died, the most suitable of his kinsmen mounted the throne, and his suitability was generally determined by the power he already wielded. But in the eleventh century, members of the Scottish royal family did not wait for a king to die naturally before seizing the crown.

However, the establishment of the law – or at least the custom – of primogeniture in the twelfth century was not enough to ensure the peaceful transition of the Scottish crown. In 1290 the royal family died out in the senior line, and a dozen contenders from among the last monarchs' distant cousins vied for the throne, in civil war. Edward I, King of England, was called in to adjudicate between the claimants and in 1292 awarded the crown to John Balliol. But Balliol's acknowledgement of England's suzerainty was against him in Scottish eyes, and he was deposed in favour of his cousin Robert Bruce – Robert I.

Then again, in the next generation, the royal family died out in the male line, and the throne passed to Robert I's grandson, Robert Stewart. Of the nine Stewart monarchs, seven came to the throne as children. Their minorities entailed the choice of a regent or regents to rule for them, which inevitably sparked off violent feuding among the nobility.

Robert III was one of the exceptions, not a minor but a man in his fifties when he came to the throne in 1390. But he was an invalid, having been kicked by a horse and sustained injuries that debilitated him for the rest of his life. For the first three years of his reign, his government was dominated by his younger brother Robert, Duke of

Albany,* and when the King did attempt to rule personally, from 1393, he was so inept that he soon lost control of the kingdom. In 1399, his heir, David, Duke of Rothesay, was appointed 'lieutenant of the kingdom', but under the watchful eyes of a body of councillors, of whom Albany was the chief. History does not record the exact reason why Rothesay was removed from office, only that he was found so self-indulgent, devious and venal that he was imprisoned in Falkland Castle – with his father's approval but probably at his uncle Albany's instigation. Albany is also said to have had Rothesay starved to death, in 1402.

Robert III's heir was replaced by Rothesay's younger brother, James, who – perhaps for fear of Albany – was dispatched to France in 1406, when he was only twelve years old. Unfortunately, his ship was captured by pirates and the boy was delivered to the King of England, Henry IV. A month later, Robert III died, and James became king of Scotland *in absentia*. King Henry had no intention of sending him home. That left Albany a free hand to rule until his death in 1420. He did not make any strenuous attempt to secure his nephew's freedom.

James I remained in England, in luxurious and informal captivity, until April 1424, when he returned home at last. He had agreed to pay a vast indemnity to England, to purchase his freedom, but one sixth of it was remitted in lieu of the dowry of the English wife he took with him to Scotland.

James I wasted no time before beginning to establish his personal rule, reclaiming the Crown lands that had been lost during his absence and imposing heavy taxes, largely to cover his English payments. Though there is no doubt that James took these measures for his own immediate enrichment, he was also far-seeing in his plans for Scotland's government. The nobles had become too powerful during the interregnum; in particular, those in the north and west of Scotland had become independent of central government. James set out to curb these tendencies, largely

* The brothers were not originally both named Robert. The King had been baptised John but had chosen to take his father's name at his accession because John was held to be an unlucky name for kings (in Scotland, England and France).

through Parliament, whose representation he broadened and whose workload he increased, with a batch of new laws. Inevitably his activities made him enemies.

James and his queen spent Christmas 1436 at the Blackfriars (Dominican) monastery in Perth, and they were still there in February 1437. On the night of 20 February, while James was preparing to go to bed, his domestic chamberlain, Sir Robert Stewart, admitted eight armed men to the royal apartments. On their way to the King's chamber, they encountered his page, Walter Straton, going for wine for James, and they cut him down with their swords. Alerted by the noise, the King sought some means of escape, but there was none. He started tearing up the floorboards and, though he was a corpulent man, succeeded in squeezing into the space below them. According to tradition, one of the Queen's ladies-in-waiting, Catherine Douglas, was in the room and, seeing that the door lacked a bar to hold it shut, slid her arm into the latch, only to have it broken when the intruders burst in. Not seeing the King in the room, they might have left to seek him elsewhere, but James emerged too soon from his hiding-place, and immediately they were upon him. He put up a fight – and so did the Queen, Joan Beaufort, who was wounded – but he was stabbed to death with swords and daggers.

The instigator of the royal murder was the King's uncle Walter, Earl of Atholl, who believed himself rightful king of Scotland. Add this to James I's unpopularity and Walter had reason to think (or to persuade himself) that Scotland would hail him as the next king, rather than James I's six-year-old son. In fact, Walter was nearly eighty, and his ambition may have been more for his descendants than for himself: his grandson and heir was that Sir Robert Stewart who had admitted the murderers to the royal apartments. However, lords and commons rallied to the young James II, and his father's murderers were hunted down and executed, Athol and his grandson among them.

The royal minority was, of course, an opportunity for the nobles of Scotland to weaken the centralised government that James I had worked so strenuously to establish; without it, they were free to return to the feuding that seemed intrinsic in their way of life. It was not until 1449, when he was eighteen, that James II took control of his kingdom. Scotland was in a parlous state, racked by the nobles' feuding, their small armies raiding and ravaging from the Highlands to the Borders – which were also the prey of the English.

James II had apparently studied the policies of his late father; he achieved a considerable measure of success when he himself used them. But he was a man of action as well as an administrator: in 1452 the King stabbed to death the eighth Earl of Douglas, the most land-wealthy man in Scotland; three years later the Douglas estates were annexed to the Crown, after members of the clan had raised a rebellion. It was a turning-point in the reign, a proof of James's strength; he was even popular – or at least admired – among the nobles he forced to abide by his laws. But James died at the age of twenty-nine, accidentally killed at the siege of Roxburgh in 1460, and yet again Scotland had a child king: James III was nine years old.

And James III was another Scottish king who was murdered. He survived the first intrigues and rebellions of his nobles, the destruction of his 'low-born' favourites, the depredations of the English, only to die, at the age of thirty-two, as a result of a nobles' rebellion. He had engaged them in battle at Sauchieburn, near Stirling, on 11 June 1488 and was facing defeat when suddenly his horse bolted from the field (so it was said; the King may have been fleeing). After falling from his horse, James staggered to the nearby house of a miller and there, in the kitchen, he was murdered – by a man who was never identified.

The new king, James IV, was only fifteen years old. It seems that, though he had been a prisoner of his father's enemies at the time of their rebellion, he had sympathised with their cause; now he felt a strong sense of guilt for the King's death. He is known to have gone through the whole of his later life wearing a metal belt under his clothes, a permanent weight on him, a reminder of the sin that all his penances and pilgrimages could not purge from his conscience. Like his predecessors, James IV did not live into old age: he was only forty when he was killed at the Battle of Flodden, at war with the English, in 1513.

Like the unexplained deaths of King Edward V and his brother Richard in England in the late fifteenth century, the murder of Henry Stuart, Lord Darnley, in Scotland in 1566 has become one of history's most cherished 'whodunits'. The names of the instigator and perpetrators of Darnley's murder are known: what remains a mystery is the degree of guilt of Darnley's wife, Mary, Queen of Scots.

Mary had been queen since 14 December 1542, when she was only six days old. Between 1548 and 1561, she had lived in France, latterly as the consort of King François II. After his death in 1560, Mary returned to Scotland, and on 29 July 1565 she married Darnley, who was her cousin and some five years her junior. He soon found out that the title of king, which Mary bestowed on him, had minimal substance and that, when his wife did not thwart his ambition to rule, her nobles did. Chief among his enemies was Mary's half-brother James Stewart, Earl of Moray; before Mary's return from France, he had been one of the most powerful men in the kingdom, and he thoroughly resented the pretensions of the young, untrained, untried Darnley. A month after the royal wedding, Moray led a rebellion, was firmly trounced and fled to England. However, the elimination of such a rival did nothing to promote Darnley in his wife's small circle of councillors.

The couple sparred incessantly; Mary was arrogant, Darnley petulant. Soon, too, Darnley came to resent the influence of the Queen's Italian secretary, David Rizzio, but then his confidential position in Mary's household, coupled with the suspicion that he was a papal spy, caused Rizzio to be generally hated. It was bad enough that Mary was a Catholic, in Presbyterian Scotland; now it was feared that Rizzio would harden her heart against her 'heretical' subjects. Mary was not a fanatic in the strain of her Guise uncles (see p. 91), but she was still regarded with mistrust by her Protestant nobles, even though she had hitherto been commendably tolerant of their religion. Rizzio's political influence was also a constant irritant to the lords of Mary's Court and council; Darnley felt himself more hard-done-by than anyone.

On the evening of Saturday 9 March 1566, Queen Mary and five close friends, including Rizzio, sat down to supper in the palace of Holyroodhouse in Edinburgh: not in one of the vast state rooms but in a small, very private chamber. (It can still be seen today, looking much as it did in 1566.) Supper was on the table, and the Queen's guests were being served when suddenly Lord Darnley appeared among them, having come into the room by a small staircase connecting with his own apartments on the floor below. It was unusual for Darnley to figure in his wife's intimate suppers, but her guests made him politely welcome. Not so the next man to enter, by the same privy stairs: Patrick, Lord Ruthven, came clad in armour.

'Let it please your Majesty that yonder man David come forth of your privy chamber, where he hath been overlong.'

When Ruthven drew his dagger, it was as if he had given a signal, for at that moment five more men entered the room. Rizzio clung to Mary's skirts, but they dragged him away, out of the room, and his cries could be heard until he was killed, his body pierced by the swords and daggers of his assailants.

Years later, when Mary wrote an account of that night, she alleged that Darnley had meant that she should be killed at the same time and, since she was pregnant, that their child should die with her, leaving her husband to reign in Scotland. When the candles were extinguished during the scuffle with Rizzio, had Lady Argyll not saved the last one, Mary might well have been killed in the pitch darkness – 'accidentally', of course.

The Queen wept when she was told of Rizzio's death but soon regained control of herself. 'Enough of grief,' she said; 'I will study revenge.'

Left alone, Mary passed the night to some effect, for by morning she had formulated a plan that served her well. She was conciliatory towards the lords who had supported Ruthven, putting them off their guard, and she played on Darnley's natural cowardice by persuading him that both their lives were now in danger from those who had killed Rizzio. That night they fled Edinburgh and took refuge in Dunbar Castle. Mary summoned her friends and on 18 March she re-entered the capital at the head of some 8,000 loyal Scotsmen. Her enemies dispersed.

On 19 June Mary and Darnley's child was born: a son, the future King James VI.

Relations between Mary and Darnley deteriorated again that summer, and in November, when her councillors suggested that she seek a divorce from him, the Queen was amenable – at first, that is: on reflection, divorce was impossible. In those days, the word 'divorce' meant 'annulment': some pretext would be sought to 'prove' that Mary and Darnley's marriage had in fact been illegal; this would mean that their son was illegitimate. Mary could not afford to lose her heir.

In January 1567 Darnley fell ill – of smallpox, it was said; it was probably syphilis. Although Mary believed that her husband had again been plotting against her (perhaps to kidnap their son), she joined him in Glasgow, intending to move the invalid back to Edinburgh. Their party paused just outside Edinburgh, at a house hard by an old church, the Kirk o'Field; Darnley himself chose it for his final few days of convalescence before entering Edinburgh. He moved in on Saturday 1 February. The Queen went on, into the city, but she returned to spend the Wednesday night at Kirk o'Field. The couple's relationship seemed improved.

Darnley was to go home to Holyroodhouse on Monday 10 February and initially Mary intended to spend Sunday night at Kirk o'Field. However, late that evening she decided to go on to Holyrood without her husband (remembering that there was to be a masque there, to celebrate the wedding of two members of her household). It would be unreasonable for her to return all the way to Kirk o'Field that night only to leave it again next morning. So Mary rode away, leaving her husband to spend his last night at Kirk o'Field.

'His last night': it was, in fact, the last night of his life. At about two in the morning, an explosion tore through the house. So loud was the blast that it was heard in Edinburgh: the Queen heard it and sent to find out what had happened. But it was not the explosion that killed Darnley. His body was found in the garden; it bore no mark of the blast but nor was there a sword or dagger wound. He had been strangled. Nearby lay his servant William Taylor, also dead.

When Darnley's father, the Earl of Lennox, heard the news, he thought he knew where the blame lay: the murder was the work of his daughter-in-law. Lennox drew up a document in which he laid out the history of the couple's marriage, from Mary's love-at-first-sight attraction to Darnley, through her cooling-off (which Lennox attributed to Rizzio's malign influence) to her actual presence, disguised as a man, at the murder of her husband. She had, Lennox said, taken James Hepburn, Lord Bothwell, as her lover, and she had accompanied Bothwell and his men to Kirk o'Field that night.

Over a year later, when the lesser characters in the drama were rounded up, some details emerged. Bothwell had indeed been the instigator of the murder, but whether other lords – even Lord Moray, who had suddenly left Edinburgh the day before Darnley's death – had been involved was never elicited. Bothwell had supervised the laying of the gunpowder at Kirk o'Field. The fact that Darnley was found outside, unharmed by the explosion, must be laid to his having heard something, taken fright and left the building, with his servant, only to be set on by the men who then killed him. This was included in Lord Lennox's account of Darnley's murder, which he must have put together from various sources, since he had not been there at the time.

Whatever the means, one thing seems clear: Darnley had been murdered by Bothwell, perhaps because he sought to become Mary's third husband, perhaps in revenge for Darnley's betrayal of those who had killed Rizzio (of whom Bothwell was one) – probably from a combination of both motives. Whether, as Lennox suspected, Mary had known of the murder plot (let alone been present at Darnley's death) can never now be proved. She spent the rest of her life denying it.

It has been suggested that the Earl of Moray was behind the plot and that he had intended that Mary should die with Darnley, in the powder explosion that would leave no traces of its perpetrators. Had Mary died, Moray would have been the prime candidate to become her son's regent during his infancy. His absence at the time of the murder would leave him apparently guiltless. In fact, his name was never breathed when Bothwell's men were rounded up.

Bothwell himself stood trial for the murder, on 12 April, Lord Lennox having insisted on it. But Lennox himself was absent (fearing to enter Edinburgh, packed with Bothwell's men), and without his voice for the prosecution, Bothwell was acquitted.

On 24 April, as the Queen was riding from Linlithgow to Edinburgh, her small party was suddenly surrounded by a force of some 800 men, with Bothwell at their head. He took her by force to Dunbar Castle, and there he raped her, as persuasion that she should marry him, for only marriage could leave her name untarnished. Or so it was said.

Mary's enemies always asserted that the abduction and apparently forced marriage were only a cover for Mary's real determination to marry the man who had long been her lover and who had killed her husband just for this.

Mary and Bothwell were married on 15 May 1567. Exactly a month later, the couple were heading an army that faced a far larger force mounted by Scotland's lords at Carberry Hill, some eight miles east of Edinburgh. Over the rebels' army floated a banner on which Lord Darnley was depicted lying dead under a tree, his baby son kneeling beside him. But the day passed without a show of arms; it was taken up with challenge and counter-challenge to single combat between the leaders of the two parties. That evening Bothwell rode away; he knew what his fate would be if he fell into the hands of his enemies. He left his wife to certain capture. (Bothwell was subsequently outlawed; he managed to escape to the Orkneys and thence to Norway, where he died – insane and in prison – in 1578.)

The remaining story of Mary, Queen of Scots, is quickly told. She was held captive in the island fortress at Lochleven, where she was forced – under threat of having her throat cut – to sign a deed of abdication in favour of her son, who became King James VI of Scotland. When she escaped, she found friends to support her but was again defeated and on 16 May 1568 entered England. Her cousin Queen Elizabeth granted her refuge but it soon became clear that Mary was not a guest but a prisoner of the English. Enquiries into her suspected complicity in Darnley's murder were inconclusive; England's queen refused to meet the woman who had claimed that kingdom for herself; Mary was left in comfortable confinement in the provinces as year succeeded year.

However, the Queen of Scots was not friendless. She had supporters in Scotland, 'the Marian lords', who kept hope alive of her restoration until their stronghold, Edinburgh Castle, fell in 1573. Mary also had friends in England. As a Catholic and as the senior cousin of Queen Elizabeth, she was the hope of every English Catholic who prayed for the restoration of their Church under a Catholic sovereign. If Mary could only outlive Elizabeth, there was a strong chance that she would succeed her on the English throne. And there were those who did not scruple at planning to shorten Elizabeth's natural life (see pp. 98–100). During the twenty-odd years of Mary Stuart's captivity in England, her hopes were raised time and again as news of various plots and conspiracies was passed to her.

In fact, Mary's 'secret' correspondence with English Catholics and with foreign powers was well known to Burghley and Walsingham, the statesmen who of all men in England had the most to lose if Elizabeth Tudor should ever be murdered and replaced on the throne by her cousin Mary. However, it took them a long time to convince their queen that Mary actually approved the plots in which her (Elizabeth's) death was a necessary feature. But in the 1580s, as evidence mounted of the rising impetus of Catholic treason, Elizabeth was forced to listen to her councillors; the murder of William, Prince of Orange, in 1584 (see pp. 95–6) gave Burghley and Walsingham an even more powerful argument. Then, in 1586, a vital piece of evidence came into their hands: letters in which Mary apparently approved a plot to kill Elizabeth. It was a part of the intrigue originating from an idealistic and energetic young man called Francis Babington, one of Mary's Catholic supporters. Elizabeth was to be killed, Mary enthroned – and Mary's own handwriting proved that she was implicated.

Of course, the former Queen of Scots could not be indicted for high treason, since she was not a subject of the English Queen, but an ideal solution was conveniently at hand – and not accidentally, for Burghley and Walsingham had had Mary's downfall in mind for some time. That solution was the use of an Act of Parliament passed in 1585, which declared that, should Queen Elizabeth be murdered, not only the killer but also the person who benefited from her death – that is, the person who claimed the throne – would be subject to the death penalty if that person could be proved to have known of the plot in advance. That was why proof of Mary's foreknowledge of the Babington plot was so important.

In October 1586 the Queen of Scots was brought to trial before a specially appointed tribunal that met at Fotheringhay Castle in Northamptonshire. Both Houses of Parliament backed up the tribunal's judgment: Mary was guilty, and she must die for her crime.

It was 1 February 1587 before Elizabeth could bring herself to sign her cousin's death warrant. The next day she changed her mind and tried to prevent its being taken to the Lord Chancellor to have the Great Seal affixed – too late: it had already been done. Walsingham was ill; Burghley took command: he summoned a meeting of the Council and persuaded its members to take responsibility for issuing the death warrant, keeping it secret from the Queen.

On 8 February, at Fotheringhay, Mary, Queen of Scots, was beheaded. When Elizabeth heard the news, she raged at everyone around her. Even her old friend Burghley found it wise to leave Court for a time. But surely Elizabeth's horror was tempered by relief: the chief claimant to her throne, the only one for whom men would risk their lives, had been removed.

The term 'judicial murder' refers to the killing of a person judged guilty of a capital offence by an illegal court or by a properly constituted court but without the safeguards that protect the defendant, such as a properly mounted defence: Mary Stuart was allowed no such defence at her trial. Another factor in 'judicial murder' is conviction on insufficient or fabricated evidence, under pressure from the authorities: it seems likely that, even if evidence against Mary was not deliberately manufactured, at the least she was entrapped into condoning Queen Elizabeth's murder. And in everyone's mind, although it was not part of the charges against Mary Stuart, was the murder of Lord Darnley, some twenty years earlier, in which his wife's part had never been fully explained or her innocence proved.

James VI, son of Mary and Darnley, was only thirteen months old when he came to the throne of Scotland. He was brought up amid open discussion of his mother's suspected role in his father's death, and protected from any contact with her or her former friends. His first regent, Mary's half-brother, the Earl of Moray, was murdered by a Hamilton, a member of the Marian party, in January 1570, shot dead in the main street of Linlithgow. In August 1571, his second regent, his paternal grandfather the Earl of Lennox, was murdered during a Marian attack on the town of Stirling. Throughout James's childhood and youth, Scotland was riven by clan feuds as well as by the nobles' unceasing rivalry for places in the regency council.

With such a heredity and upbringing, it is not surprising that James became timid, neurotic, unstable and terrified of violence – to the point at which he even disliked hearing accounts of foreign wars. He also feared supernatural forces: he was avidly interested in witchcraft and in the early 1590s convinced himself that Scottish witches were conspiring to bring about his death (see p. 80).

On 5 August 1600 James went hunting near Falkland and then went to dine with John Ruthven, Earl of Gowrie, at Gowrie House near Perth. The Earl's younger brother Alexander, Master of Ruthven, aged nineteen, was a favourite of James, who had a penchant for attractive young men, but the family had a history of bad relations with the royal family. Two generations earlier, an Earl of Gowrie had been one of Rizzio's murderers, and his son had been beheaded in 1584 after his 'Ruthven Raid' had effected the capture of the young King, who was held a virtual prisoner for a year before he regained his freedom.

The events that followed the dinner at Gowrie House are known only from King James's own account. He said that he had gone there on the invitation of the Master of Ruthven, who had told him a story of a man with a crock of gold, who should be investigated. After dinner, the King and the Master went off together, passing through several chambers (each locked behind them by the Master) until they reached a room in a tower, where there was indeed a man waiting for them, but no sign of gold. The man wore armour. The Master of Ruthven threatened James with death, reminding him of the execution of his (Ruthven's) father. James reasoned with him, and did so to such effect that Ruthven calmed down and went off to find his brother. The man in armour was obviously troubled by the assault on the King, and James managed to persuade him to open a window – just in time, for Ruthven returned and renewed his threats. A fight ensued, but the King managed to hold his own and to reach the window, shouting for help.

Meanwhile James's party had been told that he had already left, and they went out to the courtyard to take horse. That was when they heard James's cries. The first to reach him was his page, John Ramsey, who saw the King and Ruthven still grappling. Ramsey stabbed Ruthven with his dagger. Among the men now filling the room was the Earl of Gowrie. Seeing his brother, he tried to escape but he was cut down.

Even at the time, the King's story was disbelieved. How could the Ruthvens have hoped to get away with killing him? And what did they expect to gain from it – apart from the satisfaction of revenge? Was that enough to warrant their risk? On the other hand, the suspicion that James himself engineered the incident, in order to justify the murder of the Ruthven brothers, is also hard to believe. He was so timid, so fearful of cold steel, that he could never have nerved himself to provoke a fight. Is it possible that the King, a latent homosexual, made advances to the Master of Ruthven, was rebuffed violently and called for help? In any event, the presence of the man in armour – never identified – remains an element of mystery.

The Ruthven brothers were named traitors. Their bodies were quartered and sent out to be displayed, as a warning to others. The earldom of Gowrie was held forfeit, and all the Ruthven estates were taken into royal possession.

If James is to be believed, this was his closest encounter with violence. But it was not his last. In January 1603, on the death of his cousin Elizabeth Tudor, he became James I, King of England, and three months later he rode south, to take possession of his new kingdom. In November 1605, the King learned of a large-scale plot to kill not only him but members of his family and his lords and commons. This was the Gunpowder Plot (see pp. 101–5). At the time, its discovery and thwarting were seen as providential; they have been celebrated annually ever since.

With James's removal to England, Scotland became of secondary importance to the Anglo-Scots (later British) monarchs. Larger, richer England became their powerbase.

CHAPTER FIVE

MURDER BY MAGIC

To the people of the Middle Ages, murder by magic was a fact. No one doubted that a witch or sorcerer could conjure up the Devil and harness his power to procure a death. Witchcraft and poisoning seemed inseparably linked, and so they remained until the Enlightenment of the eighteenth century began to put superstition to flight.

Witchcraft and wantonness were also linked. It was all a matter of women's fallen nature. They were the daughters of Eve, the original woman who had succumbed to the temptation of the Devil and who in her turn had tempted man to sin.

In 1388, Sibilia de Forcia, dowager Queen of Aragon, was accused of having attempted to kill her stepson, King Juan I. Her witchcraft had failed to kill him, but his brief reign was marked by his persistent ill-health. The Queen was tortured, but she made no confession, and the pleas of the papal legate won her reprieve. She was briefly imprisoned, then allowed to enter a convent.

In 1419, Jeanne of Navarre, widow of King Henry IV of England, was accused of having used witchcraft to seek the death of her stepson Henry V. Jeanne was convicted – without a trial – largely on evidence given by her chaplain, who admitted that he had helped her in her nefarious practices. All the Queen's property was confiscated and she was imprisoned – but only briefly: in 1422, a few weeks before his death (by natural causes), Henry V released her and restored her property. Jeanne lived on until 1437, when she joined her late husband in an ornate double tomb in Canterbury Cathedral. Nevertheless, between 1441 and 1485 there were further allegations of witchcraft in royal circles (see pp. 74–6).

An interesting factor in the stories of Sibilia de Forcia and Jeanne of Navarre is that, though both were stepmothers of kings, neither had a son with a rival claim to the throne. Had Sibilia or Jeanne sought to kill her stepson to promote her own son, her crime would be understandable: as it is, the lack of any motive but malice makes the charges against them dubious.

More intriguing, of course, is the introduction of witchcraft as a means of murder. Although there were occasional convictions of men for witchcraft, it was a charge more usually levelled against women.

In the Middle Ages, witchcraft appeared in many guises. There were 'wise women', skilled in midwifery and herbal medicine, who could be bribed to produce an aphrodisiac or some means of terminating pregnancy. Then there were the fortune-tellers – usually men, who as learned clerks or priests could make predictions of the future based on the planets' movements. Their work verged not only on heresy but on crime, for they were often called upon to predict someone's death, the client perhaps having expectations of a legacy; this was only one step away from using magic to kill. Then there were the witches who were said to be able to conjure up the dead, or even to summon Satan and his demons from Hell, and to have sold their souls to Satan in return for their magic powers.

Murder by magic was alleged to take several forms. For example, more powerful than a simply recited spell was the making of an image of a man or woman in wax or clay, over which a spell would be said while pins were inserted. (This was called 'sympathetic magic'.) Another method was the 'Black Fast': the witch would take no meat, milk or dairy products for a period during which she would concentrate her will on killing a certain person. In 1538 one Mabel Brigge was executed in York for trying to kill King Henry VIII by the Black Fast; it was alleged that she had already killed one man, who had broken his neck during the period of her fast.

There were laws against witchcraft, of course. As early as the reign of King Alfred, the death sentence had been imposed for murder by witchcraft. However, it was notoriously difficult to prove that witchcraft had been the actual cause of death.

It has been suggested that medieval witchcraft was a survival of the pre-Christian religion in which the powers of Nature were worshipped and invoked for good or ill. In this case, it was not Devil-worship, as the late-medieval Church insisted, when witchcraft had become linked with heresy. In fact, the uniformity of witch rites and coven organisation throughout Europe does suggest some ancient source common to all. Also, there were remnants of the 'Old Religion' in, for example, the fertility dances, May Day festivals and Hallowe'en traditions that survived for centuries in rural areas. It seems that the Christian who knelt in church on a Sunday may well have come there from an all-night ritual-cum-feast-cum-orgy at an ancient site of worship, such as a stone circle.

Circumstantial evidence suggests that Jeanne of Navarre was a member of a coven of witches at the English Court, for the wives of two of her stepsons were also supposedly witches.

The first was Eleanor Cobham, wife of Humphrey, Duke of Gloucester. He was the younger brother of King Henry V and guardian of the infant King Henry VI, his nephew: this must be borne in mind when considering the charges against the Duchess, for Gloucester was both heir presumptive to the crown and the most powerful man in England during the King's minority, making many enemies.

Eleanor was arrested on 25 June 1441 at the King's Head tavern in Cheapside, London, from which she was watching a military review. On 25 July she appeared before two bishops and the two archbishops in St Stephen's Chapel, Westminster, and was remanded in custody until October, while a commission looked into allegations against her.

When, in October, the Duchess stood trial before a Church court, it appeared that the sum total of charges against her were four: that when she was a lady-in-waiting to Gloucester's first wife, she had procured a love-potion to enchant him, with the result that he had married her; that she had used witchcraft in an attempt to become pregnant, after several years of childless marriage; that she had consulted an astrologer to learn 'to what estate she should come in the future' – since her husband was heir presumptive to the throne, that could only mean that she had wanted to know if he would succeed Henry VI; fourthly – and this was the only one of the charges the Duchess refuted – it was said that she had tried to 'encompass the death' of the King.

Evidence against the Duchess was supplied by two priests (the astrologers) and one other woman, Margery Jourdemain, called 'the Witch of Eye', who had supplied the love-potion and supposed means to help Eleanor become pregnant. Margery had already been tried for witchcraft ten years before but had been cleared; this time she was convicted and sent to the stake at Smithfield. Of the two priests, convicted of treason, one was hanged, drawn and quartered, the other died in prison.

Presumably because of her high rank, the Duchess's life was spared. Her sentence, proclaimed on 9 November, was in two parts. First, she was to walk, on three occasions, through the streets of London, bare-headed and bare-legged, in a coarse, short gown, carrying a two-pound candle to be placed on the altar of a stipulated church. On each occasion the Lord Mayor, sheriffs and leaders of the craft guilds accompanied her, and crowds turned out to watch the fun. Then, having tasted public humiliation, Eleanor must disappear into total seclusion, a prisoner in distant castles, such as those on the Isle of Man and in Flint, where she died in about 1454.

As to the Duke of Gloucester, his reaction to his wife's crime and punishment was never recorded. It seems likely that, whether Eleanor practised witchcraft or not, the charges against her were brought to discredit Gloucester himself, to attack his power in government (see p. 48).

The second of the royal duchesses to be called a witch was Jacquette of St-Pol, second wife of John, Duke of Bedford, another younger brother of Henry V. He had died in 1435 and Jacquette had then 'married beneath her', becoming the wife of Sir Richard Woodville. As such, she might have lived out her life in obscurity, but her daughter Elizabeth, herself a young widow, attracted the attention of King Edward IV – and married him, secretly, on 1 May 1464. When the marriage was proclaimed, it was a matter for wonder that the King had condescended to marry a mere knight's daughter. This was remembered in 1469, when Edward was temporarily dethroned and his enemies were amassing charges against her friends and relations. It was then that Jacquette was accused of having used witchcraft to procure her daughter's marriage. Before she could be taken to court, however, Edward had been restored, and she was speedily vindicated.

Edward IV died in 1483, leaving as his heir his son, a boy of twelve, King Edward V. Soon after, the young King's uncle Richard, Duke of Gloucester, usurped the throne, becoming King Richard III, and Edward V disappeared into the Tower of London, never to be seen again (see pp. 53–5). Richard revived the old claim that witchcraft had brought about Edward IV's marriage, and it was now said that Elizabeth had been associated with her mother's wiles. At the same time, Richard declared that the Queen had caused his left arm to wither, but since it was well known that his arm had been in that state since his birth, this charge was ignored. In fact, Elizabeth Woodville's reputed witchcraft was never a matter for trial, and somehow she came to terms with her brother-in-law and adorned his Court until his overthrow in 1485. Thereupon her eldest daughter married his successor, Henry VII, and carried her Plantagenet blood into the Tudor dynasty.

Had Henry Tudor failed in his attempt to depose Richard III in 1485, he would certainly have been called a traitor. Having succeeded, he wielded the power in government that constituted the rightful authority in the kingdom. As Sir John Harington wrote, in the next century:

> Treason doth never prosper. What's the reason?
> If treason prosper, none dare call it treason.

England's Statute of Treasons of 1352 (framed with a glance back to the murder of Edward II in 1327) set out the terms in which treason was defined. The first of its clauses, the most important, are still in force today. Thus treason was – and is – '. . . when a man doth compass or imagine the death of our lord the King or of our lady his queen or of their eldest son and heir; . . . or if a man do levy war against our lord the King in his realm or be adherent to the King's enemies in his realm, giving them aid and comfort in the realm or elsewhere . . .'.

A further clause does not refer to the monarch but states that treason has also occurred '. . . if a man do violate [have sexual intercourse with] the King's companion [wife] or the King's eldest daughter or the wife of the King's eldest son and heir . . .'. The importance of this clause lay in the possibility that, by taking a lover, a queen consort or a princess of Wales might have a child by him whose eventual accession to the throne would curtail the dynasty's rule. Even the suspicion that she was unfaithful to her husband and that her children were not his would be sufficient to let a cousin challenge for the crown, to prevent the subversion of the dynasty, thereby opening the way to civil war in the kingdom. (In the case of the unmarried eldest daughter of a monarch, who must succeed any childless brother or brothers on the throne, the fear was that she would be raped by or forced into marriage with a would-be usurper.)

King Henry VIII, who reigned between 1509 and 1547, rid himself of two queens whose conduct laid them open to suspicion of adultery. In 1536 his second wife, Anne Boleyn, and her supposed lovers were charged with treason, and in 1541 a bill of attainder was passed against his fifth wife, Katherine Howard. Anne and Katherine – who were cousins – and their alleged lovers were executed.

Whether either of these queens was guilty is extremely dubious. Both had enemies eager to denounce them; neither had been totally prudent in her relations with other men; neither gave King Henry the son for whom he was so eager.

Henry VIII was obsessed by the fear that England would return to the civil wars of the previous century – the Wars of the Roses (see pp. 49–54), between rival branches of the royal house. He had married Anne Boleyn because his first wife, Catherine of Aragon, had not given him a son after many years of marriage. When the Pope refused to annul his marriage with Catherine (because the Pope was then a virtual prisoner of Catherine's nephew), Henry renounced the authority of Rome over the English Church and had his Archbishop of Canterbury pronounce the annulment on his own authority. Thus Anne Boleyn's name came to be associated with the infamy of Henry's conduct to his first wife and with the tremendous upheaval in England caused by the Henrician Reformation of the Church.

Even in her heyday as Henry's wife, Anne Boleyn was reviled; after her fall, it was perhaps inevitable that rumours should have circulated that she was a witch. How else could she have lured the King from his wife and his Church? It was said that Anne was marked as a witch by having a rudimentary sixth finger on her left hand and several large moles on her body, one of which, on her neck and always covered by a necklace, served to suckle the Devil.

Both Anne Boleyn and Katherine Howard strenuously denied that they had been unfaithful to the King. Anne also denied a further charge levied against her under the Treason Act of 1352: that she and her lovers had conspired to kill the King, one of them to be rewarded by marrying Anne when Henry died.

Both queens went to their execution after having been tried and convicted by due process of law, so that their deaths cannot strictly be called murder – though there can be little doubt but that both were innocent of the charges against them and that they were the victims of enemies who played on Henry VIII's obsession with the safety of his throne.

Elizabeth Tudor, Queen of England (daughter of Henry VIII and Anne Boleyn), reigned between 1558 and 1603. She was one of the best-educated women of her time, yet she believed in astrology. (So did the French queen Catherine de' Medici, patron of Nostradamus, whose predictions stretched centuries ahead of his own time.) However, that paradox is not so strange, for whenever there is a breakdown of orthodox religion, there is a surge of interest in the occult. In the sixteenth century, though, when an astrological chart was cast to predict someone's lifespan, it could be viewed as both heretical and potentially criminal.

Thus when Elizabeth, during the lifetime of her half-sister Queen Mary I, had not only her own but Mary's and Mary's husband, Philip II of Spain's charts drawn up, it was strongly suspected that she was harbouring treasonable intentions. Elizabeth was already, in 1555, in custody at Woodstock in Oxfordshire; that April she was summoned to the royal palace at Hampton Court and interrogated by her brother-in-law. She was fortunate that no worse resulted than her return to Woodstock. Her fortune-teller, Dr John Dee, was imprisoned.

When Elizabeth came to the throne, in 1558, Dee was asked to consult the stars as to a propitious date for her coronation, but he was more than an astrologer: he was a famed astronomer, mathematician and geographer, and his dabbling in the occult and in the popular 'science' of alchemy (which attempted to transmute base metals into silver or gold) was only a sideline. Although his occult practices caused him to be denounced as 'a companion of hell-hounds, a caller and a companion of wicked and damned spirits', he was also a clergyman and, by favour of Elizabeth I, chancellor of St Paul's Cathedral in London.

Nevertheless, it remained an offence for any of the Queen's subjects to have her horoscope cast to determine the date of her death, not only in the early years of her reign, when she feared deposition in favour of her cousin Mary, Queen of Scots (see pp. 97–9), but also in the 1590s, when her natural death was expected. Thus in 1563 the old laws on witchcraft were reinforced with a new Act of Parliament that made witchcraft a matter for the criminal courts, not the Church, asserting that anyone who 'shall use, practise or exercise any witchcraft, enchantment, charm or sorcery, whereby any person shall happen to be killed or destroyed, . . . and their counsellors and aiders . . . shall suffer pains of death as a felon or felons'. But in England, unlike most of the countries on the Continent, convicted witches were hanged, not burned.

When the Queen felt the weariness of death come upon her, at the end of 1602, she consulted Dee and was warned to avoid Whitehall Palace, so she moved her Court to Richmond, but she died there, in January 1603.

As Elizabeth lay dying, two of her ladies-in-waiting discovered (or, more likely, were shown by a housemaid) a playing-card nailed under the seat of her chair. The card portrayed a Queen of Hearts, and the iron nail pierced the forehead. The superstitious ladies dared not remove nail and card, '. . . remembering that the like thing was used to the old Countess of Sussex and afterwards proved a witchcraft, for which certain persons were hanged, as instruments of the same'.

Such credulity was general throughout Europe. Witches were still being burned to death by the hundreds on the Continent. Catholic and Protestant nations were equally fearful of and merciless to those suspected of witchcraft.

King James VI of Scotland, who ruled there between 1567 and 1625 and who reigned in England as James I between 1603 and 1625, knew more of witchcraft than any other monarch of his day. In fact, he wrote a treatise on witchcraft, his *Daemonologie* of 1597. He believed that witchcraft stemmed from Devil-worship, that witches met to practise rites that were a travesty of Christian worship and that the Devil himself appeared to them. The Devil gave them the poisons and potions they supplied to those who consulted them, and the wax figures they used to kill their enemies. James asserted that there were more witches than sorcerers – that is, more women than men involved in witchcraft – because women were as weak as their mother Eve had been when she was first tempted by Satan in the guise of a serpent. There was apparently nothing the King enjoyed more than to be present at a witch's trial and to hear accounts of occult antics and evil-doing.

King James believed that he had himself been the subject of witches' malice. A coven of witches at North Berwick, discovered and brought to trial, revealed that they had thrown cats into the sea, tied to parts of dead human bodies, in order to raise storms at sea when the King was *en route* to and from Norway for his wedding in 1589.

The North Berwick witches named Francis Hepburn, Earl of Bothwell, as their leader, but though he was imprisoned, he escaped. Few people but the King himself believed in Bothwell's guilt, and had the Earl lain low, he might have been allowed to live in peace. But on 27 December 1591, he suddenly burst in on James in Holyroodhouse, chasing the King to a tower chamber. He did no damage and subsequently escaped again. However, in June Bothwell besieged the King in Falkland Palace, and in July he suddenly appeared in James's privy chamber, kneeling with a drawn sword before him. James cried, 'Treason!' and made for the Queen's room but found the door bolted; then he turned to face the Earl – who melodramatically held out the sword and told the King to kill him. At that moment courtiers entered, and James felt safer. He would forgive Bothwell, he said, if the Earl would stand trial for witchcraft. But Bothwell never did stand trial. Released, he went on to make trouble time and again until, in April 1595, he went into exile. It was a strange episode, never fully explained.

Despite James's own experience of witchcraft's malevolence and despite the assertions he made in the *Daemonologie*, over the years the King's close observation of witch trials led him to modify his opinions. He came to realise that not everyone accused of witchcraft was necessarily guilty, and to appreciate that there was often malice in the accusations that citizens would level against their neighbours, accompanied by downright lies under oath.

'I am glad of the discovery of your little counterfeit wench,' the King wrote to his elder son, Prince Henry Frederick, when the boy also evinced interest in witchcraft. 'I pray God ye may be my heir in such discoveries. Ye have oft heard me say that most miracles nowadays prove but illusions, and ye may see by this how wary judges should be in trusting accusations without exact trial, and likewise how easily people are induced to trust such wonders.'

However, King James's understanding had become far more liberal than that of the vast majority of people of his time. The witchcraft scare that crossed the whole of Europe in the late fifteenth and entire sixteenth century, and which was transported to America in the seventeenth century, was slow to abate. A great many people, mainly women, were hanged or burned to death before the 'Enlightenment' permeating philosophy and religion began to modify superstition. Nevertheless, it was not until 1751 that England saw the last of its anti-witchcraft laws.

In the late 1670s, 'the affair of the poisons' kept the city of Paris and the royal Court at Versailles in a buzz of excitement, as revelations showed how deeply Parisians and courtiers had become embroiled in the toils of black magic.

The Palace of Versailles was an awe-inspiring place, a vast building stretching over acres, hall succeeding hall, chamber after chamber, staircases rising in graceful flights, the interior sparkling with crystal and gilding, the gardens stretching out in orderly array. The palace was peopled with the most beautiful women, the most elegant men, the richest and most spendthrift aristocrats whose 'attendance' on the King obliged them to pass their days in an idleness they made interesting with a constant interchange of partners and exchange of gossip. At the hub of the Court, Louis XIV lived like an Oriental sultan, with a harem of women who might pass just a night or a whole decade in the enviable glory of being a royal mistress.

At Court, there was talk of poison long before 'the affair' broke in 1676. Back in 1670, the King's sister-in-law Henrietta, Duchess of Orleans (sister of Charles II, King of England and Scotland), had died suddenly: well one moment, the next clasping her side in agony. It was probably peritonitis, but poison was suspected, largely because her husband was bisexual and his latest homosexual lover was known to be jealous whenever Orleans paid any attention to his wife. Other supposed poisonings followed. In 1671 the Foreign Minister had his wife arrested on suspicion of trying to poison him; she was put into a convent but still he died a month later, of no known cause. In 1673 the Count of Soissons died, convinced that he had been poisoned by his unfaithful and avaricious wife. Two years later his cousin the Duke of Savoy suddenly died – again, of poison? Every sudden and unexplained death in high society was now the subject of speculation.

The real horrors began to come to official notice in 1676. First, priests of Notre Dame warned the Paris police chief, Nicolas de la Reynie, that recently many people had been confessing to having used poison to kill. Under the seal of confession, no priest could name anyone or give details of circumstances; the most any priest was allowed to do was to alert La Reynie to the prevalence of murder by poison. At the same time there was a spate of attacks on midwives and abortionists throughout Paris, coupled with allegations that babies were being kidnapped and sacrificed to the Devil. Then came the trial, that same year, of Marie-Madeleine d'Aubray, Marquise de Brinvilliers. She had apparently killed her father and two brothers and tried to kill several other members of her family, including her husband. Fortunately for him, his wife's lover, who knew what she was doing and who feared to become her second husband, had administered an antidote to the Marquis, saving his life not once but five or six times. It transpired that Madame de Brinvilliers had perfected her methods by testing poison on the hospital patients she visited. She was beheaded and her body was burned.

Towards the end of her life, Madame de Brinvilliers claimed – without adding details – that she was not the only member of the aristocracy who had resorted to the use of poison.

La Reynie was a detective whose methods were in advance of his time: he gathered evidence, analysed it and made a pattern from apparently disparate events. He discovered that there was an occult underworld in Paris that had definite connections with the Court. There were fortune-tellers working openly (in fact, the King himself had had his horoscope drawn by a virtually official royal astrologer), and there were 'wise women', as often abortionists as midwives; there were also apothecaries who supplemented their wares with unusual items their clients might occasionally require – aphrodisiacs and poisons. Such clients also knew where to purchase special magic: a Black Mass, for example, to ensure the success of their potions. It was at such Masses that babies were sacrificed to the Devil.

In September 1677, the Jesuits who had a church in the rue St-Antoine reported to La Reynie that they had discovered an anonymous letter left in a confessional; it warned that the King and his heir the Dauphin were going to be poisoned.

There followed a series of raids on the premises of fortune-tellers, apothecaries etc, and many arrests, with torture inevitably used to elicit as much information as possible (though prisoners frequently retracted information that had been given under torture). La Reynie's expertise and the vigilance of his police led to the rounding-up of a large number of suspects. Until the spring of 1679 they were tried by the parliament of Paris; from April 1679 they went before the Chambre Ardente, a court specially commissioned by the King to deal with the poisoners. This new court, in which La Reynie was co-chairman, was to conduct its proceedings in secret, lest any detail of the methods of poisoning should become common knowledge and promote more such murders. Nevertheless, enough news escaped to keep up the level of interest, and there were always the public executions – by burning, strangulation and hanging – to attract the public.

When the underworld of Paris gave up its secrets, the extent of the royal Court's involvement emerged. Countesses and duchesses were hailed before the Chambre Ardente and, though not themselves the subject of torture and execution, several were sent away into exile, some into distant convents – though others managed to escape before their court appearance. It transpired that some of these ladies had been using aphrodisiacs to try to attract the attention and rouse the passion of the King; some had even made 'a pact with the Devil', mortgaging their souls for special favours. It was inevitable that, sooner or later, one of the King's mistresses should be implicated. The name that emerged from the examination of prisoners was that of Athenaïs, Marquise de Montespan.

The naming of the King's mistress caused the end of the Chambre Ardente. It ceased to function in 1682. The King could not allow the court to prosecute Madame de Montespan; her innocence apart (and he seems to have believed in it), the prestige of the monarchy was at stake. So instead of having the remaining 147 suspects tortured and tried, the King issued *lettres de cachet* for all of them, by which they were to be held in prison for life, without trial.

The King thought he had destroyed all the documentation that named Madame de Montespan. He had not: La Reynie's own notes remain, preserving to this day the evidence that proved how close witchcraft and poison had come to the throne of France. Nothing more ever emerged about a plot to kill the King and Dauphin, but it was that threat that had given the edge of urgency to La Reynie's investigation and the Chambre Ardente's persistence.

There is a postscript to the story of 'the affair of the poisons'. The Countess of Soissons, suspected of having poisoned her husband in 1673, was one of the great ladies called to account before the Chambre Ardente in 1680. Rumour had it that the King sent to warn her of her imminent arrest; certainly she did not wait for the summons to arrive but made for the Dutch border.

In 1689 the Countess was in Spain, where she and another homesick exile, Marie-Louise of Orleans, niece of Louis XIV and wife of Carlos II, King of Spain, enjoyed a gossip about their old friends at Versailles. The Countess offered the Queen a glass of cold milk on a hot summer day; the Queen drank it; after vomiting and writhing in agony, she died. There was a motive to hand: the Countess was a friend of the Austrian ambassador, and Austria was known to dislike the French influence at the Spanish Court; why should the Countess not have been employed to remove the French-born Queen? She was sought everywhere, but once again she was safely across a border. She died in 1708, in poverty, in Brussels.

Madame de Montespan had died the previous year. After the death of the Queen in 1683, Louis XIV married his other long-term mistress, Françoise, Marquise de Maintenon, and Madame de Montespan felt a chill set in. She left the Court in 1691 and took to good works. She was afraid of sleeping alone and had a horror of death; perhaps she had memories of a 'pact with the Devil' over the disposal of her soul. But when the end did come, she accepted the last rites of the Church and died peacefully.

CHAPTER SIX

FOR GOD'S SAKE

'Men never do evil so completely and cheerfully as when they do it from religious conviction.' So wrote the French philosopher Pascal.

That saying was certainly true in the centuries in which Christianity was spreading through Europe, challenging the pagan faiths that had prevailed 'since time immemorial'. There was persecution on both sides: pagans fighting a rearguard battle, Christians pressing their own creed on unbelievers. Everywhere Christianity triumphed in the end, but the years of transition were painful.

Rulers had the power to impose a faith on their people – by force if not by persuasion – and so religion may be added to the list of motives for killing a ruler.

Vratislav I, Duke of Bohemia at the turn of the ninth century, was a second-generation Christian, but his wife, Drahomira, was a pagan. He insisted that his heir, Václav, be brought up as a Christian and put him in the charge of his Christian grandmother, Ludmilla, but Drahomira was allowed to bring up her younger son, Boleslav, as a pagan. Inevitably, this led to conflict. When Vratislav died, in 921, Václav was initially unwilling to reign: he wanted to become a monk, and only the order of the Pope kept him on the throne: a Christian ruler was more valuable to the Church than a monk, as things then stood. But already Drahomira had taken the initiative, having her mother-in-law, Ludmilla, murdered and ordering the closure of all Christian churches. The Bohemians' revolt against this measure was put down by widespread massacres. However, Václav gained the protection of the Holy Roman Emperor, by paying homage to him, and for some years managed to maintain Christian government in Bohemia.

Then, in the year 929, Duke Václav received an invitation from his brother to be present at the baptism of Boleslav's infant son. So sudden and so unexpected was this ostensible change of heart that even the saintly Václav could not believe in it, and apparently he arrived at his brother's castle sure that he was going to his death. He was right. While Václav knelt at his prayers, Boleslav murdered him.

But the story has a happy ending. When Boleslav ruled Bohemia, he found that there was an advantage to be had in the support of the Holy Roman Emperor and his Church, and through the pressure of the first and the usefulness of the second, he came to live peaceably with his Christian subjects. The child who had been baptised in 929 became a monk, and his younger brother, who succeeded their father as duke of Bohemia, so resembled his uncle that he was known as 'Boleslav the Pious'. As to the murdered Duke Václav, he is better known by the German form of his name and, in error, as king rather than duke: he has come down in popular legend as 'Good King Wenceslas'.

Like the Slav lands, Scandinavia became Christian comparatively late in history. As elsewhere, Scandinavian kings awarded lands and money to the Church for building and missionary work. One, Knud IV, King of Denmark, went too far, making lavish grants of land to the Church, imposing heavy taxes on his people to fund church-building and extending the Church's legal powers. In 1086, with the country in rebellion, Knud fled to the island of Fyn. On 10 July he took shelter in the church of St Alban in Odense, where his subjects came to confront him. Unable at first to gain entry to the church, they threw stones at its windows; one hit the King on the forehead, drawing blood, but he remained kneeling in prayer. When the crowd battered down the door and swarmed in, a spear was thrown and Knud was killed. In 1101 he was canonised, but the Danes remembered him as a 'bad' king.

Knud's wife Adela managed to escape from Denmark with her son Karl and took him to the Court of her brother Robert, Count of Flanders. Lacking a son, Robert later left Flanders to Karl, who, just like his father, proceeded to over-tax his subjects and give the money to his clergy. On 2 March 1127 he was murdered at the altar of the church of St Donatien in Bruges.

Throughout the Middle Ages, religious zeal, in its most unpleasant form, was expressed in the persecution of heretics. Thousands of people perished as 'crusades' were mounted against, for example, the Albigensians in France, the Lollards in England, the Hussites in Bohemia. In the Middle Ages, religion really mattered to every man and woman in Europe. That is to say, there was genuine belief in God and regular attendance at church, though in daily life there was even less consideration for 'neighbours' than there is in the present Godless age.

Then, in the sixteenth century, a new factor entered the history of European Christianity – and that of royal murders. After centuries of being united by a common creed, its religious observances administered by the clergy of a recognised hierarchy, Western Europe was sundered by religious differences. This was the age of the Reformation: proof that men and women cared sufficiently for their faith to die for it – proof also that they cared enough to kill for it.

Until the mid-century, the Protestants (those in rebellion against the age-old Church) were the aggressive force; thereafter the Catholics went on the offensive, their resurgence now known as the Counter-Reformation. Both sides were guilty of atrocities: the torture of heretics and burning them at the stake were time-honoured responses to religious dissent; so was the massacring of large numbers of men, women and children by armies charged to uphold religious orthodoxy. What was new was the scale of the religious conflict, its duration and the unashamed horrors perpetrated 'for God's sake'. The whole of Western Europe was involved, in varying degrees, and it was not until the eighteenth century that religion ceased to figure as a prime motivation in civil unrest and international wars. However, echoes of the conflict can still be heard today – in Northern Ireland, for example.

As far as royal murders are concerned, religion became a motive in the 1560s, when the Catholic Church was beginning to mount its revival. The Papacy put pressure on Catholic monarchs to persecute Protestants; members of the Society of Jesus (the Jesuits) were sent into Protestant-ruled countries to rally the remaining 'Roman' Catholics as they came to be called; and writs of excommunication were issued against Protestant monarchs. There was more than a formality in this last resource: it had long been recognised that a monarch-turned-heretic forfeited his subjects' allegiance; now the Jesuits were specifically charged to absolve the sins of any Catholic who murdered a heretical monarch.

It is at this time that the word 'assassination' becomes valid for many of the murders of monarchs. Whatever its origins (see p. 16), the word has taken on the meaning of a murder done for a principle rather than personal gain – though the assassin may be employed and paid by someone whose motive is one of principle. Thus the murder of a monarch – or a murder instigated by a monarch – for religious reasons may be deemed an assassination, just as in later centuries political motives underlay the assassination of monarchs.

Jeanne II, Queen of Navarre, was a Protestant who reigned between 1555 and 1572 in the small kingdom that straddled the Pyrenees. Thus on one side of her realm lay ultra-Catholic Spain, where the Inquisition (Church courts) dealt cruelly with heretics; on the other was France, predominantly Catholic, though by mid-century perhaps one in twenty of the population was Protestant (there were high concentrations in some parts of the kingdom, virtually no Protestants in others). France had good reasons to protect Jeanne from Church censure, to keep Navarre a friendly bulwark against Spanish aggression.

In France, from 1560, another woman ruled: the Italian Catherine de' Medici, widow of King Henri II; she was regent for her young son Charles IX. Catherine found it impossible to keep the peace between Catholics and Protestants (called Huguenots in France). The noblemen who vied for power in her government were leaders of Catholic and Protestant factions, and religion was the prime factor in their balance of power. From 1562 France was torn apart by a series of civil wars – 'the Wars of Religion' – that defied the efforts of peacemakers and yet allowed neither side an ultimate victory. Thus for some quarter-century France suffered intermittent warfare in several regions, whole villages razed to the ground, their inhabitants massacred, with Huguenots hunted through the streets by Catholic mobs and with Catholic priests and laity tortured to death by vengeful Huguenots.

In one attempt to reconcile the two sides, in 1572, Jeanne of Navarre's son Henri was betrothed to Catherine's daughter, Marguerite. But even as Henri rode to his wedding in Paris, there came the news from Navarre that his mother was dead – poisoned, it was suspected, by fumes from scented gloves sent her by Queen Catherine. True or not, this death could feasibly be laid at Catherine's door, not just because she wished to have her son-in-law king of Navarre and in her power but because she had now gone over whole-heartedly to the Catholic cause. The Huguenot lords had gained too much power over her son, Charles IX, now in his twenties, and for her influence to remain paramount, the Huguenots must be destroyed.

On the night of the royal wedding, 23 August 1572, Catherine persuaded King Charles that, for the sake of France, the Huguenots must be exterminated. The campaign must start there and then, in Paris.

That night and through the next day, the streets of Paris were the scene of massacre – 'the Massacre of St Bartholomew's Day', it was called, with appropriate religious accuracy. Huguenots were slaughtered on the streets and in their houses, pierced with sword or dagger, bludgeoned, hanged, strangled, drowned in the Seine or the sewer canals. As the news permeated the country, it was a signal for further murders. It has been estimated that some 15,000 people were killed.

Pope Gregory XIII sent a message of congratulation to the King of France.

Two years later Charles IX died – not murdered; probably of tuberculosis. 'Blood all around me!' he was heard to murmur on his deathbed. 'Is it blood that I have shed?'

His successor was his brother Henri III. Himself childless, after the death of a younger brother in 1584 Henri was the last male member of the House of Valois, and his heir, by strict inheritance, was that distant cousin King Henri of Navarre who had become his brother-in-law in 1572.

Like his late mother, Henri of Navarre was a Huguenot, so it seemed impossible that he should ever rule the Catholic kingdom of France. The Pope – by then Sixtus V – clarified the situation by proclaiming that Henri of Navarre's religion was a bar to his inheriting. In his stead the heir was to be another cousin, Henri, Duke of Guise, the man who had commanded the Catholics on St Bartholomew's Day. Thus the next civil war was not specifically a matter of religion but, as 'the War of the Three Henris', more about the royal succession, with religious undertones. In the midst of all this, the man who actually reigned in France, Henri III, could see that, if Guise won, his own life would not last much longer, for his cousin was fervently ambitious for the crown. Wherever Henri III went now, he was surrounded by his bodyguard, called 'the Forty-five'.

On 23 December 1588, the King and the Duke of Guise were staying at the château of Blois. Early that morning, the Duke was warned that there was a plot to kill him.

'He is well guarded whom God guards,' said Guise.

Later that morning the King sent for the Duke. Crossing the ante-room to the royal chamber, he saw members of the Forty-five, bowing as he passed. Some of them followed him into the inner chamber, where others were already waiting. The King was absent. A moment's hesitation, then daggers were drawn.

'Traitor, that will kill you!' someone shouted as Guise fell beneath the slashes.

'Ho, friends!' he managed to call out, but no friends came. With his last strength, he dragged his assailants along as he staggered under them, his blood gushing out and staining the walls. Then, 'Have mercy, O God!'

When all was quiet, the King came into the room. 'My God, how big he is,' he exclaimed, regarding Guise's corpse with interest. 'He seems to be even bigger dead than alive.'

The next day the Duke's brother Charles, Cardinal Guise, was also stabbed to death.

For this latter crime, though not for the former, Henri III was excommunicated. The Guise faction – the Catholic League – held Paris against him, and to gain allies the King could see no alternative to acknowledging Henri of Navarre as his heir. Together the brothers-in-law began to regain control of the kingdom.

Henri III did not long survive. On 1 August 1589 a young friar named Jacques Clément was permitted to stand close to the King, to tell him a 'secret'. Clément drew a dagger from his sleeve and slashed at Henri's face before guards arrested him and dragged him away. The King survived the attack but that night he became feverish, with severe pains in his wound. (Was the friar's dagger poisoned?) Henri III sent for his heir, but by the time he arrived, the King of Navarre had become Henri IV, King of France.

It has been estimated that not even a fifth of Henri IV's subjects recognised him as king: he was a heretic, excommunicated by the Pope. After more than three years spent fighting the Catholic League that had taken arms against him, he faced reality: 'Paris is worth a Mass,' he said, and became a Catholic. However, the absolution granted him by the French Church on 21 March 1593 could not overturn the Pope's excommunication of Henri, and papal absolution was slow in coming. So for the time being his entitlement to the French throne remained in question.

On 27 December 1594 nineteen-year-old Jean Chastel tried to cut Henri's throat with a dagger but succeeded only in cutting his lip. According to his own testimony, Chastel had planned the assault alone, but he had recently been a pupil in a Jesuit college and admitted that he had been told there that it would be neither sin nor crime to kill the heretic who was the unlawful king. A teacher at the college, Father Guignard, was arrested. He was hanged, Chastel quartered. The Jesuits were banished from France.

It was not until 17 September 1595 that the Pope lifted Henri IV's excommunication. Thereafter, no Catholic had any excuse to deny his right to the French throne, and the Catholic League began to break up. However, French Catholics – and the Pope – were appalled when the King issued, in the Edict of Nantes on 13 April 1598, an outline of the rights of his Huguenot subjects, including freedom of worship. Henri IV's favours to the Huguenots inevitably annoyed his Catholic subjects – more than that: they came to fear that the Huguenots would wreak their revenge for the Massacre of St Bartholomew's Day. Inevitably, it was in Paris that fears were greatest. Parisians said that the King had no power to prevent a massacre of his Catholic subjects. Better, then, that the King should die than hundreds of his subjects.

In the spring of 1610 the King was in a strange mental state. He had long loved hunting and gambling; now he lost interest. He no longer pursued the Court ladies. He had premonitions of violent death.

The Queen, Maria de' Medici (Henri's second wife), dreamed that her husband had been stabbed. An astrologer warned him that 14 May would be a fatal day. However, when the Queen begged the King not to go out on that day, he replied that '. . . it was an offence to God to give credit to them [astrologers] and that having God for his guard he feared no man' – a chilling echo of the Duke of Guise.

On 14 May Henri intended to visit a friend, the Duke of Sully, who was ill, but despite his resolution he turned back three times before going out the door.

'I do not know what is wrong with me,' he said, 'but I cannot leave this place.'

The King did agree to put on a breastplate, as a defence against a dagger, but he did not fasten it. In the coach with him were seven attendants, and there were footmen and outriders alongside.

Carriage traffic was as congested in Paris in 1610 as car traffic is today. At the junction of the rue Saint-Honoré and the rue de la Ferronerie, the royal carriage was forced to a halt. That was the moment at which a pedestrian leaped up to the carriage window and stabbed the King with a knife. Henri raised an arm, and the man stabbed again, striking through the ribs into his lungs. The King coughed up blood and died.

The assassin was François Ravaillac, aged thirty-two. He had been a teacher until he was imprisoned for debt, then he had tried to gain admittance to the Franciscan order, but failed when his babble of visions raised suspicions of his sanity. In one vision he had seen the King as the personification of tyranny and had become convinced that he must kill him.

Ravaillac was unfortunate that the King's guards did not leave him to the fury of the mob who had witnessed the assassination. A trial by the parliament of Paris established his guilt. Then he was executed: the hand that had killed the King was burned off with brimstone; flesh was torn from his chest, arms and legs with hot pincers; boiling oil was poured into the wounds, molten lead into his navel; then his arms and legs were fastened to four horses and they were driven apart. Throughout the agony Ravaillac screamed and prayed.

Under torture, Ravaillac had protested that he was in no one's pay and had no accomplices. But there were suspicions that this was untrue – both at the time and still today, when the biographers of Henry IV sift the evidence and speculate on its significance.

Of course, the Jesuits (who had been readmitted to France in 1605) were the chief suspects, but there were several others. Even the Queen was not above suspicion: she had been on bad terms with her husband and, it was rumoured, feared that he would have her poisoned. More likely were the noblemen who had taken part in (or were suspected of having been involved in) conspiracies against the King in the past decade. Of these, the Duke of Epernon is the person most likely to have been Ravaillac's master, though the allegation is based only on circumstantial evidence and the testimony of a servant who had overheard a conversation about assassination and had subsequently learned that Ravaillac had been seen at the house of Epernon's mistress. The complex evidence presented by the King's biographers seems to point to there having been a conspiracy against his life, by courtiers and Jesuits, and the employment of Ravaillac to execute it. It can only be a guess that someone was clever enough to prompt Ravaillac to the murder by guile, so that he really thought that the idea had originated in his own mind.

The immediate effect of the assassination of Henri IV was the accession of his son Louis XIII, still a child and under the regency of the Queen Mother. In the long term, the Catholic majority kept their privileges and the Huguenots their hard-won rights, though only until the revocation of the Edict of Nantes in 1686.

In duration and intensity, the French Wars of Religion were out of all proportion to the small number of Protestants in France. During the sixteenth century, Spain and Italy remained staunchly Catholic; after some years of conflict, the German states of the Holy Roman Empire hit on a formula that made for peace: '*cuius regio, eius religio*' – 'the ruler chooses his people's religion.' That worked well for Germany, with its many local rulers standing between 'the masses' and their overlord, the Holy Roman Emperor. The situation was different in the Netherlands, which, from 1555, were ruled by the King of Spain through resident governors.

In the Netherlands, Spain's attempt to impose the Inquisition was as firmly resisted as Spain's burdensome taxes on the Dutch. As the years passed, the Netherlands' bid for freedom of worship became indistinguishable from their urge for freedom from Spanish rule.

As the struggle progressed, a leader emerged from the ranks of the Dutch nobility. This was William of Nassau, Prince of Orange. He was called 'William the Silent' – not because he was dumb or even taciturn but because he kept his own counsel; he was 'deep'. He was more than commander-in-chief of the Dutch armies, more than an administrator: he was the man who welded the Dutch people into a nation, even though they retained the identity of their individual states. When they first took him to their hearts, William was still a Catholic; it was not until about 1570 that he 'came out' as a Calvinist.

After nearly two decades of conflict with Spain, in July 1581 the States General (the governing body of the rebel Netherlands) formally renounced allegiance to Philip II, King of Spain, and proclaimed William head of state. Not king: he refused the title of king.

William had taken care, several months earlier, to publish his reasons for taking this momentous step, so that no one might say that he usurped Philip's power for the sake of his own ambition. In a document called *The Apology*, William asserted that Philip II had so failed in his duty as a monarch that he had forfeited all right to his subjects' allegiance. Among his charges against Philip, William claimed that the Spanish king had had his eldest son murdered (see pp. 56–7). Whatever the truth of it, there was sufficient doubt and speculation for William's allegation to gain some credence.

The Apology was published in December 1580, six months after King Philip had declared William of Orange an outlaw and offered a vast sum of money to anyone who would kill him.

The first attempt on William's life was made on 18 March 1582, when a pistol, over-charged with gunpowder, blew up in the assailant's hand, shattering it. He was immediately killed by the swords of William's bodyguards. The shot had been fired at very close range, and the bullet had struck William through the cheek and lodged in the palate of his mouth; it did not kill him but the treatment for the wound was agonising.

There were other attempts, all thwarted before a shot was fired, but William insisted on continuing to keep open house.

On Tuesday 10 July 1584 the Prince of Orange was talking to friends in the crowded corridor leading from his dining-room when a man approached him and shot him with a brace of pistols. The bullets passed through his lungs and stomach and lodged in the wall behind him. William staggered but did not fall. He was unconscious as he was carried into the dining-room and was dead before the doctor arrived.

This was the first murder of a ruler that was carried out with the use of guns, weapons that would later allow an assailant to fire at some distance from the victim but which at that time were still best used at close range.

William of Orange knew the man who had killed him. His name was Balthasar Gérard, and the previous May he had come to William, presenting himself as the son of a Protestant martyr and offering his services. Being advised to put himself under the command of the Netherlands' French allies did not suit Gérard's plan, and he remained in Amsterdam. In July, William spotted Gérard and asked why he was still in the city: because he had no money, was the reply, whereupon William sent him a sum of money – which Gérard used to buy his pistols.

On the day of the assassination, Gérard approached William as he was entering his dining-room and asked him for a passport, which William promised to supply. While the Prince was at dinner, Gérard reconnoitred the house and found an easy exit. The murder done, as William left the dining-room, Gérard managed to get out of the house, but he was taken as he was scaling the garden wall. He was found to be carrying waterwings (deflated), which he planned to use when crossing the nearby canal – he could not swim.

Balthasar Gérard's execution showed that Protestants were as merciless as Catholics. His right hand was burned off; flesh was taken from his torso with red-hot pincers; he was disembowelled while still alive; his heart was pulled out; then his head was cut off and the torso quartered.

King Philip of Spain honoured his promise to pay the reward, Gérard's family being the recipients. The King used money he had taken from William of Orange's eldest son, whom he held hostage in Spain.

The assassination did not cast the Dutch into turmoil or despair. The revolt of the Netherlands was a success, and for more than two centuries the nation was a republic, with members of the Orange-Nassau dynasty as its selected heads of state. After the Napoleonic Wars, the head of the house became the first King of the Netherlands.

One of the 'heretical' monarchs targeted for assassination was Elizabeth Tudor, who reigned in England between 1558 and 1603. Although her father, Henry VIII, had defied the Pope and created the independent Church of England, by no means all his subjects had become Protestants. Exact numbers of English Catholics in Elizabeth's reign are not known, but it has been estimated that there may have been as many as a quarter of the population who did not attend Anglican services or who attended only occasionally, to avoid paying the recusancy fines.

Elizabeth I let it be known that she had no desire to 'make windows in men's souls', meaning that she regarded everyone's religion as his own business. After all, with only minimal facilities for Catholic worship and by dealing severely with those who sheltered the remaining priests, it was reasonable to expect that, when the pre-Reformation Catholics died out, in the natural course of time, their children would conform to the Church of England. Given the atmosphere of 1558, that might be a reasonable assumption. Then, however, the Catholic Church on the Continent engaged in the conference known as the Council of Trent, concluded in 1563, which set in train the strategies of the Counter-Reformation.

Allied to the problems of religion in England was the problem of the royal succession. Catholics could argue that, since Rome had not sanctioned the marriage of Elizabeth's parents, she was illegitimate and thus could not inherit the throne; those of that mind looked to Elizabeth's Catholic cousin Mary, Queen of Scots, as the true queen. Mary did not make the sort of claim that is backed by an invading army but nor did she dissuade those who called her England's queen as well as Scotland's. Thus, to be a Catholic in England was, it appeared, to be a potential traitor to Queen Elizabeth. In fact, the vast majority of Catholics were as law-abiding as their Protestant neighbours. However, after 1568, when Mary fled Scotland and became her cousin's prisoner, a small minority of English Catholics first mounted an abortive insurrection (in 1569) and then began to engage in conspiracies that involved Elizabeth's death and Mary's accession to the throne. Mary was also the niece, through her late mother, of the French Catholic leader, the Duke of Guise, and it was he who put a price on Queen Elizabeth's head, to be awarded to her killer.

In 1570 Pope Sixtus V excommunicated the English queen, and in 1571 the first of the main conspiracies designed to effect her deposition or death was discovered. The senior Catholic peer, Thomas Howard, Duke of Norfolk, was the plot's figurehead, but it was co-ordinated by a Florentine banker, Roberto Ridolfi, and had Spanish backing. Elizabeth was to be murdered and, in the ensuing confusion, Spanish troops were to invade England and place Mary, Queen of Scots, on the throne. On discovery of the plot, minor conspirators were subjected to torture, to gain information, and Norfolk was tried, convicted of treason and beheaded.

As the years passed, other plots came to light, proving – so it was said – the disloyalty of English Catholics. There was a pattern to the plots: generally it was given out that someone had confessed, betraying his fellows, and that the plotters had been arrested before they could make their move; trials followed, then sentence of death of the leaders, but also a strong measure of mercy for the minor players, calculated to reinforce the loyalty of those Catholics who had no taste for treason.

But there is another way of looking at those plots. It was convenient to the Queen's Secretaries of State, William Cecil, Lord Burghley, and Sir Francis Walsingham, to foster suspicion and fear of England's Catholics and of the Queen of Scots. Walsingham was Elizabeth's 'spy master', maintaining a network of agents and informants, some of them living under cover as Catholics, at home and abroad. Walsingham collected and analysed their information and, it is alleged, employed picked men to encourage the development of each plot until its hatchers had made 'enough rope to hang themselves'; then they were arrested. In this way, Burghley and Walsingham sought to speed up the elimination of the Catholic faith from England. Norfolk's execution, for example, was a cornerstone of their strategy, for after his death there was no natural leader among the Catholic peers and gentry.

Revelation of the plots 'proved' to Queen and Parliament that there was a real threat to Elizabeth's life and to the security of her realm, thus justifying the anti-Catholic legislation that the Queen had been loath to introduce in the early years of her reign: recusancy fines were increased and it became a matter of treason to harbour a 'Mass-priest', especially a Jesuit, for the Jesuits were known to be henchmen of the fire-breathing Pope.

In 1583 discovery of the Throckmorton plot revealed another foreign-backed conspiracy, with the implication of the Spanish ambassador. The assassination of William the Silent, Prince of Orange, in July 1584, confirmed Englishmen's fears of the murderous intent of Catholics on the lives of Protestant rulers. Out of these fears came the Bond of Association, a pledge signed first by Elizabeth's courtiers, subsequently by nobles, gentry and townsmen throughout England and Wales, to the effect that all of them constituted a corps of bodyguards to defend the Queen and pledging that, if she were murdered, they would hunt down and punish not only her killer but also the person who would benefit from her death – that is, her successor on the throne. When the bond was considered for enactment by Parliament, Elizabeth herself demanded a revision of the original: the beneficiary of her death was not to be convicted unheard but to stand trial, albeit to suffer the death penalty not merely for implication in the conspiracy to murder but even for foreknowledge of it.

In 1586 the Babington plot came to light. Several young men had conspired to kill Elizabeth and enthrone Mary – the usual story, but this time implemented by documentary proof that Mary had known of and approved plans for Elizabeth's murder. This was the factor, under the 1585 legislation, that brought her to trial.

Initially Queen Mary denied the right of an English court to try a Scotswoman and of commoners to try a queen. When she did deign to appear before the commissioners sent to Fotheringhay Castle, she returned glib answers-that-were-no-answers to their questions. But she was adamant that she had never sought her cousin's death.

Inevitably Mary was found guilty of 'imagining and compassing Her Majesty's death'. Probably she was, just as she was probably a party to the murder of her second husband (see pp. 65–6). Still, her execution has been called 'judicial murder', because of the possibility that documentary evidence against her had been fabricated to dispel any uncertainty of the circumstantial evidence, and that men had been tortured into 'confessions' that implicated her. Thus it might be argued that Mary,

Queen of Scots, died not as a criminal meriting capital punishment but because it seemed essential for the security of England and the safety of Queen Elizabeth. She was beheaded on 8 February 1587, in the great hall of Fotheringhay Castle.

Yet still Queen Elizabeth was not free from fear. Seven years after Mary's execution, nearly six years after the defeat of the Spanish Armada, hopes of peace with Spain were dispelled when it was discovered – or alleged – that Philip II, King of Spain, had planned the English Queen's death at the hands of Dr Roderigo Lopez, her Portuguese physician. (Philip was also, by then, King of Portugal.)

Lopez was one of many Jews who had fled Spain and Portugal in recent years, when the Inquisition was as active against Jewry as against Christian Protestants. In England, he had acquired a clientele in the highest echelons of the kingdom and had become the Queen's personal physician in 1586.

Lopez's accuser was Robert Devereux, Earl of Essex, who had personal reasons for victimising the physician. Essex aspired to the power that Lord Burghley had accumulated over three decades and which Burghley was planning to pass on to his son, Robert Cecil. To forestall Burghley, Essex must discredit him, and he intended to do so by demonstrating that Burghley had failed to uncover Lopez's machinations. But examination of Lopez failed to elicit any indication of guilt, and the Queen was furious with Essex – 'a rash and temerarious youth', she called him.

Essex was not deterred. Now he charged Lopez with having planned to murder the Queen, by poisoning her. Threatened with the rack, Lopez confessed – and then, in court, retracted the confession. But he was inevitably found guilty and sent to the public ritual of hanging, drawing and quartering. Two Spaniards suffered with him, his supposed confederates.

Essex continued in his attempts to undermine Lord Burghley's power and, after his death in 1598, to prevent Burghley's son Robert Cecil from accessing power, but without success. In 1600 Essex mounted a *coup* ostensibly designed to put the age-weary Queen in his custody and make him her 'Lord Protector' but which did not rule out her murder. It is significant that, on the night before the *coup*, Saturday 7 February, he paid the actors of the Globe Theatre to stage Shakespeare's *Richard II*.

On the morning of Sunday the 8th, Essex rode at the head of an armed force into the City of London – a mistake, for it gave time for the city of Westminster to be fortified, and the Londoners refused to turn against the Queen. Before the day was out, Essex was in custody. On 19 February he was tried on a charge of high treason; on the 25th he was beheaded.

As with so much in the reign of Elizabeth Tudor, the Essex plot is not all it seems on the surface. At his trial the Earl charged Robert Cecil with plotting to have the Infanta Isabel of Spain succeed Elizabeth as queen (as supposedly the principal of the descendants of King Edward III). Thus Essex posed as the Protestant champion against the allegedly turncoat Cecil, who would have 'sold out' Protestant England to Catholic Spain. In fact, Essex could bring no evidence to support his allegation, showing that there had been no justification for his attempted *coup*.

Queen Elizabeth was approaching seventy; she had reigned for almost forty-five years when she died, on 24 March 1603. She had survived the assassination plots, to die naturally, in her sleep.

Had the Gunpowder Plot of 1605 succeeded, it would have been the most spectacular and probably the most far-reaching royal murder in European history. In fact, it would have gone far beyond being a royal murder: it would have been a massacre of the nation's leaders – not just the King but also his queen, his sons, his lords spiritual and temporal, judges and members of the House of Commons.

The Gunpowder Plot did not succeed, but the magnitude of its ambition was so great, and its discovery (apparently) so breathtakingly dramatic, that it is still recalled annually:

> Please to remember the 5th of November,
> Gunpowder, treason and plot.
> I see no reason why gunpowder treason
> Should ever be forgot.

King James VI of Scotland had been chosen by Elizabeth I of England as her heir, and soon after her death he came south to survey his new kingdom; he liked it so much that he made it his home.

Himself a Presbyterian (Calvinist), the new King James I of England had married a Lutheran, Anne of Denmark – at least, she was a Lutheran until the year 1600, when she was secretly received into the Catholic Church. Of course, it could not long remain a secret, and when the couple arrived in England in 1603, English Catholics were delighted, expecting an appreciable measure of toleration. At first, the King seemed amenable. However, there had been too much blood spilled, in England and abroad, for English Protestants to sanction any increased measure of toleration for Catholics. Where the King would have had the recusancy laws employed more laxly, his judges – prompted by the clergy – became ever stricter. At length, public opinion caught even the King's attention: reneging on promises he had made on arrival in England, he began calling for stringent enforcement of the law.

Nevertheless, it was not this change of heart that put the King – and so many others – into mortal danger on 5 November 1605. The Gunpowder Plot had been devised as early as 1603 by a Catholic who had not waited to see what James would do for his Catholic subjects before he planned that the Stuart dynasty should supply not toleration of Catholics but government by Catholics. As the plot developed, it came to combine the death of the King and his elder son with the capture of his younger son (later his daughter): the new child monarch would be 'protected' by the plotters, who would constitute the government, since they had already dispatched (to Heaven or Hell) the Lords and the Commons.

Robert Catesby, the plot's prime mover, was so resolved on his enormous enterprise that he actually prevented his friend Thomas Percy from carrying out his own plan to murder the King. They, and the men gradually gathered to help them, did nothing precipitately. For one thing, they had to wait for the State Opening of Parliament. After James's first Parliament met in February 1604, the next was not called until the autumn of 1605. In the meantime the plotters collected a large supply of gunpowder and, renting a house near the Houses of Parliament, began to dig a tunnel that should enable them to place the powder where it was needed. The tunnel filled with water and was useless, but as luck would have it they were then able to rent a cellar that led directly under the House of Lords, and there they stashed their barrels.

At the same time, the conspirators made preparations for the capture of the child Prince Charles – until they were thwarted by the King's decision to take the boy to the Opening of Parliament, along with his elder brother, Prince Henry Frederick. Then Charles was replaced in the plan by his sister Elizabeth, born in 1596, who was living in the house of Lord Harrington, near Coventry. The plotters aimed to place armed men round the house, ready to capture the Princess and take her to London to proclaim her queen. Coventry conveniently lay in an area full of Catesby's own friends.

An obvious major problem was the possibility – probability – that the nation would not accept the new government, even though, in the chaos following the massacre, there would be no immediate alternative. But it would take weeks before news of the massacre had permeated the country, and if London could be secured, and the mechanism of government, the plotters stood some chance. Catesby and his friends planned to post proclamations throughout the cities of London and Westminster to the effect that King and Parliament had been killed because they had planned to unite England and Scotland (a possibility under debate at the time and of which the King was widely suspected). As news left the capital of the demise of King and Parliament, copies of the proclamations would go with it. Catholics would be rallied to the support of the new government, and though Catholic foreign powers could not be persuaded to lend their support to such a project before the fact, the plotters were confident that, once in power, they would be afforded all the foreign help necessary to subdue dissidents at home.

The Opening of Parliament was set for Tuesday 5 November 1605.

On the evening of Saturday 26 October, the Catholic Lord Monteagle received an anonymous letter, semi-legible and cryptic but clear enough in its advice that he should not go to Parliament on 5 November. That night Monteagle presented himself to Robert Cecil, Lord Salisbury, the King's chief minister, and thereby set in train the investigation that led to the thwarting of the plot.

Or did it? Had not the plot been known from the very beginning, through the vigilance of the spy service that Robert Cecil inherited from his father, Lord Burghley, and from Sir Francis Walsingham? That is the version of the story that challenges the simpler, long-accepted one. It is said that this was another of the Catholic plots nurtured by the English government and denounced, at the last moment, in order to raise anti-Catholic feeling in the country and so justify the imposition of ever-sterner measures against Catholics.

Whatever its antecedents, the Gunpowder Plot was effectively ended in the early hours of 5 November, when one of the conspirators, a Yorkshireman named Guy Fawkes, was discovered in the cellar below the House of Lords, carrying the means to fire the gunpowder – 'slow' matches and touchwood. On the Friday Catesby and several of his friends were besieged in a house near Stourbridge, and he and three others were killed in an exchange of fire with the force sent to take them.

Torture was used, first on Guy Fawkes, then on his associates, and having learned all they could by this means, the government brought them to trial on 27 January. Four men were hanged, drawn and quartered on 30 January, four more the next day.

The opening of Parliament, postponed until January 1606, was an occasion for general thanksgiving, and members unanimously agreed to declare 5 November a day of national celebration in perpetuity. They also passed two Acts of harsh measures against Catholics. As Lord Salisbury said, it was essential that something be done '. . . to demonstrate the iniquity of Catholics, and to prove to all the world that it is not for religion but for their treasonable teaching and practices that they should be exterminated'.

By 'extermination', Salisbury did not mean that England's Catholics should be massacred, as the Huguenots had been in France in 1572; rather, he relied on their slow suffocation by withdrawing the fresh air that blew in from Rome, with the itinerant priests, while recusancy fines impoverished those of the Catholic gentry and nobility who remained faithful.

And so England's Catholics continued to suffer and to decrease in number (largely by the natural deaths of those unable to come to terms with necessity) until in 1650 the recusancy Acts were repealed. This boon was the result not of a monarch's liberalism but of the advent of Parliamentary rule that replaced the monarchy and which favoured an unprecedented latitude of religious toleration. While Parliament ruled, Catholics were not allowed publicly to worship in their own way but they were not molested when they did so privately.

And King James I, chief target of the Gunpowder Plot? He was left with shattered nerves, refusing to dine in public, rarely leaving his private rooms, surrounding himself with Scotsmen he had known for years. The discovery in 1606 of another plot – the Franceschi plot, less flamboyant than the Gunpowder Plot and nowhere near the point of execution – frightened him further.

To the end of his life, James lived in dread of violent death. When he heard of the assassination of Henri IV, King of France, in 1610, the number of palace guards was increased, and when the King drove out in his carriage, he was surrounded by armed men. He took to wearing a padded doublet that was supposed to deflect knife or gunshot.

One night, a cannon was fired in Gray's Inn Fields, by some City youths. A couple of miles away, in Whitehall Palace, King James heard the explosion, sat up in bed and shouted 'Treason!' Courtiers and servants came running, the Earl of Arundel with a drawn sword, ready to fight would-be regicides.

It is hard to blame James for his neurosis. His father and grandfather had been murdered, his mother beheaded for her suspected involvement in potential regicide (see pp. 63–9). This and his own experience accounted for his terror of violent death.

The restoration of the Anglo-Scottish monarchy in 1660 brought to the throne a man who had spent most of the past decade in Catholic France and whose mother and sister were overtly Catholic. Charles II, King of England and Scotland, did not take the final step, of formal conversion to Catholicism, until he was on his deathbed in 1685, and he could not prevail against his Parliaments' measures against Catholics. However, in 1670 he signed secret clauses in the otherwise public Treaty of Dover, in which he promised to promote the Catholic faith in England in return for a financial subsidy from France, and from 1672 he protected his brother James, Duke of York, when he began to live openly as a Catholic.

The conversion of the Duke of York infuriated the bigoted Protestant element in government and Parliament, for James was heir presumptive to the throne. At the same time, the fact that the

King's friends and councillors included several Catholics focused anti-Catholic feeling on Court circles. In 1678 the politician poet Andrew Marvell published a pamphlet claiming that there was a Court plot 'to change the lawful government of England into an absolute tyranny and to convert the established Protestant religion into downright popery'. Religious feeling ran high that year throughout the nation, but especially in London, where citizens were quick to pass on rumours and avid to debate the latest news.

That summer the century-old fear of the Jesuits resurfaced too, in relation to a plot to kill the King and to enthrone his brother, the overtly Catholic Duke of York. In the midst of the furore, in October, a London magistrate at work on the case was found dead, pierced by a sword, on a suburban road; the public imagination inevitably linked his death with the 'Popish Plot'.

The man who had let loose the allegations and suspicions was a fraudulent clergyman named Titus Oates. In the autumn of 1678 he tasted fame and power – the power to bring Catholics to trial and death and to rally both rabble and solid citizens to an anti-Catholic frenzy. It was Titus Oates who accused the Queen, Catherine of Braganza, of attempting to poison the King. Catherine was, of course, herself a Catholic.

Trial followed trial, and there were several executions, including those of five Jesuits alleged to have plotted the murder of the King, at a meeting at which Titus Oates said he had himself been present, though witnesses came bravely from France to swear that he had been with them on the date of the Jesuits' alleged 'consult' in London. In July Sir George Wakeman, the Queen's physician, was found 'not guilty', vindicating the Queen herself by association; but the Duchess of York's 'secretary' – her confessor – went to the scaffold.

In the winter of 1678–9 it seemed probable that James, Duke of York, would become a victim of the flying accusations. King Charles could not persuade his brother to make token submission to the Church of England but, fearing imminent impeachment, James agreed to leave the country. In the spring of 1679 the Duke and his Italian Catholic wife took up residence in the Spanish Netherlands; in October they moved to Scotland, where they largely remained until 1682.

Plot and counterplot became entwined. In the matter of the Meal Tub Plot of October 1679, it is hard to tell who was really at fault. A Catholic claimed to have discovered a Presbyterian plot against the life of the Duke of York; then he admitted – or he was paid to pretend – that he had been bribed by the Duke to fabricate evidence of such a plot. It only led to more suspicions of Catholics. And still the trials and executions continued. The Catholic Archbishop of Dublin was one of those implicated – and executed – in 1681.

The Protestant cause was the rallying point of the Whigs, a party strong in Parliament and led by Anthony Ashley Cooper, Earl of Shaftesbury, who urged exclusion of the Duke of York from the royal succession. Although York had Protestant daughters who might have been called to take his place, Shaftesbury won over the King's eldest illegitimate son (he had no legitimate children), James, Duke of Monmouth, with promises of support whenever the crown should be tossed into play. Then, in the autumn of 1682, Shaftesbury suddenly fled the country, just as a warrant went out for his arrest.

It seems likely (though it cannot be proved) that the King had got wind of a rebellion, planned by the Whigs to break out in London on 17 November. That was the anniversary of Elizabeth Tudor's accession to the throne in 1558, which was celebrated by an annual festival in which effigies of the Pope and his cohorts were paraded through the streets – an ideal moment to rally a mob. But the festival was banned that year.

Whether the Whig leaders intended to kill the King and Duke is not known; it seems likely. However, there were others who did. In June 1683, one of the plotters informed on the others. They had, he said, been prepared to assassinate the King and Duke on their way home from the races at Newmarket in April. Rye House, at Hoddesdon in Hertfordshire, lay on the main road to London, and it was planned that, when the King's coach approached it, a haycart would pull across the road, blocking it, and the King and Duke be shot by hidden musketeers. The plot had been foiled by an accident at Newmarket: some stables were destroyed by fire, the races curtailed, and the royal brothers went home a week early, before the plotters' preparations were completed.

Not only the Rye House conspirators but several of the Whig leaders in parliament were arrested now. One of them, the Earl of Essex, committed suicide in the Tower of London before he could be brought to trial; others were found guilty of high treason and executed. Only Monmouth, the King's son, went free, having been frank about the crimes of the others and denying that he had ever intended his father's death. But he went into exile, in the Protestant Netherlands. Back in January, his friend Shaftesbury had died there.

In the aftermath of the Rye House Plot, Charles II felt sufficiently in control to free the Catholics who had been imprisoned on the 'evidence' of Titus Oates and his ilk, and to imprison Oates himself.

On 5 February 1685 Charles was received into the Catholic Church and on the 6th he died. His Catholic brother came to the throne as King James II of England, VII of Scotland.

James survived on the throne for only some three years. His army thwarted Monmouth's bid for the throne in 1686, and many died for their adherence to 'the Protestant Duke', but in 1688 James's nephew and son-in-law William III, Prince of Orange, dethroned him and he went into exile.

William III and his wife-and-cousin Mary II (James II's elder daughter) came to the throne in a blaze of goodwill on all sides. True, the Toleration Act of 1689 excluded Catholics, but the penal laws against them were laxly enforced – except in Ireland, where James had staged an insurrection in 1689.

In exile on the Continent, the former King was surrounded by those who always looked to his restoration, and by 1696 this coterie had formulated a plan to kill William III and, with French help, invade England. In fact, the Jacobites could not hope to mount an invasion without French help but the French were determined not to give that help until the invasion had begun and shown some signs of prospering. The plot – and thus also the invasion – was foiled when one of the plotters found his conscience too heavy and confessed. The story he told showed how detailed had been the plan to assassinate William.

The King enjoyed hunting in Richmond Park. Returning home, he would take the ferry to the north shore of the Thames and then travel by coach to Kensington Palace, with only a small armed escort. The plotters surveyed the route and decided to take their places either side of a narrow lane coming up from the Thames to Turnham Green. When the coach was in the lane (with the soldiers in front and behind because it was too narrow for them to ride abreast the coach), the hidden men were to halt the coach by shooting the horses, then turn their muskets on the split guard, leaving the King at their mercy.

The plot was revealed a couple of days before it was due to be put into effect, on 13 February 1696. The conspirators were arrested and the Navy and volunteer militia of the coastal counties put on alert for the sight of a French fleet in the Channel; of course, it never materialised. Throughout the nation, men flocked to sign *The General Association for King William*, a bond promising to protect the King and swearing vengeance in the event of William's future death by violence.

But William III lived out his natural lifespan and in 1702 was succeeded by his sister-in-law, Anne. With her death in 1714, the rule of the Stuart dynasty came to an end, and neither of the Scottish risings on behalf of James II's Catholic son and grandson, in 1715 and 1745, managed to unseat the Hanoverians who succeeded to the British throne.

That was not, of course, the end of religious intolerance or of the disabilities with which Catholics – like other religious dissenters – had to live, but it was the end of the assassinations for religious purposes that had threatened English and Anglo-Scottish monarchs for some century and a half.

At least, that is how it seemed until, in 1979, a member of Britain's royal family was killed in Ireland, where religion and politics are still as closely entwined as they were three centuries ago.

CHAPTER SEVEN

KILLING NO MURDER

Killing No Murder was the title of a pamphlet distributed in England in 1657. In forceful and witty language, it set out to justify the killing of a ruler – a killing which, it argued, was neither sin nor crime: a killing that was not murder.

That pamphlet should not be mistaken for an apologia for the 'judicial murder' of King Charles I, eight years earlier. Rather, it advocated the killing of Oliver Cromwell, the Lord Protector, head of the government of the republican Commonwealth that had replaced the age-old monarchy. *Killing No Murder* sought to justify the killing of Cromwell as being in the public interest. It was characteristic of the seventeenth century that a pamphlet should be the means of disseminating this view: it was a message for the masses, not a proposition for consideration by philosophers.

Tyrannicide had long been a subject for philosophical debate: was it justifiable to depose a tyrant (or an unworthy ruler) and to kill him so that he might never regain power? In England in the eleventh century Henry de Bracton, in the twelfth John of Salisbury and in the fourteenth William of Occam made major contributions to the debate. But it was the Italian Thomas Aquinas, troubled by the paradox of a God-appointed king who resorted to evil, who placed the problem in the international arena of controversy, in the thirteenth century. Aquinas insisted that, while it might be justifiable to kill a usurping monarch, even the worst of tyrants must go unharmed if his title to power could not be disputed, since legitimate secular power derived from God.

In 1408, when Jean, Duke of Burgundy, was on trial for the murder of Louis, Duke of Orleans (see pp. 41–2), he was represented by a theologian named Jean Petit. Petit based the Duke's defence on the authority of previous philosophers' works but came to the then novel conclusion that it was not only justifiable but praiseworthy to kill 'a traitor and disloyal tyrant'. Petit's pleading can scarcely be said to have won Burgundy's subsequent acquittal, for the Duke was never in danger of being punished for his admitted murder. However, the case Petit stated was a landmark in the development of the debate on tyrannicide. That is not to say that it was generally accepted. In 1413, taking advantage of Burgundy's overthrow, Charles, Duke of Orleans (son of the murdered Duke), had the celebrated cleric Jean Gerson denounce Petit's thesis: a tyrant must be brought to justice, he declared, not killed before he had a chance to repent. Orleans used his influence to have France's highest churchmen declare Petit's justification of tyrannicide suspect of heresy, and the Church Council that opened at Constance in November 1414 condemned it.

A century later, Martin Luther urged Protestants to obey lawful authority however harsh or unjust it might be. Jean Calvin insisted that, as all earthly power derived from God, disobedience to a ruler was disobedience to God. Neither of the great Reformers would countenance tyrannicide. The sixteenth-century Jesuits, on the other hand, did manage to make a case for tyrannicide – one that the Catholic Church now condoned. The Spanish Jesuit Juan de Mariana, in his *De Rege et Regis Institutione* (1599), laid out the reasons for killing a tyrant, however lawful his kingship might be. A private citizen was justified in killing a monarch whom his subjects had declared unfit to rule, said Mariana – unfit, that is, by being a tyrant or heretic. However, after the assassination of Henri IV, King of France, in 1610, Claudio Aquaviva, general of the Jesuit Order, repudiated Mariana's thesis, instructing Jesuits that they were not to teach or advise anyone that it was lawful, on any pretext, to kill a monarch or plot his death. Nevertheless, Mariana's assertion that a nation's representative body might rightfully declare a monarch a 'public enemy' and depose him was in line with the general thinking of the time, by then Protestant as well as Catholic.

The judicial deposition of a monarch – as a 'tyrant' – occurred twice in Scandinavia in the sixteenth century. In 1523 Christian II, King of Denmark and Norway, was deposed, and in 1568–9 Erik XIV, King of Sweden. Christian II remained at large (and troublesome) until 1532, when he was imprisoned until his (natural) death in 1559. In 1568 Erik XIV was replaced on the Swedish throne by his brother, Johan III, and in January 1569 formally deposed by the kingdom's four Estates. Erik had suffered periods of insanity, and Sweden's nobles had had no choice but to dethrone him. Even so, there were at least three attempts to restore him, including one, in 1574, which aimed to kill King Johan. But already, in 1569, Johan had gained Church approval for the execution of Erik if he were proved to be involved in any plot against the throne; in 1575 this was extended to allow for him to be killed if there were any attempt to free him from captivity. The former king died on 24 February 1577 after a brief illness. Recent examination of the corpse presents the strong likelihood that he was poisoned.

A more obvious step along the road to 'public regicide' occurred with the execution of Mary, Queen of Scots, in 1587 (see pp. 99–100). After her trial and conviction, she might have been brought to London, to die on Tower Hill in the sight of thousands of witnesses, but her execution was staged in the great hall of Fotheringhay Castle, in Northamptonshire, with at most some 300 onlookers. Elizabeth of England would have liked her cousin's death to have been even more private. After Mary's conviction, her gaoler, Sir Amyas Paulet, received word that a loyal subject of Queen Elizabeth might prevent the necessity for an execution – that is, Paulet was invited to murder Mary in her cell. Ostensibly this was desirable lest Scotland be antagonised by the execution of its former queen; in fact, Elizabeth shrank from having her cousin's death accredited to her, lest she herself should one day fall victim to 'judicial murder'.

Paulet did not take the hint. 'I am so unhappy as to have lived to see this unhappy day,' he wrote, 'in which I am required by direction from my most gracious sovereign to do an act which God and the law forbiddeth. . . . God forbid that I should make so foul a shipwreck of my conscience, or leave so great a blot on my poor posterity, to shed blood without law or warrant.'

'Law or warrant': in other words, authorisation by the nation's leaders, which Mariana subsequently declared one of the essential requisites of tyrannicide. (The alternative was divine inspiration.) But would any monarch at the mercy of his people recognise the authority of a court set up to try him? This was the problem that arose when Charles I, King of England and Scotland, was put on trial in 1648.

The King's stance was based on the ancient belief that a monarch was a person chosen by God to represent Him on earth and that subjects' obedience to a monarch reflected their obedience to God. The 'Divine Right of Kings' was a concept that Charles had imbibed from his father, James VI and I, whose view of his calling could not have been more exalted: '. . . kings are justly called gods,' James wrote in his *Basilikon Doron*, 'for that they exercise a manner or resemblance of divine power on earth. For if you will consider the attributes of God, you shall see how they agree in the person of the king.' It was unfortunate for Charles I that he believed in his sacred, mystic appointment at a time at which his subjects were beginning to define kingship by its duties rather than its rights and to speak of the contract implicit in the relationship between a monarch and his people.

However, Charles's subjects did not make war on him and subsequently behead him because he was unrealistic, anachronistic or vainglorious. The nation, under Parliament's leadership, took up arms against Charles in 1642 and killed him in 1649 because he had offended against the things closest to human hearts, religion and money, and Parliament took the lead because the King had denied Parliament's rights.

Charles I's insistence on Anglican orthodoxy and his leniency towards Catholics (his French wife was a Catholic) infuriated his Puritan subjects – the vast body of nonconformists who sought the separation of Church and State. The economic basis of the Civil War is harder to define: in some measure, it reflected the resentment by the increasingly wealthy and educated middle class of the land-owning aristocracy, in whom political as well as economic power was still largely vested. More specifically, Charles had sought to circumvent Parliament's power to vote taxes by the use of financial ploys that had no legal precedent. This was one of the many ways in which he had alienated his Parliament, which in practical ways came to act out the political theories that claimed rights and powers for the elected representatives of the people – limited rights and powers, they seem in modern terms, but repugnant to the man who claimed absolute authority for himself.

When the nation divided, in the summer of 1642, before the first skirmishes of the Civil War were fought, many of those who became

Royalists ('Cavaliers') whole-heartedly disapproved of the policies of Charles I but could not bring themselves to wage war on him – an action that constituted treason according to the 1352 statute. Had the Royalists been victorious in the Civil War, there would have been a spate of treason trials of the leaders of the Parliamentarian ('Roundhead') army and its political masters. As it was, after six years of war, Charles was the loser, and it was he who was indicted for treason, for having waged war on his subjects.

As the law stood, there was no provision for charging a king with treason, since treason had always been defined as a crime against the monarch himself. However, earlier in Charles's reign, in 1644, when Archbishop Laud was tried under a bill of attainder, it was stated in his prosecution that 'treason may be against the realm as well as against the king.' Hitherto the king and his kingdom had been seen as one entity; their division allowed for a situation in which a king might be a traitor to the realm.

This was the stance taken when Charles I was impeached as 'a tyrant, traitor and murderer and a public and implacable enemy to the commonwealth of England'. He had had, it was said, 'a wicked design to erect and uphold in himself an unlimited and tyrannical power to rule according to his will and to overthrow the rights and liberties of the people'; in pursuit of this aim, he had 'traitorously and maliciously levied war against the present Parliament and the people therein represented'.

The trial of Charles I has been called illegal (and so his execution has been called 'judicial murder') because no case for the King's defence was presented. But this was Charles I's own responsibility: he refused to recognise the authority of the court and thus refused to plead either 'guilty' or 'not guilty'. Of course, since no court had ever been convened in England to try a reigning monarch, there could be no appeal to precedent to justify either the existence or the constituent parts of the court. Parliament acted as it thought best, assembling a commission to try Charles, but inevitably the King refused to recognise its members' right to stand in judgment of his actions.

In treason trials, under Common Law, a refusal to plead was treated as if the defendant had pleaded 'guilty'; that is, it eliminated the need for presentation of a case for the defence. Obviously, there were men in the commission whose consciences would have been easier had the King been given the chance to present his case, but his refusal to plead deprived them of that salve to their conscience. Charles knew full well what he was doing.

The court sat on Saturday 20 January 1649 and on Monday and Tuesday the 22nd and 23rd. Each day Charles was offered – and refused – the chance to enter a plea. On the 27th he heard himself convicted and sentence passed: he was to be beheaded.

Never for a moment, apparently, did Charles I doubt that he had been in the right in all his dealings with his subjects, in peace and in civil war. When two of his children were brought to bid him farewell, he impressed on the elder, the thirteen-year-old Princess Elizabeth, that he was going to die 'a glorious death . . . it being for the laws and liberties of this land, and for maintenance of the Protestant religion'.

In preference to Tower Green, which was large and open, the square in front of the Banqueting House of Whitehall Palace was chosen as the site of the scaffold: the area was small and easily controlled by armed guards. At about 2 p.m. on 30 January Charles stepped onto the scaffold. He was not given the chance to address the crowd that had gathered, for soldiers stood between the people and the scaffold; but he spoke to those who stood around him. This was his chance to protest his innocence and to explain his actions – and to forgive his enemies.

Then King Charles I lay down on the ground, his head on the low block, and the executioner waited while he said his last prayer. When Charles made a pre-arranged sign, the axe fell on his neck.

A young man in the crowd recorded his impressions: 'The blow I saw given and can truly say, with a sad heart, at the instant whereof, I remember well, there was such a groan by the thousands then present as I never heard before and desire I may never hear again.'

The execution had been delayed until the afternoon by the necessity for Parliament to pass a bill prohibiting the proclamation of Charles's successor on the throne. With his death, the monarchy was to die also.

Was the execution of Charles I murder? He would have said so, since he would not admit that he had merited capital punishment or that those who had convicted him had the right to do so. At the time, Royalists said the same. Even today, there are those, generally 'Anglo-Catholics', who refer to the King as 'Charles the Martyr', going so far as to dedicate their churches to his memory.

In 1649 it seemed impossible that the monarchy would ever be willingly restored; the defeat of the nominal King Charles II at the Battle of Worcester in 1651 apparently confirmed that. Yet in 1660 Charles II was warmly welcomed home, crowned king and accorded scope for personal rule scarcely less than that his father had claimed. The Commonwealth had been a noble experiment – admirable, above all, in its religious toleration – but its ideals had been marred by the imperfections of human nature and by a perpetual vying for power between Parliament and army.

As far as the theme of royal murders is concerned, the significance of the restoration of the monarchy lies in the retribution meted out for the 'judicial murder' of Charles I. Of the fifty-nine signatories to his death warrant, forty-one were still alive in 1660. Fifteen now fled the country; nine were tried for regicide and hanged, drawn and quartered (along with four other men, including a minister who had preached against the King). Some regicides claimed to have been misled or to have been weak in giving the verdict expected of them, against their conscience; one of them actually said that his hand had been held to write his signature. Of those who escaped execution, some were sentenced to life imprisonment, others set free, though they had to undergo the annual humiliation of being drawn on a hurdle to Tyburn.

The corpses of the three most important signatories, Oliver Cromwell, General Ireton and John Bradshaw, president of the regicide court, were exhumed from their place of honour in Westminster Abbey, exposed on gibbets at Tyburn and then thrown into the ditch in which common criminals' bodies were piled.

It was generally felt that, in view of the enormity of the crime, the regicides had been treated with considerable mercy by the son of the man they had allegedly murdered.

The overthrow of Charles I and his government and the King's execution were accompanied by a host of political treatises offering justification for such extreme measures, and the action of a monarch's responsibility and accountability to his subjects became a central factor in the philosophy of politics.

'L'état c'est moi,' said Louis XIV, King of France: 'I am the nation.' He was also the government, for all appointments were in his gift, and he was vigilant in controlling policy and administration. His great-grandson and successor, Louis XV, was, however, responsible for taking France into a disastrously expensive (though ultimately successful) war and was threatened (albeit without effect) by a parliament's refusal to sanction taxation unless a limit were placed on royal powers.

Philosophers and statesmen were not the only critics of royal government. In 1757, Robert-François Damiens, a servant in his early forties, told at his trial for attempted regicide how he had heard his masters blaming the King for the parlous state of France and had decided to do something about it. In January 1757, he stabbed Louis XV with a pen-knife. The King bled a good deal and was thoroughly frightened (expecting death, he was given the last rites and begged his wife's forgiveness for his infidelities) but he survived. When Damiens was told that, before his execution, he would have his right hand cut off and its wound seared with boiling pitch, he remarked laconically, 'It's going to be a hard day.' He died in front of a crowd of thousands, some of whom had made the journey from Britain to watch the spectacle.

During the next reign, that of Louis XVI, political, fiscal and social discontent escalated – justifiably, for the King's ineptitude was as great as his intolerance of attempts to relieve him of any part of his power. Open and forceful opposition to royal despotism began in May 1789 with an attempt by the Third Estate (Commons) of the States General to become an assembly representing, and legislating for, the French people, but neither this concession, in June, nor the King's acceptance of a constitution, limiting his power, in September 1791, could end 'the French Revolution', as it came to be called. Had Louis been scrupulously obedient to the new terms under which he reigned, he – and the French monarchy – might have survived.

While the extent of the treason for which Charles I was indicted covered many years of his reign, Louis was charged with crimes that dated only from the establishment of the new constitution; before that, the French king had been held to be 'inviolable'. Under the terms of the new constitution, Louis was certainly a traitor, having vetoed legislation in contravention of his constitutional rights, supported counter-revolutionaries against the government, corresponded with *émigrés* outlawed by the new regime and negotiated with the foreign powers that had recently invaded France. All this was proved against Louis XVI at his trial in December 1792. He was convicted and sentenced to death.

There was one major difference between the executions of Charles I and Louis XVI, in 1649 and 1793 respectively: Charles I went to the block a king, Louis XVI was only 'Citizen Capet', the French monarchy having been abolished in September 1792, after he had been declared a traitor to his realm. His execution, on 21 January 1793, was the punishment of a criminal, it was claimed; still, the monarchs of Europe called it murder.

Nearly a century and a half earlier, Charles I had died in the traditional way, the axe wielded by a masked man; Louis's head fell under the blade of a guillotine, a machine that was a symbol of the new democracy: before the Revolution, only aristocrats were beheaded, commoners were hanged, but the revolutionaries had voted to end the use of hanging and introduced the efficient and 'merciful' device invented by Dr Joseph-Ignace Guillotin.

In October 1793, Louis's widow, Marie-Antoinette of Austria, went to the guillotine, the following May his sister, Madame Elisabeth. It was the time of the 'Reign of Terror': some 14,000 people were guillotined in the year following Louis XVI's death. Fewer than ten per cent were aristocrats, about six per cent clergy, the rest a broad spectrum of people who had been charged with sedition against the new regime.

In July 1793, six months after the death of Louis XVI, his son, the twelve-year-old Dauphin – or Louis XVII, as royalists called him – had been taken away from the rooms in the tower of the Temple prison in Paris in which his mother, aunt and sister were lodged. For the next six months he was in the care of a shoemaker and his wife. After their resignation in January 1794, he was confined in one room, under guard, and soon after, inspectors found him silent, withdrawn, unwilling to make any unnecessary movement; by May he was ill; in June he died.

The Dauphin was not murdered: the autopsy done on his body after death showed that he had died of scrofula, a form of tuberculosis almost certainly attributable to living-conditions of the meanest sort. And it seems too that he had lost the will to live.

Whether the deaths of Louis XVI and members of his family were judicial murder or capital punishment is still debated. At the time, they caused amazement and horror throughout Europe, even in those nations in which monarchy and democracy were seen as incompatible. In France, it was as if the violence of revolution demanded the ritual sacrifice of the figureheads of the old regime, so that the new regime might be legitimately born.

CHAPTER EIGHT

RUSSIA

The murders of Russia's early rulers bear a striking resemblance to those of rulers of other European nations, in motive, method and result. However, no other nation had to undergo Russia's agony of being ruled by a man who was inherently cruel and merciless, relishing the pain of others – not just killing his enemies but devising new torments to prolong their pre-death agony, for his own enjoyment, and making others watch them. No ruler in European history, not even Adolf Hitler in Germany, was ever as evil as Tsar Ivan IV of Russia – Ivan 'the Terrible', as he is known, though he might be better named Ivan 'the Terrifying'. In later centuries, Russian rulers and members of their families were murdered for that familiar prize the crown, but their stories come as a welcome anticlimax to the hell of Ivan IV's reign, in the second half of the sixteenth century.

As elsewhere in northern Europe, Russia's history begins at the blurred line between legend and fact. For example, when Prince Igor, ruler of Kiev, was murdered while he was collecting tribute money from the tribe of the Drevliane in the year 945, his killers were allegedly punished by his widow, Olga, by her sending over their village a flight of sparrows with lighted matches attached to their tails, to burn the Drevliane out.

Two generations later, three brothers, Igor's grandsons, vied for the throne. Yaropolk killed Oleg, then Vladimir killed Yaropolk, to become sole ruler of the principality of Kiev. When Vladimir died, in 1015, allocating his lands to the sons of his many marriages, the eldest, Sviatopolk 'the Accursed', increased his holdings by killing his half-brothers Sviatoslav, Boris and Gleb but was then overthrown and killed by another half-brother, Yaroslav, who reunited Kievan Russia and extended it.

The history of medieval Russia is one of intermittent war between the three principal states, Kiev, Novgorod and Moscow. The supremacy of Kiev was challenged by the rise of Novgorod, then both were eclipsed by Moscow.

One of the weaknesses of Kiev was its frequent civil wars, waged by members of the ruling family, laying waste to the land and devastating the capital city. In 1169 Prince Andrei Bogoliubski came down from the north and sacked Kiev, then, taking power himself, moved the capital to his own city of Vladimir, between the rivers Volga and Oka. But that transfer was only brief: in 1174 Andrei was murdered by his own nobles. They set on him when he was unarmed but he was able to beat them off; the nobles were even in retreat when they heard the Prince moaning at the pain of his wounds; realising that he was no more to be feared, they returned and killed him.

The last blow to Kiev was dealt in 1240 by the Mongols, the great 'Golden Horde' of invaders from the east who stormed through Europe in the thirteenth and fourteenth centuries, penetrating as far as the Baltic and Adriatic Seas and challenging even the Holy Roman Empire. In Russia, Mongol rule lasted some two and a half centuries. Novgorod submitted to the Mongols and was allowed to keep its independence, as long as it paid tribute to the Khan; Moscow retained its native princes too. One of them, Yuri, married a sister of the Mongol Khan in 1317 or 1318. But Moscow was at war with the principality of Tver, and when the Mongol princess was captured and died in prison in Tver, Yuri accused Prince Mikhail of Tver of having her poisoned. Mikhail was called to the court of the Khan, tried, convicted of murder and executed. Yuri's triumph was brief: in 1322 the Khan named Mikhail's son Dmitri Grand Prince – the ancient title taken by the most powerful of Russian princes, which was now in the Mongols' gift. Three years later, Dmitri had Yuri murdered.

In the second half of the fifteenth century, Ivan III of Moscow was Grand Prince, and he also claimed to be 'ruler of all Russia', for his power extended from the White Sea almost to the Black Sea, from the Baltic to beyond the Urals, after his defeat of the Mongols in 1480. In

1472 he had married Zoë (in Russia, Sophia) Palaeologina, niece of the last Emperor of Byzantium. The ceremonial of his Court, based on Byzantine tradition, was designed to impress on the nobility his exalted position, to reinforce their awe of him and their obedience.

Another element of Byzantine Court life allegedly brought to Russia by Sophia was the use of poison. For centuries, Byzantium had been a byword for its monarchs' heedless dispatching of over-ambitious relations – as an alternative to having them blinded or castrated, to diminish their will to reign. Now Sophia was suspected of having her stepson Ivan poisoned (Ivan III's son by his first marriage) in order to promote the claim of her own son Vasili to be heir to the throne. But the younger Ivan was survived by his son Dmitri, and in 1497 a plot was discovered against Dmitri's life too. Sophia and Vasili were both implicated, and both were 'disgraced' – not imprisoned but kept under guard in their apartments. Five years later, however, Dmitri alienated Ivan III's favour, and Vasili was restored and raised to the rank of co-ruler with his father. When Ivan III died, in 1505, Vasili succeeded him.

And so to Ivan IV – Ivan 'the Terrible', Vasili's son, who was only three years old when, in 1533, Vasili died. Ivan was the first Tsar of Russia – the word 'tsar' (meaning emperor) deriving from the Roman 'Caesar' and coming to Russia via Byzantium.

Admittedly Ivan had an unhappy childhood, if that may be used as a plea in mitigation of his crimes in adulthood. His mother, who acted as regent, was poisoned when he was eight years old, and during his minority his Court was constantly depleted by the murder of nobles vying for power, at the hands of their rivals. However, even in early childhood, Ivan showed the traits that later made him feared throughout Russia. The boy delighted in torturing animals and in watching the torture of political prisoners; he was only eleven years old when he committed his first rape.

When Ivan took power into his own hands and was crowned Tsar, in 1547, he began to establish a reputation as a lawgiver and promoter of trade and industry. He was devoted to his young wife, Anastasia

Romanova, and was even regarded by his nobles as somewhat over-pious. Then, in 1559, Anastasia died, and inevitably Ivan suspected that she had been poisoned by his closest councillors, who resented her influence over him. Thereafter the Tsar was prone to sudden fits of rage, exacerbated by drunkenness: hysterical crying, shouting, falling to the ground, banging his head on the floor. At war in Lithuania and Poland and against the Tartars in southern Russia, he took thousands of prisoners and himself supervised their torture, flogging and rape, relishing their screams as their eyes were torn out. The process of killing was often deliberately prolonged. Not only men but women and children were flayed, impaled and disembowelled, mauled by wild bears, buried alive, roasted over fires and frozen in icy rivers. When Ivan sacked Novgorod, in 1569, as many as 60,000 people may have been killed; the fortunate ones died in battle.

One source of Ivan's inventive punishments was the Dracula myth, which first entered Russia in a 1502 publication but which was popularised in Ivan's reign. 'Dracula' was in fact a fifteenth-century prince of Wallachia, Vlad V Dracul ('Dracul' meaning 'dragon' and referring to the Order of the Dragon conferred on his father by the Holy Roman Emperor). He was also known as 'Vlad the Impaler' from the most notorious of his methods of dealing with his enemies: impaling them on spikes. His sadism was horrific; the stories about him encompass every form of torture, including enforced cannibalism – mothers eating their children, husbands their wives, cooked and uncooked. At least that was never alleged of Ivan the Terrible.

In 1565 Ivan instituted the corps of Oprichniki, a specially recruited force of men who virtually policed the countryside but who were themselves immune from the law, free to punish and kill anyone who opposed them. But even the Oprichniki were not immune from Ivan's paranoid suspicions. After the sack of Novgorod, he claimed that the Oprichniki had betrayed him: in 1570 they were disbanded and their leaders tortured and killed.

Ivan's fear of assassination was not unwarranted. In 1567, for example, while he was engaged in the Lithuanian war, his nobles planned to hand him over to his prime enemy, the King of Poland – in whose hands he would inevitably have died. But the plot was discovered, and, predictably, retribution was horrible. It was almost always the nobles whom Ivan treated the most harshly, those with the potential of banding together effectively against him, those who might use their access to the Tsar to kill him. But every class of society in Russia was the Tsar's to use as he would; he had unlimited power. It has been estimated that hundreds of thousands of people were killed during his reign.

Ivan IV's heir was his eldest son, another Ivan, his willing companion in every evil pleasure. For some years, the Tsar felt no reason to mistrust his son, and the Tsarevich survived to the age of twenty-seven before he fell foul of his father; even then, there is nothing to show that Ivan IV killed his son in more than a momentary anger. The story went that, in November 1581, the Tsar discovered his daughter-in-law, who was seven months pregnant, wearing clothes other than those prescribed by the Church for expectant women: it took so little to trigger his rage. He knocked her down and kicked her as she lay before him. The younger Ivan tried to go his wife's aid, but the Tsar lashed out at him with his iron-tipped staff. Three days later, the Tsarevich died of his injuries. The baby was born dead, and the Tsarevna died soon after.

For years Ivan IV had been given to bouts of self-hatred and self-recrimination, though they did nothing to mitigate his bloodlust. After the death of his son, he was never at peace. He lived only three years more, indubitably insane.

When one man has supreme power in a nation, the danger that that man might be a homicidal maniac must be just one in several million. Yet Ivan IV of Russia was such a man, and under his rule Russia lived through a nightmare. If ever the murder of a ruler might be justified, it must surely have been that of Ivan 'the Terrible'. Tragically, he was allowed to live.

After Ivan 'the Terrible', Russia enjoyed a brief respite from its miseries under his son Feodor I, an ineffectual young man content to abide by the decisions of his advisers. He was childless; his heir was, presumably, his half-brother Dmitri of Uglich, though as the son of Ivan IV's seventh wife, Dmitri's eligibility was questionable, for the Church allowed only three legal marriages.

When, in 1591, Dmitri died, Boris Godunov, leader of Tsar Feodor's councillors who himself coveted the throne, was suspected of having had him murdered. However, there were witnesses who claimed that the nine-year-old had been playing when suddenly, before they could go to his aid, he fell down in an epileptic seizure, accidentally cutting his own throat with a knife.

Thus, when Feodor died in 1598, Boris Godunov succeeded him. Then began 'the Time of Troubles'. A drought was followed by a famine; the people became desperate, defending their food supplies, defending their meagre crops or fighting to gain the food that would keep their families alive, scavenging and looting, killing for their own survival. Then came epidemics worse than any known since the Black Death. In Moscow alone, over 100,000 people died.

The people said that these calamities were God's punishment for their accepting Boris as their tsar. Some claimed that Boris had killed Dmitri of Uglich to take the throne for himself; others said that Dmitri was still alive, that Boris had passed off another dead child as Dmitri. A man calling himself Dmitri of Uglich began to gather a following in Lithuania and Poland. In October 1604 he invaded Russia with a sizeable army; in April 1605 Boris Godunov conveniently died; in June Dmitri entered Moscow and was hailed as tsar. Boris's widow and his heir, Feodor II, were strangled.

Whether Russia's leading nobles believed in Dmitri's claim or not, it suited them to accept him, to be rid of Boris Godunov. The mother of Dmitri of Uglich claimed to recognise her son in the young man, and Prince Vasili Shuisky, who had headed the commission inquiring into reports of the boy's death, now said that he had been wrong in believing the epilepsy story.

Imperial or commoner, Tsar Dmitri was an intelligent man who rapidly learned the art of governing, though he shocked his courtiers by his air of informality and by his habit of wandering through Moscow unprotected, in disguise. But his reign was brief. His main failing was that he was bound in gratitude to the Poles who had increased his army in 1605. Ostensibly to save the Tsar from the Poles, in May 1606 Vasili Shuisky led armed men into the Kremlin, but when they had taken the palace by force, he declared that Dmitri was, after all, an impostor. 'The False Dmitri', as he came to be called, tried to save himself by leaping from a window, but he was badly hurt in the fall and was taken prisoner, inevitably to be killed.

To prove to Russia that Tsar Dmitri had been an impostor, Shuisky had the body of the child Prince brought from Uglich to Moscow, for burial among his ancestors. Thus he demonstrated that the ancient reigning dynasty was now extinct.

Vasili Shuisky's reign lasted from that summer of 1606 until the summer of 1610, and he passed most of those years in attempts to put down assaults on the crown on behalf of further pretenders. The main one was 'the second Dmitri', his origins obscure (a Lithuanian gaol was mentioned) but accepted by 'the False Dmitri's' widow, who subsequently bore him a son. Living with his army and occasionally engaging tsarist forces, the new Dmitri outlived Shuisky, who was childless, so that Russia drifted in uncertainty while Poles and Swedes made inroads in the west. Then, in December, the second Dmitri was murdered by one of his own adherents, apparently in revenge for another killing.

In July 1613 a sixteen-year-old was crowned Tsar. He was Mikhail Romanov, a young nobleman who had to be strenuously persuaded to accept his destiny. His first challenge was to impose order in Russia, eliminating the rebels and pretenders of recent years. In 1614 the four-year-old son of the second Dmitri was one of those who was hanged for the sake of future peace in Russia.

The violence witnessed by Peter I, Tsar of Russia, when he was a child, accompanied by the threat to his own life, might have acted on him as similar childhood traumas had on Ivan IV. In fact, though Peter was always subject to violent rages and was unquestionably cruel by modern standards, he also had a strong vein of human sympathy and understanding, a rational view of his own power and purpose and a vibrant energy, focused on Russia's welfare, that have made him the most admired of the Romanov tsars.

Peter came to the throne at the age of nine, in April 1682, at the death of his half-brother, Feodor III. Feodor's full brother, Ivan, aged sixteen, should have been his successor, but Ivan was weak in both physique and intellect. Peter's mother, Natalia Narishkina, became his regent, supported by her ambitious family. Inevitably, this elevation of a section of the nobility alienated other nobles from the government, and they immediately began to gather round the Tsarevna Sophia, the 25-year-old sister of Feodor and Ivan. Sophia had all the qualities of a potentially successful ruler.

Moscow seethed with the rumour that Natalia had had Tsar Feodor poisoned, to promote her own son, and that she was planning to kill his brother Ivan. Sophia's supporters fed the *streltsi* – the palace guard – with these rumours, and in May 1682 they marched on the Kremlin, crowding into the courtyard in front of the palace and calling for the blood of the Narishkins. Courageously, Natalia appeared on the Red Staircase above the courtyard, accompanied by both Peter and Ivan. Appeased, the soldiers might have dispersed, had not their commander joined the group on the Red Staircase and threatened them with punishment if they did not immediately leave the Kremlin. Those nearest the staircase seized the man and threw him over the balustrade, to be impaled on the pikes of the men below – in full sight of the nine-year-old Peter.

Not satisfied with one death, the *streltsi* roamed through the palace, seeking out the Narishkins and their friends. The Tsarina's kinsmen spent two days in hiding, hearing the screams of those who fell victim to the *streltsi*. On the third day, in fear of her own life and that of her son, Natalia was forced to hand over her brother Ivan, a particular object of hatred. Whatever his former sins, he died bravely, having resisted the torture intended to make him confess to having murdered Feodor III. His arms and legs had been broken by the time the guards gave up and dragged him into Red Square, where he was hacked to death.

A hastily convened assembly of nobles and the representatives of the people declared Ivan and Peter joint rulers of Russia. A few days later, at the demand of the *streltsi*, Sophia was declared regent. With a mixture of guile and sheer force of character, she strengthened her position and set about stabilising Moscow and ruling Russia. Ivan was firmly under her control; Peter and his mother were sent into the country.

By the summer of 1689, when he was seventeen years old, Peter had already shown his half-sister that he would not be another Ivan.

A clash seemed certain, but which would make the first move?

Then Peter received a warning, delivered one night by two loyal guardsmen, that Sophia was planning to have him murdered. He panicked, running out of the palace in his nightshirt, taking horse and hiding in a wood, in which he was found by friends who brought him clothes and begged him to return. He would not. Hysterical with fear, he rode on to a nearby abbey and asked for shelter.

1 September was New Year's Day in the old Russian calendar, and according to custom crowds gathered in Red Square in Moscow. Sophia came out to address them. She had never intended fratricide, she said, and she asked them to judge her only on her record as regent. She spoke to no effect. Within a few days the army had deserted her, and senior churchmen were approving Peter's independence. Even before Peter entered Moscow, Sophia had been enclosed in the convent in which she was to spend the next fifteen years.

Despite Peter's triumph in 1689, it was to be nearly a decade before he embarked on those reforms that were his monument. Initially he gave over the government of Russia to his mother and a select group of ministers, while he undertook a strenuous study of warfare and its allied crafts, such as smithing and gunnery but especially shipbuilding, which came to dominate his life. After his mother's death in 1694, he took on more work but in 1697 left Russia forthe West, to study – and work with his bare hands – in shipyards in the Netherlands and England. On his return in 1698 he at last began to set in train the reforms that reshaped Russian government and to build the navy on which he had set his heart.

First, though, Peter eliminated the power of the *streltsi*, perhaps thereby purging himself of the nightmares that must have haunted him since 1682. More recently the *streltsi* had mounted rebellions that he suspected had been instigated by his half-sister Sophia. They had been put down, in his absence, with what he regarded as insufficient severity. The same could not be said of his measures. Hundreds of men (and several women whom their forced testimonies implicated) were put to torture in an attempt to trace the highest culprits, but Sophia's name was not among those screamed out by his victims. Then the executions began: a total of 799 *streltsi* were beheaded, hanged or broken on a wheel. Their bodies decorated the public thoroughfares of Moscow, and the grim cold of winter preserved them for months.

Peter had learned more in the West than shipbuilding, and on his return to Russia he instigated reforms in government, trade and industry, commerce, education, medical care and other spheres of life; he even tackled the reform of the hidebound Orthodox Church. His energy, inventiveness and capacity for creating order from ancient chaos were phenomenal. But Peter lacked one gift: he had no satisfactory son whom he might train to succeed him and to continue his work.

By his first wife, Peter had one son, Alexei, born in 1690, but as the boy grew to manhood it became clear that he was by no means the heir his father wanted. Alexei was gentle and timid, academically accomplished but lacking energy, uninterested in warfare and above all terrified of his father. Influenced by his mother and by the churchmen who feared Peter's reforms, Alexei harked back to the old Russia, before Peter began to 'westernise' its government and society. By 1715, Peter so feared the reversal of his policies when his son should come to reign that he wrote to Alexei threatening to disinherit him if he did not soon offer proof of his loyalty. However, when Alexei volunteered to renounce the succession, Peter would not accept it: it would be all too easy for Alexei to claim, when Peter died, that that renunciation had been made under duress. Nor would the Tsar accept his son's subsequent offer to enter a monastery: again, religious vows made under duress could be annulled.

In the autumn of 1716 the Tsarevich took advantage of his father's absence abroad to leave Russia. He presented himself at the Court of his late wife's brother-in-law, the Holy Roman Emperor Karl VI, begging asylum. Although Karl realised the danger of provoking war with Russia, he took pity on the young man – perhaps with an eye to the gratitude of a future tsar – and sent him to live in hiding in the Tyrol. But Peter's agents found Alexei there, and later they discovered him in his new hideout, in Naples. Promised a pardon if he returned to Russia, threatened with retribution if he did not, Alexei was lured home.

The Tsarevich arrived in Moscow at the end of January 1718. On

13 February he renounced his right to the throne and promised to uphold that of his three-year-old half-brother, another Peter.

However, that was not the end of it. Alexei's friends and his mistress were induced to testify against him, revealing that he had become the focus of all who opposed Peter's reforms, in expectation that the next tsar would reverse them. These testimonies were enough to have Alexei arrested and imprisoned, to stand trial before a court composed of statesmen, military officers and senior churchmen.

This last fact is extremely interesting. It seems strange that the Tsar should think it necessary to have public approval of (indeed, public demand for) the elimination of his son. Russia had progressed a long way under Peter, but by no means as far as this 'power-sharing' between monarchy and people. The answer seems to be that Peter chose this public method of dispatching Alexei in order to avoid rumours of his survival and the appearance of men pretending to be the Tsarevich, such as had occurred in the previous century, with 'the false Dmitri' and his like.

On 19 June 1718 Alexei was lashed with twenty-five strokes of the knout; on the 24th he suffered fifteen more. As a result, he confessed to all the charges of treason brought against him, and he was sentenced to death. But more was wanted, and on 26 June he was tortured again, apparently in his father's presence. That day he died.

The death – the virtual murder – of Alexei Romanov recalls those of Ivan IV's son Ivan in 1581 and of the heir of Philip II of Spain in 1598 (see pp. 56–7). But neither of those princes was tortured in public and sentenced to death: Alexei was deliberately submitted to the extremity of pain and may well have been fortunate that it killed him before he could undergo the refinements of agony in which Russian executioners specialised.

Peter I's sons by his second wife predeceased him, as infants, but since he had claimed the power to name his own heir, he might choose from several members of the family, including Alexei's infant son, the only male in a dynasty of daughters. But, on his deathbed in 1725, Peter left it too late. He managed to write the words 'I leave everything to' – but no more. At his death, his wife, a German peasant who had formerly been the Tsar's mistress, took the throne as Catherine I. In her reign and later, Peter's reforms were not developed

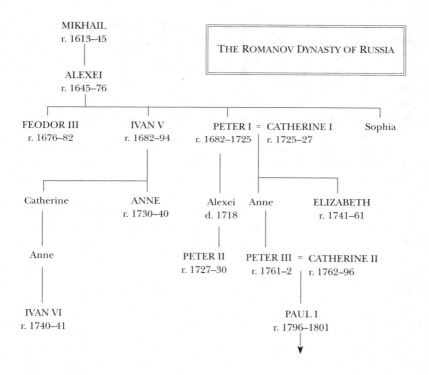

as he had hoped but nor were they reversed, and the Russia that he had envisaged was still largely intact when it was challenged by revolution in 1917.

Catherine II was responsible for – even if she did not order – the murder of two tsars, one of them her husband.

Like Catherine I, this Catherine was German by birth, but she was no peasant. As Princess Sophia of Anhalt-Zerbst, she had been brought to Russia at the age of fourteen to marry the Grand Duke Peter, nephew and heir of the Tsarina Elizabeth (a daughter of Peter the Great). Catherine (as she was named in Orthodox baptism) found her husband uncouth, unintelligent, usually unwashed, totally uninterested in her. Even in her teens, she had sufficient appreciation of danger to put up a façade of frivolity that gave Peter, his aunt and the Court the impression that she was an empty-headed nonentity. Once Catherine had succeeded in supplying an heir, in 1754, she had more freedom. Neither the Tsarevich nor the Tsarina seemed to care that she began to take lovers, through them building up her popularity with the young noblemen who were the officers of the regiments of guards.

The main danger to Catherine in those years was her husband's long-term mistress, Elizaveta Vorontsova, who had her own ambition to be tsarina. Peter spoke freely of intending to divorce his wife when he became tsar.

Tsarina Elizabeth died on Christmas Day 1761. Fortunately for Catherine, Tsar Peter III had pressing business to attend to before he embarked on a divorce: himself born a German, he was eager to end Russia's war with Prussia and to turn its armies against Denmark, which had appropriated his own German lands. This was fortunate, because Catherine was pregnant – and not by her husband. In April she gave birth to a son who was rapidly smuggled out of the palace; Peter never knew of his existence. Two months later, Catherine's friends were ready to make their move, having won over a large part of the army. When Catherine rode into St Petersburg on 28 June, one regiment after another swore the oath of loyalty to her as reigning Tsarina. At the rural palace of Oranienbaum, Peter heard the news with stupefaction. Presented with a deed of abdication, he made no protest before signing it. He was held at the country manor of Ropsha, in the charge of Alexei Orlov, brother of Grigori Orlov, Catherine's current lover, who with his brothers had masterminded the *coup*.

On the evening of 6 July 1762 Catherine received a message from Alexei Orlov. A few words scribbled on a dirty piece of paper told her that her husband was dead, killed in a drunken brawl with his guards.

If Catherine had expected this – had ordered Orlov to arrange it – cannot now be known. It would have been only sensible to have Peter killed, lest any future dissidents attempt his release and restoration.

Nor is there any evidence to link Catherine with the death of another tsar, two years later, though it would be absurd not to suspect it. Long before Catherine's *coup* and Peter III's death, Ivan VI had reigned between October 1740 and December 1741, before he was two years old. The great-grandson of Ivan V, he succeeded his great-aunt Anne, Tsarina between 1730 and 1740. When he was deposed (in favour of his cousin Elizabeth), the child was held in prison, growing up amid the most abject neglect, scarcely able to speak, knowing nothing of the world beyond his cell as Elizabeth, Peter and Catherine reigned. Certainly Ivan knew nothing of the plot hatched by Vasili Mirovich, in 1764, which involved his rescue, the deposition of Catherine II and Ivan's restoration as tsar. Mirovich was a guards officer whose ambitions were greater than his intellect and whose backing was pathetically insufficient for success. He and his followers managed to enter the fortress of Schlüsselburg and overpower the garrison, but before he could reach Ivan's cell the young man had been killed by his gaolers, who had long-standing orders to kill him before he could be rescued. Mirovich was subsequently captured, tried and executed.

With the help of these two murders, Catherine II – Catherine 'the Great' – reigned for more than thirty years. A German who had become thoroughly Russian, a woman who could rule men more effectively than any other since Elizabeth I of England, she overcame tribulations and disasters that would have broken a lesser monarch, and her reign has always been remembered with a veneer of glamour and glory.

Tsar Paul I, son of Catherine II (and probably of Peter III), was born in September 1754 and for eight years scarcely saw either of his parents, because soon after his birth his great-aunt the Tsarina Elizabeth had him carried away to a nursery under her own supervision. But somehow Paul came to cherish a devotion to his father, and after Peter's murder he hated his mother. Even in the last years of Catherine's reign, when Paul was in his forties, the Tsarina denied him an active role in government, ignoring her son's very real abilities and aspirations. He became convinced that she would pass him over and have his eldest son, Alexander, declared her heir –

even that his mother would have him murdered. But Paul survived, and at Catherine II's death in 1796 he succeeded her.

Five years later, Paul was murdered by a group of men who had decided that his rule was intolerable. They were certainly not representative of the great majority of Russians. To the serfs and peasants, the Tsar was their 'little golden heart', the man who had ordered their exemption from labour on Sundays and who had toured his dominions extensively, leaving a lasting impression on people who regarded him as ranking just below God. To the gentry and nobility, however, Paul was a despot. He had introduced a strict censorship on works written in Russia and banned the import of books from abroad; even correspondence with foreigners must be cleared by his censors; it was practically impossible to obtain permission to travel abroad. In the cities, imperial agents spied on all and sundry and reported to the government; anyone suspected of sedition was deported to Siberia.

These measures were Paul's reaction to the French Revolution and to the growth of the democratic ideals of the West. In an attempt to centralise government, under his own direction, the Tsar began to build up a bureaucracy answerable only to superiors in its own hierarchy and ultimately to himself; ironically, Russia's ancient aristocracy saw its own power being undermined by a despot rather than by democracy.

In foreign affairs, Paul was equally high-handed. He withdrew from the alliance of European nations against France and as the new century opened was in negotiation with Napoleon Bonaparte. Although Russia was nearly bankrupt, the Tsar planned to invade India, ostensibly to distract Britain from a supposedly imminent attack on Russia through the Baltic, in fact with an unrealistic eye to Russian rule in India. It was alleged (by a not disinterested France) that Paul's Indian ambitions led to his murder, in 1801, backed by the British ambassador in St Petersburg, under orders from London; but of this there is no evidence.

Early in 1801 Paul picked up rumours that there was a plot hatching, involving his murder and replacement on the throne by his eldest son, Alexander. He asked the Governor-General of St Petersburg, Count Peter von der Pahlen, if he had any evidence of it. Certainly, said Pahlen, and he was himself a party to it, in order to keep an eye on the conspirators.

That was partly true: Pahlen was among the leaders of the plot, but not as a renegade – he was in deadly earnest.

The Tsar also asked Pahlen if his own elder sons, Alexander and Constantine, were involved. No, said Pahlen. He lied. The Tsarevich and the Grand Duke Constantine had given their approval to the removal of their father from the throne, on condition that he was not to be murdered.

Despite Pahlen's assurance, Paul continued to suspect his own family. One day he found a copy of Voltaire's *Brutus* lying on a table in Alexander's apartment; it was open at the page describing the murder of Julius Caesar. Paul sent his son a history of Russia, open at the page describing the events leading up to the death of Tsarevich Alexei in 1718.

Hating St Petersburg's Winter Palace, because of its associations with his mother, Tsar Paul had had a new residence built in the city, the Mikhailovski Palace; he moved in early in 1801, taking his family with him. The Tsarevich and the Grand Duke Constantine were held there under virtual house arrest.

When Paul confronted Pahlen with his suspicions of a plot, the Count did not panic. He was only awaiting a change of the guard at the palace before putting his plan into effect: when the Semenovski Regiment, led by the Tsarevich's friends, went on duty, the opportunity would occur. However, Paul was already suspicious of the Semenovski Regiment. On the evening of Monday 11 February he told the colonel on duty at the Mikhailovski Palace that the officers of the regiment were all 'revolutionaries at heart' and that he had signed an order for the regiment to leave the palace – and the city – before six the next morning. But by then Paul was dead.

On the evening of the 11th, Pahlen took care to be at the side of the Tsarevich while his colleagues set the imperial *coup* in train. He had told his co-conspirators to capture Paul and take him to the Peter and Paul Fortress across the river. And if he resisted? they asked. Pahlen did not reply.

Late that evening, an imperial aide-de-camp admitted seven men to the palace. Some of them were so drunk that two of the leaders, Platon Zubov and Count Leon Bennigsen, went on ahead to the imperial apartments; on the way they encountered two hussars and the Tsar's valet, whom they overpowered. The two men entered Paul's bedroom.

The Tsar was not in bed, but he was in his nightshirt, nightcap and dressing-gown. Bennigsen told him that he was under arrest, by order of 'Tsar Alexander'. Paul stood as if stunned. Although he had long expected some attempt to dethrone him, now that it had come, he was stupefied. Crossed swords hung on the wall, but had he made any move towards them, Bennigsen and Zubov would have killed him before he reached them. There was a door leading to the Tsarina's bedroom, but it offered no means of escape; the Tsar habitually kept it locked so that his wife should not surprise him with his mistress.

Hearing a noise outside, Zubov left the room. Bennigsen continued speaking – not even menacingly – to the Tsar. Then the other five men burst into the room. Bennigsen left.

The furore brought Paul to life. He tried to put his desk between him and the drunken, noisy intruders. They chased him round it until he was caught. Then someone tried to strangle him with a scarf, someone hit him with a snuffbox.

'Gentlemen, for heaven's sake, have mercy!' the Tsar pleaded. 'Give me time to say my prayers.'

But then he was killed. One of his assailants had found a malachite paperweight on the desk and pressed it down on Paul's throat until he stopped breathing.

Bennigsen returned to the room. Cold sober, he supervised the others as they dressed the Tsar's body and tidied the room. Then Pahlen arrived.

The new Tsar, Alexander I, was informed that his father was dead. It was given out that Paul had died of apoplexy (a stroke), but Alexander must, of course, have known better. He must surely have realised that Pahlen had always intended to have Paul killed. Certainly Paul's widow believed that her eldest son bore some blame for his father's death: Tsarina Maria Feodorovna thought, momentarily, of claiming the throne herself, as the two Catherines had, as consorts of Russian tsars; she was dissuaded from doing so. One of Paul's first acts as tsar had been to decree that his dynasty should be subject to the law of male primogeniture.

Alexander I did not turn against the men who had put him on the Russian throne, denouncing them as murderers, but nor did he reward them. Even Pahlen faded into obscurity.

The new reign was hailed with expressions of hope that were soon fulfilled. Alexander countermanded the invasion of India and made peace with Britain. He recalled from internal exile the liberal statesmen whose ideals he shared. He planned to give Russia a constitution and, once it was functioning, to abdicate. In the meantime, he abolished the secret police, returned powers to local government and restored age-old privileges enjoyed by the nobility that his father had denied them. He even made an effort to begin the emancipation of the serfs, although it was to be by purchase, at a price that very few could afford.

However, Alexander's first years as tsar were overshadowed by the problems of Europe. Although he had immediately sought to placate Britain, he was also anxious to keep the peace with France, and a treaty was signed between France and Russia that autumn. Then, in the spring of 1804, a personal matter entrenched Alexander's antipathy to Napoleon Bonaparte.

On 21 March 1804, a member of the exiled French royal family, Louis-Antoine of Bourbon, Duke of Enghien, was shot by a firing-squad at Vincennes. He should not have been in France; members of his family were forbidden to enter the country. But Enghien had been kidnapped, captured by a troop of French cavalry that had crossed the German border by night and dragged him out of Schloss Ettenheim. Once in France, he was charged with having plotted against the new regime; he was inevitably found guilty. When Alexander of Russia, among other European sovereigns, sent a protest to Napoleon about the virtual murder of the Duke of Enghien, he received a trenchant reply. Who was Alexander to take the moral line, when he himself had failed to punish his own father's killers?

Again the nations of Europe aligned against France, and in November 1805 Alexander rode into battle at Austerlitz, only to flee from the field a few hours later, leaving thousands of Russians dead. In 1812 he had his revenge, when the Russian winter thwarted Napoleon's invasion of the empire; and in 1815 Alexander celebrated the final downfall of the 'little corporal' who had been defeated at Waterloo.

By then, Russians who had looked to Alexander for democratic reforms had long been disappointed. Throughout the years of war, he had needed the support of the nobility, the chief opponents of reform, and now he could not withstand them. The Church, too, had a strong hold on him, and the Russian Orthodox Church was always the prime agent of conservatism. The last decade of Alexander's reign witnessed the birth of secret societies pledged to revolution and reform. Had Alexander lived up to his early ideals, such societies would never have existed. As it was, they were the parents of many more, gathering members rapidly as the Tsar's regime took on ever more trappings of despotism. The secret police, whose organisation Alexander had originally disbanded, were brought back into being, their numbers increased, to infiltrate the groups of 'revolutionists', as they were then styled.

In his last years, Alexander was gripped by religious obsessions, seeking seclusion and silence. In the autumn of 1825 he was at Taganrog, a small town on the Sea of Azov, far from his palaces, his ministers and public scrutiny, when on 19 November he died, allegedly after a brief illness.

A decade later, a man called Feodor Kuzmich was wandering through Siberia: a holy man, much revered by the peasantry. He refused to say anything about himself, but from his bearing, his language and his knowledge he was obviously of high rank and extensive education. People who had seen the late Tsar Alexander claimed that Feodor Kuzmich was his double – or that he was the Tsar himself. His poverty, his sympathy, his humility: all these things spoke to Russians who were themselves poor and powerless. During the lifetime of Feodor Kuzmich and after his death in 1864, he was regarded as a saint, one of those who, like the saints of old, had been a great sinner and had renounced his former life to make atonement for his sins.

Had the death of Alexander I been staged, so that he might disappear and purge himself of half a lifetime's burden of guilt, blaming himself for the murder of his father?

Perhaps the greatest sin was Alexander's reneging on his ideals, which left millions of Russians in serfdom, the entire empire in the toils of an outworn, inefficient, unjust system of government.

CHAPTER NINE

MARKSMEN, MADMEN AND THE INFERNAL MACHINE

In the eighteenth century, the pistol (a much improved version of the heavy, unwieldy, unreliable handguns that had been in use since the sixteenth century) became the main murder weapon. It had the advantage of being small enough for concealment before the crime; it had a range – albeit still limited – that enabled its user to attack from some distance and to have the chance to attempt an escape, though the gunman must be proficient in shooting for his bullet to be lethal. In one respect the gun never replaced the sword: it was a weapon of conscious aggression or defence, not part of the ensemble that distinguished the nobility and gentry from commoners.

As early as 1582, a gun had been fired at William 'the Silent', Prince of Orange. It was over-charged with gunpowder and, though he was severely injured, it failed to kill him. By 1758, when three men shot at Jose I, King of Portugal, the pistol had become a weapon of real power, and men had mastered the art of marksmanship.

However, motives for royal murders at this period were no different from those of the Middle Ages. That of the King of Portugal, in 1758, sprang from nothing more than a personal quarrel with a nobleman. The murders of Gustav III, King of Sweden, in 1792, and of Paul I, Tsar of Russia, in 1801, were in the conventional tradition of tyrannicide: the murder of a monarch by conspiring noblemen. If Napoleon Bonaparte may qualify for inclusion here, while he was yet First Consul of France, the attempt on his life in 1800 (see pp. 145–46) was the work of French royalists – in other words, an attempt to replace one ruler with another. Such motives have become familiar.

The eighteenth century also had its murder attempts by 'lunatics', as they were called at that time, as did the nineteenth century, but then that is a hazard endured by monarchs even today.

On the night of 3 September 1758, Jose I, King of Portugal, was driving home in his carriage when his coachman found the road blocked; when he turned the coach into a side road, three men sprang out of the darkness, firing pistols. Wounded in the arm, shoulder and chest, the King shouted to the coachman to drive him straight to his surgeon's house, and this may have saved his life, for more armed men were waiting on the original route – one that was well known, for it led from the King's mistress's house to his palace.

It was not hard to trace the instigator of the attempt on the King's life. Jose de Mascarenhas, Duke of Aveiro, had private grievances against the King, and he had involved other members of the nobility in his plan. The Duke and eight others, one a woman, were publicly executed the following January. In September 1761, a Jesuit named Gabriel Malagrida was also executed for involvement in plotting the attempted regicide, and his Order was expelled from Portugal – to the satisfaction of the King's chief minister, the Marquis of Pombal, who made what capital he could from the attempted murder of King Jose, ridding himself of his clerical and secular enemies.

On the evening of 15 March 1792, Gustav III, King of Sweden, received a letter warning him that, if he went to the Court ball that night, he would be killed. The King was seen to smile as, having read the letter, he put it in his pocket. It was to be a masked ball, held at the Stockholm opera house, and the King donned a mask that covered half his face and a black silk Venetian-style domino cloak before going to watch the dancing from a private box. Aware that he presented a vulnerable target, standing above the dancers, the King was relieved when no shot was fired. He felt sufficiently confident to go down and walk among his subjects.

The masked dancers were all in black, like Gustav, but the King was recognisable by the gleam of the decorations he wore on his coat under the domino and by what showed of his well-known features – an accident at birth had left his face with an unusual imbalance between left and right.

Having made his gesture of bravado to his enemies, the King led his party towards the exit. From somewhere close to him, a shot was fired and Gustav fell. Immediately, someone shouted, 'Fire! Fire!' and everywhere there was turmoil. Fortunately, there was one man present who rapidly assumed control. As the King was carried to an ante-room, a police lieutenant named Liliensparre took command. No one was to leave the ballroom. The entire company, some 700 or 800 people, must wait and give name, address and details of what they had seen, before they were allowed to go home. It was four in the morning before the opera house was emptied.

The methods of the Stockholm police would have done credit to any modern force. Two pistols and a dagger had been found, abandoned, on the ballroom floor, and these were immediately sent to be examined by the city's arms merchants. One of them recognised one of the pistols, of British manufacture, and stated that he had recently sold it to a Guards officer named Anckarström. That name was also on the list of people present at the Court ball. In fact, in the opera house a musician in the orchestra had spoken of having seen Anckarström near Gustav just before the shot was fired. While they were waiting to be interviewed by the police, Anckarström had heard the man talking about it and had accosted him, shaking his hand and drinking his health, but that did not allay the musician's suspicions and he had duly reported everything to the police.

The King was still alive. Though wounded in the back, near his hip, and in terrible pain from fragments of the lead bullet left in the wound, he lived through twelve days before he died.

Anckarström was whipped and pilloried, and his right hand was cut off before he was beheaded; then his corpse was drawn and quartered. It was known that he was only one of a group of men who had planned the King's death, but the others were merely exiled. The deed had been too popular among the nobles of Sweden for them to vote for retribution against the conspirators. Nor was Gustav's brother Carl, who became regent for his nephew, dismayed by the turn of events; in fact, it was thought that he had given his approval to the murder. The political changes that Carl wrought as regent were in keeping with the ambitions of the noblemen who had sought King Gustav's death.

Gustav III was one of Sweden's most outstanding rulers. He had come to the throne at the age of twenty-five, in 1771, and a year later had engineered a *coup*, in melodramatic fashion, that had greatly reduced the power of the Swedish nobility. The next five years witnessed reforms in government and law that seemed to promise unprecedented democracy in Sweden. Yet Gustav was no democrat, but a monarch who felt most in control when he had the reins in his own hands. At the time of his death he was pressing the other monarchs of Europe to unite to invade France, rescue Louis XVI from the clutches of the revolutionaries and reinstate the Ancien Régime. He would have done better to work more strenuously against the reactionaries of his own country, from whose ranks came the men who plotted his death.

When Gustav IV gained his majority, he set about reversing his uncle's work and took back into favour his father's friends – now called 'Gustavians'. But he lacked the military genius of his ancestors and in 1809, with Sweden under threat of invasion by Russia and Denmark, he was deposed without difficulty and sent into exile. The King's uncle Carl, the former regent, became King Carl XIII in 1810. Elderly and lacking a son, the new King accepted as his heir Prince Carl August, commander-in-chief of the Danish and Norwegian armies.

In May 1810 the Prince was reviewing troops in Scania when he suddenly died. As ever, sudden death was viewed with suspicion. It was well known that the Gustavians had opposed Carl August's adoption as heir to the Swedish throne. Had the Prince been poisoned?

One of the Gustavians' leaders, Count Axel Fersen, was forced by his position as Grand Marshal of the royal Court to lead the Prince's funeral procession in Stockholm on 20 June. The sight of him infuriated the mob. Stones were thrown at his carriage, and then Fersen was dragged out onto the street. He managed to escape and ran into a nearby café, but men burst in after him. A troop of guards rode up, and their officer promised that Fersen would be taken to prison until he stood trial for the alleged murder, but Fersen was given only a few moments respite before the mob were on him again, killing him unhindered by the watching troops.

Whether Carl August was murdered or not, his death was significant in that the Swedes now chose as heir to the throne a Frenchman, Jean Bernardotte, one of Napoleon's Marshals. In 1815 Napoleon himself was defeated in battle and exiled to the distant south Atlantic, and the states that he had allotted to his relatives were confiscated by the victorious powers of Europe, but Sweden chose to retain its French Crown Prince, who in 1818 became King Carl XIV and whose descendants have reigned in Sweden ever since.

It is often said that the French Revolution could never have happened in Britain. There is no easy confirmation or refutation of that statement. However, it is true that Britain's ruling class felt extremely uneasy in the years following the French Revolution and that the government was vigilant for signs of discontent and dissent. The suspected threat came not from the mob but from the growing radical element in the professional and artisan middle classes, which were bonding in 'corresponding societies' and urging reform in many spheres, notably for a much extended male suffrage. The respectability of the vast majority of radicals was indubitable, but inevitably there were extremists in their ranks who looked for their inspiration to France, and the French revolutionaries' methods, even after Britain declared war on France in 1793.

In September 1794 a plot to assassinate King George III was uncovered. Some members of the London Corresponding Society had purchased a three-inch metal tube from a brass-founder and had employed a mathematical-instrument-maker to invent a way of discharging a poisoned dart from the tube, using compressed air – the dart to be aimed at George III. Even more dangerous to the nation's stability, radicals were proposing the setting-up of a national convention to represent their views. This was a direct challenge to the Parliament that so obviously did not represent them. Although radical leaders arrested on a charge of high treason were acquitted, the government's response to their threat was a series of draconian measures, including the suspension of the Habeas Corpus Act and the passing of Acts against Seditious Meetings and Treasonable Practice, which helped allay fears of revolution.

Radicals apart, the people of Great Britain largely approved of their king: not because he was personally familiar to his subjects, for he never travelled more than a couple of hundred miles from London; rather, it was because he was known to live a respectable family life, with only moderate expense, at a time at which such 'middle-class' morality and restraint were appreciated. But even the most popular of monarchs may become the victim of one sort of killer: the lone man or woman in mental disorder, whose attacks can never be predicted or guarded against.

On 2 August 1786 the King was dismounting from his horse, outside St James's Palace, when a woman approached him, apparently wanting to hand him a petition. But it was a cover for a knife, with which she tried to stab him. Onlookers would have seized her, but the King called out that he was unhurt and that no one must harm 'the poor creature'. The woman, Margaret Nicholson, was sent to a lunatic asylum, rather than prison. In the week that followed the attack, Windsor was thronged with loyal subjects, who roared their appreciation every time the King emerged from the castle.

George III was equally calm when the bullet of a deranged former soldier, James Hadfield, passed close to him and struck a wooden pillar in the royal box in the Drury Lane Theatre on 15 May 1800. The King stepped forward, where all could see him, looking around with not the slightest sign of alarm. The playwright Sheridan hurriedly wrote a verse to add to the familiar stanzas of 'God Save the King', and when it was sung from the stage at the end of the performance, the already excited audience exploded with cheers.

> From every latent foe,
> From the assassin's blow,
> God save the King!
> O'er him thine arm extend,
> For Britain's sake defend,
> Our father, prince and friend.
> God save the King!

The decade after the execution of Louis XVI, King of France, was one of turmoil in France, which gradually resolved itself as the young republic matured. From among the many politicians vying for power, a Corsican soldier emerged to lead them. Through his multifaceted genius, sheer energy and forceful personality, Napoleon Bonaparte pushed himself to the fore and became First Consul – in effect, head of state.

Across the Channel, sheltered by the British, the so-called Louis XVIII, younger brother of the last King of France, watched the rise of Bonaparte and awaited the signs of revulsion from the new regime that he could interpret as his chance to claim the throne of his ancestors. No such signs were shown; Bonaparte went from strength to strength. To further his ambition, Louis maintained a network of correspondents in France and a spy system that was managed by a red-headed, bull-necked Breton, Georges Cadoudal. It was Cadoudal who masterminded the attempt on Bonaparte's life in 1800 that came close to depriving France of its leader – and European history of its greatest genius.

On Christmas Eve 1800, Bonaparte sat relaxing in a chair by the fire after dinner. His wife, Josephine, reminded him that they were due at the opera, to attend the first French performance of Haydn's *Creation*. Bonaparte did not want to go; in that case, said Josephine, she too would stay at home. That was enough to rouse him, as she probably knew, for her husband would not deprive her of a pleasure. He drove off, while Josephine, her daughter (by her first marriage), Hortense de Beauharnais, and her sister-in-law Caroline Bonaparte prepared to follow. Josephine put on a shawl newly arrived from Constantinople, and a veteran of France's military expedition to Egypt suggested that it would look attractive arranged in the Egyptian manner; this delayed the women a few minutes.

Bonaparte's coachman, César, was drunk, and as the carriage approached a cart that was partially blocking the way, he recklessly failed to slow down, careering past it and round the corner. Moments later the contents of a barrel in the cart exploded. Fired by gunpowder, it scattered grapeshot. Had Bonaparte been travelling at a normal speed, his carriage would have caught the full force of the explosion. The carriage carrying Josephine, Hortense and Caroline caught part of the blast, which blew in the windows, showering them with glass: but they were scarcely injured. Had they arrived a few moments earlier, all would have been killed. As it was, nine bystanders were killed, twenty-six injured; several nearby houses were damaged.

In the immediate, panic-stricken aftermath of the attack, leaders of the Jacobins – left-wing republicans antipathetic to Bonaparte – were rounded up and many of them imprisoned. When the plot was traced to the royalists (and two of the conspirators guillotined), Bonaparte still refused to release the Jacobins, to prevent renewed, and now exacerbated, protest from that quarter.

In August 1803 Cadoudal himself came (secretly) to France, to co-ordinate a *coup d'état* involving the assassination of Bonaparte and the seizure of power by the royalists. Sixty men, dressed as hussars, were to join a military parade and, when Bonaparte came to review them, one was to step forward, as if to present a petition, the signal for the rest to surround Bonaparte and dispatch him with their daggers.

However, the French police and government agents were on the watch for royalist infiltration, and their vigilance was rewarded in February 1804 by the capture of Cadoudal's second-in-command, who was induced to reveal many secrets. Then, on 9 March, a policeman spotted Cadoudal himself emerging from a Paris greengrocer's and entering a carriage. He was disguised and wore a large hat, but his physique was unmistakable: a short, squat figure; a scarred, once-broken nose; one eye larger than the other. When policemen leapt onto the carriage, Cadoudal pulled out a pistol, killing one and wounding another before he was overpowered. He was thoroughly questioned before his trial and execution.

Cadoudal's plots had far-reaching consequences. Had Bonaparte been assassinated, there was no obvious successor to uphold the republic against a royalist uprising or to govern France in his stead. Suggestions, mooted over recent years, that Bonaparte take the title of emperor and that the French empire become a hereditary monarchy were now given the most serious consideration and became widely accepted. On 2 December 1804 Napoleon Bonaparte became Napoleon I, Emperor of the French.

Over the next decade Napoleon led France to military victory throughout Europe until in 1812 the snows of Russia proved too much for the Grande Armée and in 1814 the allied nations of Europe overcame him. His return from exile on Elba in 1815 resulted only in defeat at the Battle of Waterloo and his departure for more distant exile, on the Atlantic island of St Helena. And there, on 5 May 1820, he died.

Shortly before he died, the former Emperor of the French wrote a testament, in which he claimed that his death must be laid to the door of his chief enemy, Britain – in effect, blaming Sir Hudson Lowe, who had charge of him. Although a post-mortem showed that Napoleon had in fact died of cancer of the stomach, Lowe was inevitably blamed in some quarters for Napoleon's death. Visitors had long been aware that Napoleon lived in fear of being poisoned, and the rumour spread.

In recent years the doctors' diagnosis has been brought in question, as certain of their findings seem inconsistent with evidence of stomach cancer. The fact that tests on Napoleon's hair (preserved by members of his family, friends and servants) have allegedly shown the presence of arsenic is inconclusive, as arsenic was used, in small doses, as a medicine for indigestion; if Napoleon had been taking it for some years, it would understandably be found in both tissue and hair.

It seems unlikely that Lowe was responsible for the murder – if murder it was. He had always been aware of the possibility of his being blamed were Napoleon to die suddenly, as if of a one-off dose of poison; in 1820 even Napoleon's two-month illness could not dispel suspicion that the man responsible for his welfare had been ordered to kill him. The alternative is that the French found means – perhaps through one of his doctors – to have Napoleon poisoned. After all, the newly enthroned King Louis XVIII owed his elevation more to the allied sovereigns of Europe than to the people of France, and the possibility of a Napoleonic revanche must have been his perpetual nightmare. Even in defeat and in exile, Napoleon was too formidable to be ignored. When his death was announced in Europe, the majority of his former subjects openly mourned him, and many of his former enemies admitted that he had been the greatest man of their time.

❖❖❖

After the defeat of Napoleon in 1815, the French monarchy was restored, in the person of Louis XVIII, brother of the guillotined Louis XVI. But whereas Louis XVIII attempted to rule within the bounds laid upon him at the restoration, his brother and successor, Charles X, was heedless of them. Disregarding mounting pressure for political reform, in 1830 Charles was faced with a renewal of revolution and was forced to leave the country (see p. 168). Nevertheless, the French chose to retain the monarchy, and into the void stepped a Bourbon cousin, Louis-Philippe, who had formerly rallied opposition to Charles X and who now pledged himself to reign as a 'constitutional monarch' should.

Louis-Philippe's initial political propriety did not, however, safeguard his life, and he became the first European monarch of the nineteenth century to survive multiple attacks. For example, on 19 November 1832, when he was riding through Paris on his way to open a new session of parliament, a single shot was fired at him; he was unharmed. A man was arrested but later released for want of evidence. Twice in 1836 there were attempts by gunmen on the King's life. On the first occasion, a republican fired at him with a gun disguised as a walking-stick; on the second a pistol shot broke the window of his carriage, grazing him, the broken glass wounding his eldest son.

Such pistol attacks – and these were not the only ones to threaten Louis-Philippe – would become commonplace during the nineteenth century, as the weapon was improved, marksmanship practised. It was also the century of the 'infernal machine', generally a charge of gunpowder hidden in some everyday object, such as a barrel or packing-case, that could be left beside a royal route without arousing suspicion, to be detonated as the intended victim passed (as in the attack on Napoleon in Paris in 1800). However, the infernal machine used against Louis-Philippe in 1835 was altogether more ingenious.

A Corsican named Joseph Fieschi had conceived an idea for a weapon that could be used in the next revolution: a line of ninety rifles, connected, that could be fired simultaneously by one man. Fieschi was a minor civil servant who had spent ten years in prison after being convicted of fraud. After his release he had served as a police informer against working-class dissidents. Fieschi imparted his idea to Pierre Morey, a man in his late fifties who could remember the

French Revolution and who had fought at the barricades in 1830. Late in 1834, he took up Fieschi's idea, modified it (only twenty-five rifles) and proposed that the 'infernal machine' should be used to assassinate the King.

In January 1835, Fieschi and Morey were joined by Théodore Pépin, a grocer, who supplied the money that bought the guns. He also rented a third-floor flat overlooking the thoroughfare called the Boulevard du Temple, along which the King was due to ride in a procession on 28 July. Two days before the planned assassination, Fieschi brought in a fourth man, an ironmonger named Victor Boireau, who supplied mountings for the machine. Boireau also rode slowly past the house on the Boulevard du Temple to allow Fieschi to sight the guns.

That night Fieschi and Morey completed the preparations. Fieschi, who was to fire the machine, believed he could escape over neighbouring roofs but, unbeknown to him, Morey adjusted the machine so that it would explode after use, killing Fieschi; he must not be allowed to survive lest he fail to escape and then inform on his accomplices.

However, Fieschi had already set in train a rumour of the plot, by bringing in Boireau, for in his cups Boireau boasted of his part in it. Among those who heard his babble was a man called Suireau, who went home and told his father, who took the matter to the police. But all Suireau knew of the location of the infernal machine was that the flat was near the Théâtre de l'Ambigu. While some policemen went to arrest Boireau, others went to search houses around the Théâtre de l'Ambigu – the wrong Théâtre de l'Ambigu: not the one in the Boulevard du Temple but another of that name in the Boulevard de Saint-Martin (the two boulevards were then separated by the Porte du Temple, now by the Place de la République). It was a foolish, dangerous error.

The occasion of King Louis-Philippe's ride through Paris on 28 July 1845 was a military review held to celebrate the anniversary of the 1830 revolution. To many who had participated in the revolution, it now seemed a hollow victory: Louis-Philippe had long since given in to the temptation to overstep the bounds of a constitutional monarch. Republicanism was again rife. Since an incipient revolution had been put down in 1834, assassination seemed the obvious way of ridding France of its increasingly unpopular King. Louis-Philippe had refused to cancel the anniversary review, even though he knew that he would ride to it at grave risk to his life.

The King rode through Paris flanked by his sons, a military escort following behind. There was still sufficient enthusiasm for him to draw cheers from the crowd. Having safely negotiated the Boulevard de Saint-Martin, past its Théâtre de l'Ambigu, Louis-Philippe entered the Boulevard du Temple. The sound of a barrage of shots and the sight of smoke billowing from a high window gave him the chance to shout 'This is for me!' before bullets rained down. His horse was wounded and reared but Louis-Philippe was only grazed on the head. As his sons closed ranks around him, the King rose from his saddle, waving his hat and calling out 'Here I am!' to the crowd, who responded noisily.

Behind the royal family, Marshal Mortier lay dead, and in the crowd there were numerous casualties. Eighteen people were either killed outright or died later of their injuries; one of them was a girl only fourteen years old.

Fieschi was badly injured when the infernal machine was shattered, and he was quickly arrested. With Boireau already in custody, Morey and Pépin were soon apprehended. Fieschi, Morey and Pépin went to the guillotine, Boireau to prison for twenty years.

An enormous and lengthy state funeral was accorded the eighteen victims of the infernal machine. The King wept over the coffin of the young girl.

Louis-Philippe's first target for reprisals was the republican Press, who had, he believed, incited the various assassins of recent years. The French constitution ruled out censorship but there were means (such as the libel laws and those against incitement to violence) of preventing attacks on the King in the newspapers. As to royal security, the increase in the numerical strength of undercover agents and paid informers cannot even be estimated, but there is evidence that the rapidly expanded force discovered and prevented several conspiracies against the life of the King – including the manufacture of a new infernal machine. Even so, the shots fired in the two gun attacks of 1836 were not the only dangers Louis-Philippe faced in the remaining years of his reign.

In 1848, revolution broke out again (see p. 168). King Louis-Philippe, who for so long had been adamantly opposed to parliamentary reform, now offered to accept it. It was too late. Having abdicated the throne of France, he went into exile in Britain. He died in 1850.

Facing a pistol attack on his – or her – life, the victim cannot know if the ammunition used is in fact capable of killing, so that every attack must seem, at the time, to be life-threatening. Though Britain's Queen Victoria was attacked seven times and in all but one case by men firing guns, only two of her assailants had loaded their guns with shot that could kill. But the Queen could not know that. Even when she was first threatened, in 1840, when she was only twenty-one years old, she reacted with 'perfect courage and self-possession and exceeding propriety', her husband recorded.

That first attack occurred in the early evening of 10 June 1840 when the Queen (in her first pregnancy) and her husband, Prince Albert, were driving up Constitution Hill. Prince Albert saw a man on the pavement raise a pair of pistols and fire: at the second shot, the Prince pushed the Queen down. She was unhurt. The assailant, Edward Oxford, was quickly overpowered by a member of the public. He went for trial on a charge of high treason and was found guilty but was reprieved because he was thought to be insane. He was committed to an asylum for criminal lunatics and not released until twenty-seven years later, whereupon he emigrated.

The pistols Oxford used have caused some speculation. They were mounted in silver and monogrammed 'E.R.'. Were they the property of – and lent to Oxford by – 'Ernestus Rex', that is, Ernest Augustus, King of Hanover, formerly the Duke of Cumberland, Victoria's uncle? A letter allegedly found in Oxford's lodgings apparently confirmed that suspicion; if it existed, it was, of course, never published; if it was preserved, its whereabouts are now unknown; if it was destroyed, no copy has come to light. Probably the allegation was merely part of the growing myth about Queen Victoria's 'wicked uncle' (see pp. 160–62).

On Sunday 29 May 1842, as the Queen and Prince were driving

down the Mall, returning home from a service at the Chapel Royal, a man fired at them from a distance of only two paces before escaping into the crowd. Although the royal couple were convinced that the man would try again, they refused to be cooped up for safety: better risk another attack in the hope that he would be apprehended. So the next day they made a carriage excursion to the northern heights above London, going as far as the then village of Hampstead before turning back. They were nearly home, driving down Constitution Hill, when the man fired again, this time from five paces. But the Sunday alert had ensured that the road was patrolled by plain-clothes policemen, and the man was in fact standing beside one when he fired, so he was quickly taken.

John Francis, a London cabinetmaker, was tried on a charge of high treason, found guilty and sentenced to death, but on 1 July he was reprieved, because of his insanity, and sent to prison.

Two days later, a deformed sixteen-year-old, John William Bean, fired a pistol at the Queen – a pistol loaded with paper and tobacco, with scarcely enough gunpowder to fire it. His death sentence was commuted to eighteen months' imprisonment.

Francis and Bean owed their reprieve from the gallows to their insanity. Neither had loaded his pistol with lethal shots: what sane man would risk capital punishment for a project impossible to fulfil? Although they, like Oxford, were tried on the charge of high treason, this seemed inappropriate in the circumstances, and in 1842 Parliament enacted a Bill designed to reduce such crimes to the rank of 'misdemeanour'. Thus conviction would not incur a sentence of capital punishment: there were the alternatives of imprisonment or transportation to a penal colony, after flogging.

On 19 May 1849, an unemployed Irishman, William Hamilton, shot at the Queen, once more as she drove on Constitution Hill. Convicted under the 1842 Act, he was sentenced to seven years' transportation. Again, Hamilton's pistol had not been charged with shot. In fact, he had originally tried to make a pistol – out of wood and an old kettle spout. Failing, he had borrowed a pistol from his landlady, which shows how common the possession of fire-arms was in the nineteenth century.

On 27 June 1850, a retired army officer named Robert Pate mounted the Queen's open carriage and struck at her head with his stick. After a moment's unconsciousness, Victoria assured onlookers that she was unhurt, but later bruises and a black eye appeared. Only her sturdy bonnet had saved her from worse harm. That evening, when the royal party arrived fashionably late at the Royal Opera House, the performance was interrupted for 'God Save the Queen' and five minutes of cheering. Victoria herself was shocked that a man could strike any woman, let alone his sovereign, and in the presence of three of her children, all under ten. Pate was sentenced to seven years' transportation.

On 29 February 1872, a reportedly 'feeble-minded' seventeen-year-old, Arthur O'Connor, fired at the Queen with a broken flintlock pistol loaded with nothing more dangerous than plugs of paper and scraps of old leather. He had scaled the railings of Buckingham Palace and waylaid the Queen as she was about to alight from her carriage after a drive. He was seized by the Queen's Highland servant, John Brown, who just beat Prince Arthur in the race for glory. Brown received a medal and an annuity, Prince Arthur a gold pin. O'Connor received a sentence of a year's imprisonment, with hard labour, after a flogging. The Queen was horrified, fearing that O'Connor would make another attempt on her life on his release, and he was 'persuaded' to take ship for Australia. However, he did not remain there long: on 5 May 1874 he was spotted outside Buckingham Palace and arrested. A court committed him to a lunatic asylum.

On 2 March 1882 a Scotsman, Roderick McLean, fired at the Queen as her carriage left Windsor station. Two Eton boys had the presence of mind to attack him with their umbrellas and were later rewarded with the Queen's praise in front of their schoolmates. McLean was a self-professed poet who had sent his work to the Queen and had it politely returned. Some months before the attack he had been discharged from a lunatic asylum, and in the dock he stared round 'with a vacant, imbecile expression'. He was found 'not guilty on the grounds of insanity' and was to be kept in custody 'at Her Majesty's pleasure'.

This time it was not the sentence but the style of the verdict that annoyed the Queen. A year later, Parliament changed the term 'not guilty by reason of insanity' to 'guilty but insane', an absurdity not corrected until 1964.

Victoria was interested to learn that McLean's weapon was a revolver, the first to be used against a British monarch, though the first of its kind, the Colt, had come on the market as early as 1835. On the day after the attack, the revolver was brought to her by Brown, who showed her the six chambers that could be loaded with bullets (fortunately, only one had been discharged) and fired without the need for priming with gunpowder.

The incidence of insanity among Queen Victoria's assailants was not a new phenomenon. Her grandfather, for example, had been attacked by 'lunatics' in 1786 and 1800. But in what did their madness consist? McLean's original committal was as the result of brain injuries sustained in a fall in 1866; O'Connor was 'feeble-minded'; but what form did the others' madness take? Fascinated as Victorian doctors were by insanity, the study of psychology was still rudimentary.

More interesting than the incidence of insanity among Queen Victoria's assailants is its comparative absence among the assassins and would-be assassins of foreign monarchs at the same period. Could it be that some of the foreign assassins (notably those who were found to have no connection with 'anarchist' or nationalist groups) were in fact insane but regarded as being 'revolutionaries' in countries more accustomed than Britain to terrorist activities?

Nevertheless, a fear of nationalist terrorism did surface in the trials of Hamilton (in 1849) and O'Connor (in 1872), for they were suspected of having Fenian connections. The Fenians were members of the Irish Republican Brotherhood, sworn to free Ireland from its English oppressors. Their terrorist activities were originally confined to Ireland itself, with English landlords their main prey, and Queen Victoria was dissuaded from visiting Ireland until 1849, twelve years after her accession; she returned in 1861, but then there was a hiatus of thirty-nine years before Ireland was again pronounced sufficiently safe for another royal visit.

Hamilton's attack, in May 1849, came in the wake of Ireland's potato famine, which was responsible for thousands of deaths by starvation and for Irish fury against the English landlords, which had broken into widespread violence in the Continent-wide revolutionary year 1848. Albeit a brave personal venture, Victoria's visit to Ireland in August 1849 did nothing to reconcile the Irish to the English – inevitably and understandably.

By 1872, when O'Connor shot at the Queen, circumstances had changed drastically. Irish violence had spread to mainland Britain, and Victoria had lived for several years under the threat of kidnapping or assassination by the Fenians.

In the autumn of 1867, there was a panic at the Queen's Scottish retreat, Balmoral Castle, when there came a warning that Fenians planned to abduct her. She was to be held hostage against the release of Fenian prisoners, 'the Manchester Martyrs', it was said. However, the peaceful Scottish countryside was invaded by no more dangerous men than a posse of Scotland Yard detectives and Scottish policemen drafted from nearby cities. Nothing happened.

Then again, that December, came news – from such a reliable source as the Governor-General of Canada – that eighty Fenians were on their way across the Atlantic to kidnap the Queen from Osborne House on the Isle of Wight. How could the house, with gardens going down to the sea, be protected from attack by the Irishmen? Surely the Queen must return to the mainland and take up residence at Windsor or Buckingham Palace?

Let Osborne be reinforced with troops and police, by all means, said Queen Victoria, but she would not leave. She suspected, probably with some justification, that the alarm was a deliberate exaggeration on the part of members of the Government, to lure her out of the seclusion she had craved since the death of her husband, in 1861. The Queen was scathing about the precautions taken to protect her: among the suspect persons detained by her new guards was her own son Arthur.

Nevertheless, there was some justification for the fear of Fenian attacks. On 12 March 1868, the Queen's second son, Prince Alfred, who was visiting Australia, was shot in the ribs by a Fenian, apparently in revenge for the hanging of the Manchester Martyrs. The man was hanged on 21 April.

The Queen was appalled when she heard of her son's injuries. But on Alfred's return home she wrote to his eldest sister, 'I am not so proud of Affie as you might think, for he is so conceited . . . and receives ovations as if he had done something instead of God's mercy having spared his life.'

Four years later, O'Connor's attack thoroughly shook the Queen. Partly it was the nature of the attack, for not only had O'Connor penetrated the grounds of Buckingham Palace but he actually thrust his pistol over the side of her stationary open carriage, though it did not – could not – fire. Worse, she later learned that he had originally planned to hold the pistol to her head, to force her to accept a petition, as she knelt in St Paul's Cathedral two days earlier, during the service of Thanksgiving held to celebrate the recovery of her heir from typhoid. O'Connor had tried to hide in the cathedral overnight but had been discovered and removed by a verger who had no suspicion of his intention.

O'Connor had shown signs of incipient madness for some time. Also, he was the great-nephew of the Chartist agitator Feargus O'Connor, who had died insane in 1855. As well as campaigning for the universal male suffrage, annual parliaments etc outlined in the People's Charter of 1838, Feargus O'Connor had pressed for Irish independence. Arthur O'Connor had been brought up on tales of his great-uncle's exploits, and the petition he had taken to St Paul's and which was in his pocket when he was arrested was a plea for the release of Fenian prisoners. However, it was shown that his attack on the Queen was the product of his own mind, not planned or prompted by any Fenian group, which, along with the pathos of his insanity and physical defects (he had tuberculosis and scrofula), accounted for the court's leniency.

Over the next decade, Ireland's fury increased as the Home Rule movement was fiercely rebuffed at Westminster and as the Protestant landlords' depredations continued to impoverish the peasantry. A climax was reached in 1882, when, on 6 May, Lord Frederick Cavendish, recently appointed Chief Secretary of Ireland, and his Permanent Under-Secretary, Thomas Burke, were attacked in Phoenix Park, in Dublin, by a gang of Fenian 'Invincibles' who hacked them to death with knives. The Government's reaction was to abolish trial by jury in Ireland and to extend police powers of arrest.

Fenian 'outrages' were still occurring in Ireland and in mainland Britain at the end of Victoria's reign, but the Queen continued to drive out among her subjects and in April 1900, at the age of eighty, paid a three-week visit to Ireland. Cheers greeted her, but she was guarded both by ceremonial troops and by plain-clothes police officers.

❖❖❖

Like Queen Victoria, Queen Isabel II of Spain was attacked by lone assailants, not by groups of revolutionaries, but in other ways Isabel could not have been more unlike Victoria. She had come to the throne in September 1833, just before her third birthday, had been declared of age at thirteen and had married on her sixteenth birthday. While her governments stumbled from crisis to crisis, Isabel's personal life became an open scandal: none of her children was accredited to her husband, except on paper, for Isabel's husband, her cousin Francisco, was obviously incapable of satisfying a normal wife, let alone the nymphomaniac Isabel.

The first attack on the Queen, in May 1847, occurred when a young man fired a pistol at her as she drove through Madrid. No record of his motive survives, and though he was sentenced to death, he in fact suffered no worse than four years' exclusion from towns in which there was a royal residence.

The second attack, on 2 February 1852, took place inside the royal palace. When a priest, Martín Merino, approached the Queen and knelt before her, Isabel thought he was about to offer a petition and held out her hand, whereupon he plunged a dagger in her chest.

Merino, aged sixty-two, would give no explanation of his act beyond saying that 'She deserved it.' The Queen tried to have his death sentence revoked but failed. Merino was publicly unfrocked by his bishop; with his hands tied behind his back, he was mounted on a donkey, facing its tail, and led through Madrid before being hanged.

At the time, the Queen's survival was hailed with national rejoicing, but in 1868 she was forced to flee Spain as rebellion spread. One of the instigators of the uprising was the French Duke of Montpensier, husband of Queen Isabel's younger sister. He had long been suspected of coveting the throne – even of having had Isabel's first son murdered in his cradle. After the 1868 *coup*, Montpensier was mooted as King of Spain, but even if he had won the support of the generals who had taken power, he had far too many enemies to succeed. One of those enemies was the Queen's cousin Enrique, Duke of Seville, who now protested that Montpensier's ambitions constituted treason; then he fell into vulgar invective and called Montpensier 'a puffed-up French pastrycook'.

Montpensier challenged Enrique to a duel. At dawn on 13 March

1870 they faced each other at ten paces. Both fired; both missed. They fired again, with the same result. At the third attempt, Enrique again failed to hit Montpensier, and the Duke was left with a shot to fire and time to take careful aim. His last bullet pierced Enrique's brain.

In Spanish law, duelling did not constitute murder, and though Montpensier stood trial, he was sentenced to no more than a month's banishment from Madrid and required to pay an indemnity to Enrique's family. When, a year later, there was an attack on the Italian prince, Amadeo of Savoy, who had become King of Spain, Montpensier was inevitably suspected, but there was no proof of his involvement in the attack.

In fact, Amadeo reigned for just over two years, and there followed a brief republic before, in the last days of 1874, Isabel II's son Alfonso, to whom she had resigned her rights, was called back to Spain to reign as Alfonso XII.

CHAPTER TEN

CROWNED KILLERS

Although the Duke of Montpensier was not convicted of murder under Spanish law when he shot and killed Enrique of Seville in a duel in 1870, by modern standards he was certainly a murderer. Enrique had discharged all his shots; Montpensier had only to take his time and aim carefully to kill Enrique. According to the etiquette of duelling, he might have discharged his shot into the air for honours to be even. So it was surely 'cold-blooded murder'.

Perhaps Ivan the Terrible never had 'cold blood'. His murders, many of which were apparently the work of his own hands, were the product of insanity, that homicidal mania that is fortunately so rare. And what of Charles IX of France, responsible for the death of hundreds of his subjects in the Massacre of St Bartholomew's Day in 1572? Charles gave the order for the massacre under strong pressure from his mother and her confederates, but he also believed that he was doing the right thing – even the will of God. It was a policy of extermination that monarchs had inflicted on heretics for centuries and which Hitler would inflict, on a much larger scale, on the Jews of Germany and the lands he conquered.

In the Middle Ages and early modern period, the majority of royal murderers who killed - or rather ordered the killing of – kinsmen did so to gain a throne or to keep their own throne secure. Although the word 'alleged' must be applied to many of those whom history has labelled murderers (such as Richard III and Mary, Queen of Scots), there are plentiful instances of medieval monarchs who did not scruple to kill for their own advantage.

Even less easy to prove is a monarch's involvement in the assassination of a statesman. For example, the Holy Roman Emperor Ferdinand II denied any responsibility for the murder of his former commander-in-chief Albrecht von Wallenstein in 1634, though it was obviously to his advantage to be rid of the suspected traitor. But it is widely believed that Ferdinand, Prince (later King and Tsar) of Bulgaria, was the instigator of the assassination of his former prime minister Stepan Stambulov in 1895.

❖❖❖

In the 1820s, a rumour permeated the upper echelons of British society that there was a threat to the life of the young Princess Victoria. The threat emanated, allegedly, from her uncle Ernest Augustus, Duke of Cumberland. The Duke stood after Victoria in the royal succession, and so it would be to his advantage to have her die.

It seems now that the source of the rumour was Sir John Conroy, comptroller of the household of the Duchess of Kent, Victoria's widowed mother. He had beguiled the Duchess into implicit trust in him, and he sought, through her, to control Victoria, should she come to the throne as a minor. (That Victoria loathed him was of little consequence, for Conroy envisaged the Duchess's being made regent for her daughter in the hoped-for eventuality.) Conroy's ploy had two aims: to prevent the Duke of Cumberland's being chosen as his niece's regent and to isolate her, in the meanwhile, from all influences but her mother's – that is, his own.

There was enough suspicion of Cumberland in the 1820s for the rumours to seem plausible. Politically, the Duke was out of step with other members of the royal family, being a Tory, while his elder brothers, King George IV and the future King William IV, favoured the Whigs. The Whig Press made the most of Cumberland's defects and had the gall to turn an incident in which the Duke was nearly murdered into a tale in which he himself featured as a murderer.

On the night of 31 May 1810, the Duke of Cumberland was peacefully asleep in bed in St James's Palace when he was suddenly awoken. A sharp blade slashed into his head. Fortunately he wore a thick, padded nightcap, which took the force of the blade, and though he did not realise it, the tassel of his bed curtains had deflected his assailant's hand at the critical moment. However, as the Duke raised his hands to fend off the blows, another slash almost cut off his fingers.

The Duke of Cumberland was extremely shortsighted, and he could not make out the features of his attacker, but he could see the flash of the sabre he held; it was the Duke's own regimental sabre. He tried to wrest it from his assailant's hand but only sustained another injury to his fingers and his right hand. In fact, the attack left the Duke with three wounds in his neck, one in his head, five in his right hand, one in his left arm and one in his left wrist. But he was still alive, and he began yelling for his valet, Neale, who was asleep two rooms away. However, by the time Neale ran in, the would-be killer had left by another door.

Fearing that the man would return, Neale helped the Duke downstairs, to the nightwatchman's room. The outside sentries were alerted, to prevent anyone's leaving the palace. Then Neale roused the servants.

The only person who could not be found was the Duke's other valet, Joseph Sellis, who took turns with Neale to care for him. Sellis was apparently not in his room near the Duke's – at least, he did not answer when Neale rapped on his bedroom door; nor was he in his family's apartment on the other side of the palace. Some time later, the searchers returned to Sellis's room, and when they entered, they saw him lying on his bed. His throat had been cut from ear to ear, and he was dead.

The doctor who had been summoned to tend the Duke took a look at Sellis. The man had killed himself; there was certainly no sign of a struggle to suggest that he had been attacked and killed.

By the time the coroner's court convened for the inquest on Joseph Sellis, the events of that night had been pieced together. It was Sellis who had attacked the Duke of Cumberland; fearing discovery, he had killed himself only minutes later.

But why? Sellis was a Corsican (like Napoleon Bonaparte) and though there was not the slightest evidence to suggest that he had been employed to kill the Duke, he was evidently a Jacobin – a sympathiser with revolutionary France. However, there was a personal motive: the Duke had been exceedingly good to him (had even stood godfather to his youngest child) but his fellow-servants gave evidence that Sellis had been jealous of the favour the Duke also showed to Neale.

Cumberland's injuries were severe. It was a long time before he was fully recovered. One good thing came out of the incident, however: he was reconciled with his eldest brother, George, Prince of Wales, with whom he had quarrelled years before. This did not please the Duke's political enemies . . .

The first libels appeared in 1812, in a paper called *The Independent Whig*. They alleged that the Duke had killed Sellis. When prosecuted, the writer, a man named White, was found guilty and sentenced to fifteen months in prison and a fine of £200. But his initiative led to many later slurs on the Duke's character, including the allegation that he had had an incestuous relationship with his sister Sophia. In 1829 there was a rumour that the Duke was having an *affaire* with a Lady Graves, who was separated from her husband. In an attempt to scotch the rumours, Lord Graves returned to his wife, but they continued, and in January 1830 he killed himself.

Published in 1832, *The Authentic Records of the Court of England during the Last Seventy Years*, by Josiah Philips, stated that Cumberland had killed Sellis because he had surprised the Duke in a homosexual act with Neale. At the Duke's orders, Neale had killed Sellis to silence him, said Philips, and together they had concocted the story told at the inquest. In May 1833 the Duke prosecuted Philips for libel, and again he won his case: Philips was sentenced to six months in prison, a lenient sentence pronounced by a judge who was a political enemy of Cumberland. In fact, Philips escaped and managed to leave the country.

And so the story of the Princess Victoria's 'wicked uncle Cumberland' and his plots against her life were believed in some quarters. Years later, when the elderly Queen Victoria read an account, by Lady Conroy, of the suspicions against the Duke of Cumberland, the Queen made margin notes refuting the allegations and stating that they were Conroy's invention. When she came to the throne, in 1837, the eighteen-year-old Queen had immediately made it clear that neither her mother, Conroy's pawn, nor the man himself had the slightest power over her.

As for Cumberland, when Victoria became Queen of Great Britain, he became King of Hanover. His elder brothers had worn both crowns, but no woman could reign in Hanover, so Cumberland inherited that kingdom. Unlike others of his family, he was a thoroughly respectable monarch, both personally and politically, but the old stories of his murder of Sellis and his plots against Victoria have been retold time and again. Mud sticks.

❖❖❖

On 26 May 1829, a young man presented himself to a cavalry officer living in Nuremberg, handed him a letter of introduction and asked to become a cavalryman. He gave his name as Kaspar Hauser. The letter was signed by a man describing himself as Hauser's foster-father; it gave no information about his family or origin. Nor could the young man himself tell anything definite. He said he had been brought up in a dark room, that his food was delivered overnight, while he slept, and that he had never got a good look at the man who came to teach him to read and write; the man had brought him to the outskirts of Nuremberg and then deserted him.

Kaspar Hauser became quite a celebrity in Nuremberg and in July 1829 was given into the care of a Doctor Daumer, who undertook his education and was amazed at his rapid progress. Then, on 17 October, Daumer's wife came upon Hauser lying unconscious in the cellar of her house; he had a wound on his forehead. All he could say was that a tall, dark man had attacked him; he could not see the face but thought he had recognised the voice as that of his childhood keeper. Four years later, on 14 December 1833, there was another attack. Hauser had been lured to a secluded spot where he met a man who showed him a silk bag – and then dropped it; when Hauser bent to pick it up, the man had stabbed him in the chest. This was the story he told before he died three days later.

The mysterious life and death of an unknown young man seems far distant from the foregoing royal murders. The link is this: during Kaspar Hauser's lifetime, rumours began to circulate in Nuremberg that he was the son of the late Grand Duke of Baden. The story went that he had been 'snatched from his cradle' soon after his birth in 1812 and replaced by another baby, so sickly that it died. The substitution was supposedly the work of the Grand Duke's step-grandmother, the Countess of Hochberg, who wanted her own son to succeed him. The substitution of a dying baby for the healthy one would ensure this. (Presumably the Countess drew the line at infanticide.)

So Kaspar Hauser, as the baby was named, was brought up in secrecy and seclusion. In 1830, according to plan, Leopold of Hochberg succeeded in Baden, though the Countess had not lived to see the success of her machinations. Did the new Grand Duke instigate Hauser's murder in 1835, fearful that he could somehow be proved to be the rightful heir to the grand duchy? Some six months before Hauser's death, a judge who had been enquiring into the rumours of his origins had died suddenly – of a heart attack, it was said; of poison, it was suggested. Had he come too close to the truth?

Was Kaspar Hauser the rightful Grand Duke of Baden or was he merely an ambitious nobody with a clever self-advertisement? Perhaps he even inflicted those two wounds on himself, to revive waning interest in him; if so, he went too far, for the second wound festered and killed him.

The story of Kaspar Hauser is far more complicated than this outline, and it is puzzling to sift through its obscurities and through the irrelevant data amassed since 1833. More than a century and a half after Hauser's death there is a lengthy list of books on him, in several languages; two films have been made about his strange life and mysterious death. His gravestone epitaph calls him 'the enigma of his time', and he remains an enigma.

Whoever else might be given 'the benefit of the doubt', it seems certain that Ludwig II, King of Bavaria, murdered Dr Bernhard von Gudden on 13 June 1886. Gudden was the psychiatrist who had been given charge of the King when he was deposed, having been pronounced insane, a few days earlier.

Ludwig II had given signs of incipient insanity since childhood. He became King of Bavaria at the age of eighteen, in 1864. From the start he showed reluctance to undertake affairs of state, and increasingly he sought seclusion in the fairytale castles he had built in the Bavarian alps: there he was virtually inaccessible to members of his government, ignoring the state papers that pursued him. When he did want company, he preferred the society of soldiers and servants – male servants, for he was homosexual. His behaviour became ever more bizarre: when alone, he would talk and laugh; sometimes, in company, he would break into a dance, sometimes into noisy rage.

The King's sudden anger was a danger signal to his servants. When the psychiatrist Dr von Gudden was employed to assess the King's sanity, early in 1886, he collected reports from members of the royal household that showed that the King had many times assaulted them. For the slightest annoyance he would order a servant flogged or imprisoned – he tried to strangle one of them when he failed to trap a bird that had escaped from its cage. It was alleged that a young postillion's death was due to the beating he had taken from the King.

When these and other symptoms of madness were assessed, Ludwig was declared insane – as his younger brother Otto had been a decade earlier, though Otto was now declared king in Ludwig's place, with an uncle as regent.

On 12 June 1886 Ludwig and his entourage arrived at Schloss Berg on Lake Starnberg, where he was to be incarcerated. After the stress of the past few days, he seemed acquiescent. The next day, Whit Sunday, Ludwig and Gudden went for a morning walk in the grounds, accompanied by two male nurses. Keeping his appointment to walk with Ludwig again at 6 p.m., Gudden told the nurses they would not be needed this time. He and the King would be back by eight, he said.

They were not. Dr Muller, Gudden's assistant, sent out men to look for them. It was 10.30 p.m. before the King's hat, coat and umbrella were found, beside the lake. Then came the discovery of the bodies of Dr von Gudden and King Ludwig, in the shallows. Though no official statement was made, it was said that Gudden's neck bore marks of strangulation; the King's body was unmarked. This suggests that he strangled Gudden and then drowned himself.

It has been argued that Ludwig might have killed Gudden in the hope of effecting an escape. In that case his drowning is inexplicable, for he was a strong swimmer, and his body was found close to the shore. The only doubt can be whether Gudden tried to prevent Ludwig's suicide and so the King turned on him or whether Ludwig knew that he must kill Gudden before he could be free to kill himself.

The person who grieved most for King Ludwig was his cousin Elisabeth, a Bavarian princess who had married Franz Josef, Emperor of Austria. Although she by no means shared her cousins' insanity, Elisabeth was unstable and self-absorbed ('an ageing, rather inarticulate Ophelia', said a courtier), and she was guilty of her caste's unforgivable sin: putting self before duty. These traits were inherited by her son Rudolf, Crown Prince of Austria.

Rudolf was another of the princes of Europe who seemed destined for power and pleasure but whose character blighted his life. His misfortune was not insanity but the inability to accept the restraints that accompanied the privileges of rank. He was certainly not the only man to be married to a woman he did not love and to turn to a succession of mistresses; nor was he the only heir to a throne who chafed at his exclusion from affairs of state. By the time he was in his late twenties, the Crown Prince had contracted heavy debts and a venereal disease that would prevent his fathering a son for the imperial succession. Resentment and self-pity ate away at him.

In one respect, the Crown Prince gave himself the illusion of involvement in the affairs of the Empire: he committed himself to the separatist aspirations of Hungary and corresponded with Hungarian dissidents. However, every man he met, every letter he wrote, was known to the government, through the secret police.

Rudolf was not only ill but deeply depressed. Although he and his wife, Stéphanie of Belgium, were on the coolest of terms, he suggested a suicide pact to her; when she refused, he made the same proposal to his then mistress, Mitzi Kaspar. The Crown Princess tried to alert the Emperor to the danger but failed; Mitzi Kaspar took her story to the police, only to be turned away with the warning that she must not divulge her secret to anyone else. Then, late in 1888, the Crown Prince found a woman so infatuated with him that she would consent to die with him. This was the eighteen-year-old Baroness Marie Vetsera, who affected the English name Mary.

On the morning of 30 January 1889, servants at the Crown Prince's hunting lodge at Mayerling found their master shot through the head, and beside him on the bed the body of Mary Vetsera, who had also been shot.

In the days that followed, Europe learned only what the Austrian Emperor would allow: that the Crown Prince had shot himself; the death of Mary Vetsera was ignored and the fact of her presence at Mayerling withheld. It was alleged that the Crown Prince's suicide was due to insanity, probably caused by a malformation of the brain, revealed in the autopsy; that was the only way of persuading the

Catholic Church to afford him Christian burial. Nevertheless, rumours sped through Austria and thence into the rest of Europe: Rudolf had been shot in a duel; he had been killed by the father of a girl he had seduced; he had been killed accidentally in a fight; he had been assassinated for some political motive.

The simplest solution seems the most likely: that, having found a willing partner for suicide, the Crown Prince ended a life that had become a burden. Medical evidence showed that Mary Vetsera had been dead some six to eight hours longer than Rudolf. He must have sat alone through the night next to the body of the woman he had killed, before killing himself.

CHAPTER ELEVEN

PROPAGANDA BY DEED

In the first half of the nineteenth century, nationalism and liberalism (the determination to give 'power to the people') came to dominate Europeans' aspirations. The theses of eighteenth-century political philosophers and the success of the French Revolution were positive encouragement for the liberals; the repression of democratic trends, after the fall of Napoleon, only hardened their resolve. At the same time, the peoples of Europe ruled by foreigners began to press for their liberty. In Ireland, the foreigners were the English, who were seen as rapacious landlords heedless of the needs of their tenants and as religious heretics domineering a Catholic nation. In Poland and Finland, Russia was the overlord and the enemy. In northern Italy, it was Austria. Nationalism, like liberalism, inspired Europe's 'revolutionists', as they were then called.

In 1830, revolution broke out in France, challenging the repressive measures imposed by the restored monarchy, and the monarchy fell, though a 'liberal' Bourbon cousin subsequently took the throne. An uprising in Brussels, against Dutch rule, brought into being the new kingdom of Belgium, with a constitutional monarchy. In Germany, several states secured constitutions. For some ten months in 1830–31, Poland maintained its independence of Russian rule, until it fell – inevitably – to the military might of 'the great bear'. By 1831, states in northern Italy were also in revolt.

In 1848 France again erupted into riots and political demonstrations, this time turning out its Bourbon monarch for ever. Insurrection spread to the various states of Italy and Germany and to Austria and its dominions, again with pressure for constitutions and representative assemblies. In Poland and Hungary, demands for independence of the Russian and Austrian empires were countered with harsh reprisals.

After 1848, the forces of conservatism and counter-revolution restored order, and governments recruited thousands of agents to keep dissidents under surveillance. Many of these agents 'went underground', posing as revolutionaries themselves and in some cases acting as *agents provocateurs*. Whatever the morality of their profession, they were often responsible for preventing acts of terrorism, saving the lives of potential victims – and not only those of the monarchs and politicians of Europe.

Even before the revolutionary years 1831 and 1848, Italy had become the proverbial hotbed of political ferment, flares of rioting and organised terrorism, fostered by secret societies. In fact, as for centuries past, there was no such country as Italy, but a collection of states from Austrian-held Piedmont and Venetia in the north to the Bourbon kingdom of 'the two Sicilies' in the south. But there was a feeling throughout the peninsula that Italian unity must come, and with it a liberal constitution.

Mazzini, Cavour, Garibaldi: these are the names honoured in the history of Italy's unification, but there were thousands of others who devoted their lives to the cause. All over Italy there were groups of dissidents against the various regimes, from aristocrats and intellectuals to peasants and bandits. Some of the secret societies were loosely grouped together, crossing the boundaries of the kingdoms, duchies and Papal States. Chief among them were the Carbonari, whose movement had begun in Naples after the restoration of the Bourbon monarchy. Most of the societies' members were law-abiding citizens who did nothing more than argue politics over café tables; others flouted the censorship laws by distributing pamphlets and pasting up posters; but there were also some who were prepared to take up arms in local revolts – and, of course, in the larger rebellions of 1831 and 1848. The few (the very few) who adopted the 'theory of the dagger', using mass terrorism and individual assassination as weapons of revolution, were, however, sufficiently active to give Italy a continent-wide reputation for political violence.

In 1833, Giuseppe Mazzini, leader of the Young Italy party that replaced the Carbonari as Italy's main revolutionary force, was confronted by one Antonio Gallenga, who offered to kill the King of Sardinia. Mazzini was by no means averse to the idea of regicide, having first established that Gallenga's motive was political and not the result of any personal grudge. His target, Carlo Alberto, King of Sardinia, was an unfortunate monarch: in his youth he had displayed such liberal tendencies that he was something of a hero to the revolutionaries; as king, he was mistrusted by his conservative subjects but at the same time alienated his former admirers by becoming more reactionary.

Gallenga planned to take up a position in one of the long corridors of the royal palace in Turin along which the King passed daily, in slow procession, on his way to the chapel. Mazzini provided the weapon, his own stiletto paper-knife. But Gallenga was thwarted: the visit of the Duke of Modena to Turin that autumn saw an increase in police activity in the city, and when the house of a friend was raided, Gallenga fled.

The police and their secret agents were particularly vigilant in Naples, where there were intermittent rebellions, in an attempt to restore the 1820 constitution, and where plots against the life of King Ferdinando II were frequently uncovered before they could be realised. Others were not prevented, such as that in September 1849, when a man carried a bomb into the royal palace, to be set off during a papal blessing; somehow, the bomb detonated too soon and no one was injured. And in 1856, at a military review, a soldier tried to stab Ferdinando with his bayonet; he wounded the King, but the pistol case attached to Ferdinando's saddle took the main force of the blow, and he was sufficiently calm and courageous to remain in place throughout the review.

Italian nationalism – and resentment, in northern Italy, of Austrian dominion – was paralleled by that growing in Hungary, which had been under Austrian rule for more than three centuries. In February 1853, the Hungarian Janos Lebényi stalked the Austrian Emperor Franz Josef on the fortifications of central Vienna and stabbed him in the back of the neck. But the knife was deflected by the Emperor's thick collar, and he survived the attack. In 1867, Hungary did win a measure of self-government as outlined in the Austro-Hungarian Ausgleich (Compromise), but it was the work of Hungary's moderates, not her revolutionaries.

In Italy, revolutionary activity was often a scapegoat for acts of common banditry but also in one instance for plain murder. In 1854, when Carlo III, Duke of Parma, was murdered by a rival for his mistress's favours, it was given out that he had been assassinated by revolutionaries. His reputation as a womaniser was too well known for that to gain much credence; in fact, many preferred to believe the version of the story that had the Duke murdered in a brothel.

Louis-Napoleon Bonaparte was the nephew of the Emperor Napoleon and in his youth was an idealist of the 'liberty, equality, fraternity' school. In 1831 he joined the Romans in their revolt against the Pope's temporal rule, a prelude to a brief career in France that led to his deportation to America. Inevitably he returned to Europe, inevitably presented himself in France, and he was imprisoned there between 1841 and his escape in 1846. As a champion of the working class he was elected to the revolutionary parliament of 1848, and before the year was out he was elected president of the Third Republic. Despite his obvious ambitions, in 1852 it was politely said that he 'accepted' the title of Napoleon III, Emperor of the French.

Not surprisingly, the Italians looked to such a man for support in their own struggle for liberty. However, as president of France he had to placate the strong Catholic element in his army and government, and in 1850 he sent a French force to restore Pope Pius IX, thereby ending the Roman Republic that had resulted from the 1848 revolt. As emperor he maintained an army in Rome to keep the Pope in power. Thus, to his former friends in the Carbonari and to members of Young Italy, Napoleon III appeared a traitor.

The career of Felice Orsini, leader of the men who in 1857 planned to assassinate Napoleon III, was more characteristic of the revolutionary of popular fiction than of the thousands of Italians who worked for liberation. Born in 1819, he was the son of one of the founder members of the Carbonari and himself became a member of the Young Italy movement. As a lawyer and author, he was one of the movement's leading intellectuals but was nonetheless also an activist and was elected to the parliament of the short-lived Roman Republic. Five times he was imprisoned, in 1855 sentenced to death for high treason; his prison escape that September made him famous far beyond Italy.

Orsini's was not the first attempt to kill Napoleon III. In 1853 the Emperor watched from a theatre box as police arrested fifteen men in the audience below; they were carrying daggers and were to have struck at Napoleon after the performance. In 1854 a bomb was found on a railway line over which he was to travel the next day. In 1855 an Italian fired three shots at him on the Champs Elysées. In April 1857 three Italians tried to waylay his unguarded carriage late at night, as the Emperor left the house of his Italian mistress. Now, in the autumn of 1857, Orsini laid his plans from his place of safety in Britain, where he was earning a living by lecturing. At the end of November he crossed to Belgium, carrying British-made explosive devices (variously called grenades and bombs) and went on to Paris, where he was joined by three fellow-conspirators, Pieri, Gomez and Rudio.

On the evening of Thursday 14 January 1858, Inspector Hébert of the French Sûreté was about to enter the opera house on the rue Lepelletier when he recognised Pieri. When Pieri was searched, he was found to be carrying a grenade, a revolver and a dagger.

Pieri had been spotted in the crowd waiting to see the Emperor and Empress, who were expected at the opera house to attend a gala performance in honour of a retiring Italian baritone. The programme was a mixed one – opera, drama and ballet – but it was united by the theme of royal murder: scenes from Rossini's *William Tell* and Auber's *La Muette de Portici* (*Masaniello*), an extract from Alfieri's *Maria Stuart* and a ballet depicting the murder of Gustav III of Sweden. Presumably that is why Orsini had chosen that occasion for the assassination of Napoleon III.

As the imperial coach drew up outside the opera house, Gomez hurled the first grenade. It landed among the Lancer escort. Orsini's and Rudio's followed. One grenade exploded under the Emperor's carriage. A maelstrom of staggering, screaming people surged forward, their cries mingling with the screams of wounded horses.

Now the police forced their way through and pressed close as the Emperor and Empress alighted from the carriage, fearful of gun-shot and dagger-thrust. Inside the theatre, Napoleon and his Spanish wife Eugénie took stock of each other. The Emperor's nose was slightly grazed; the Empress had a bleeding cut on her left eyelid. Napoleon wanted to go out to the wounded.

'Don't be a fool!' Eugénie hissed, and he turned back.

Inside the theatre, the orchestra was already playing the *William Tell* overture when the sound of explosions was heard. The music ceased. News of the attempted assassination preceded the imperial party, and the Emperor was greeted with cheers.

During the performance, Napoleon received reports from the police, and pieces of metal were brought in, as evidence of the grenades. The Empress put these souvenirs into her reticule.

By midnight, when the imperial procession returned to the Tuileries, the news had permeated Paris, and thousands of citizens turned out to take the Emperor safely home.

Of the 28 Lancers who had comprised the imperial escort, 13 were wounded, as were 31 policemen. From a total of 156 casualties, 10 people later died, 3 were blinded. Orsini himself had been struck by a fragment of the third grenade, and he joined other victims in a pharmacist's shop demanding first aid. Although all three men left the scene of their crime without detection, Gomez was found sobbing in a restaurant, a loaded revolver on the table before him, and Rudio was arrested in the hotel room he had shared with Pieri. From Gomez's hotel, the police traced the way to the rooms Orsini had taken nearby. He was asleep, his pillow bloodstained from his wound. Thus before dawn on the 15th all three had been arrested and joined Pieri in custody.

Since none of Napoleon's assailants was a Frenchman, the charge against them was not treason but only attempted parricide (the killing of a head of state). None of the four disputed the charge. At their trial, Orsini was the only one of them to present the court with a political apologia for his act, his legal training standing him in good stead. He also wrote to Napoleon III, proclaiming the wrongs suffered by Italians, reminding him of the human rights that the Emperor had himself enunciated and begging his help for Italy. Napoleon recognised in Orsini a great patriot and a man of high principle and was willing that he and his comrades should be reprieved from the death sentence, but his government would not allow it. Gomez and Rudio's sentences were reduced to transportation to the French penal colonies, but on 13 March Orsini and Pieri went to the guillotine.

In the aftermath of this attempted assassination, the fact that the grenades had been made in Britain, along with Britain's long-term protection of foreign dissidents and conspirators, raised anti-British feeling in France. Prime Minister Palmerston felt it necessary to introduce a parliamentary bill against conspiracy to murder, largely to show foreign Governments that the British Government did not condone such activities. This gave Palmerston's political opponents the opportunity to revile his Government as pandering to a foreign power, and in the face of parliamentary condemnation, the Prime Minister felt that he 'could not with honour or with any advantage to the public service carry on the Government': he resigned. In France, a Law of Public Safety was passed, one of the most stringent measures against French dissidents in half a century.

Italy felt the strongest effects of the attempt on the Emperor's life – and in a strange way: far from being alienated from Italian nationalists by their attack on him, Napoleon III came to see the urgency of the Italians' cause. In a secret meeting with the Italian leader Camillo Cavour at Plombières in July 1858, Napoleon pledged France to joining Piedmont in a war against Austria (if Austria could be shown as the aggressor), Austria's Italian lands to be split between them when victory was accomplished. In the event, the war of April–July 1859 ended in a truce between France and Austria without Piedmontese agreement. Nevertheless, the outcome was significant in paving the way for Cavour in the north and Garibaldi in the south to secure the unification of Italy, under a constitutional monarchy, in March 1861. The old republican Mazzini refused to countenance the monarchy, and he continued to feature in abortive conspiracies until his death in 1872.

Mazzini was the last of the great liberal theorist-activists to champion the use of regicide.

As for Napoleon III, Orsini's attempt on his life was not the last time he encountered danger. On 6 June 1867, he was driving with Tsar Alexander II in the Bois de Boulogne when shots were fired. One hit an equerry's horse, the second burst in the pistol's barrel. In fact, the assailant's target was the Tsar, not the French Emperor, for he was a Polish nationalist. 'Long live Poland!' was a cry heard throughout the streets of Paris during the Tsar's visit, for the city was a mecca for Polish émigrés.

Wilhelm I, King of Prussia, made a third with the Tsar and Emperor in Paris that month, all enjoying the wonders of the city's Exposition Universelle. The next time the King was in France, it was as a conqueror, the victor of the brief Franco-Prussian war of 1870–71. On 18 January 1871, at Versailles, he was proclaimed Emperor (Kaiser) of Germany. Napoleon III, who had been captured at the battle of Sedan, went into exile, living out his last years in Britain, dying in 1873.

On a May afternoon in 1878 the former King Wilhelm of Prussia, now Kaiser of Germany, was driving with his daughter along the avenue Unter den Linden in Berlin when a man fired at him. In fact, he fired three times, without success, before the Kaiser's coachman and outrider overpowered him. He was executed three months later, his counsel's plea of insanity having failed.

On 2 June, in the same circumstances, another attempt was made on the Kaiser's life. This time he was shot in the head, back, arms and hands before his assailant, Karl Nobiling, a doctor of philosophy, shot himself in the head. Unlike Nobiling, the 81-year-old Kaiser survived, and he was even heard to say that the attack was the best physician he had ever had, for it gave him a new zest for life. He lived ten more years.

On 23 October that same year, two shots were fired at Alfonso XII, King of Spain, as he drove through Madrid. His assailant was hanged before a crowd of 50,000.

And then on Sunday 17 November, when Umberto I, King of Italy, was driving through Naples with his wife, son and prime minister, a man leapt up onto the open carriage and struck him in the shoulder with a dagger. Prime Minister Cairoli threw himself at the assailant and took the next dagger-thrust in his thigh. By then, the King was beating the man with the flat of his sword, and Queen Margherita was hitting him with her bouquet; a guard overpowered him. Public demonstrations in several cities proved the people's loyalty to the monarchy, but in Pisa and Florence bombs were thrown, killing three. Giovanni Passannante, an unemployed cook, was sentenced to death for the attempted assassination, but Umberto himself commuted the sentence to one of life imprisonment*.

In all four cases, the would-be assassins were labelled socialists or anarchists.

Across the length and breadth of Europe, men – and, increasingly, women – debated liberation from tyranny, self-government for each nation, political rights and the fairer sharing of material things. Thus they were called 'socialists', later 'communists'. A substantial number found in favour of the use of terrorism as a means of destroying current systems of government, to usher in their planned utopias. 'Propaganda by deed', as such terrorist acts were called, was perpetrated in virtually every country in Europe before the century was out. The assassination of autocratic and reactionary monarchs was a widespread objective. The ends justified the means.

If the religious background of assassination attempts was too vast a subject for more than a cursory glance here, how much more so the philosophical basis of the revolutionary movement in Europe in the late nineteenth century. There was no single philosophy underlying the aims and methods of revolutionary activists, who were indeed often at variance with each other, their groups continually splitting after heated disagreements. Although, in the long term, the German Karl Marx would emerge as the most influential political theoretician of the nineteenth century, in their time the best known were the Russians Herzen, Bakunin and Nechaev, the first a liberal, the second an anarchist, the third a nihilist. For most people, of course, the distinction was thoroughly blurred, and the terms 'revolutionary' (or 'revolutionist'), 'anarchist' and 'socialist' were applied haphazardly.

---

* As Passannante's prison was an underground cell, in which he was chained, in solitary confinement, it is unsurprising that he was found insane a decade later. He died in an asylum in 1910. After an examination for signs of abnormality, his brain was 'pickled' and, until 2007, displayed in a museum in Rome.

From the novels of Turgenev, through Conrad and Zola to the purple prose of cheap 'shockers', the revolutionary became a recognised character in the repertoire of villains. He was stereotyped by his black beard and thick-lensed glasses, invariably an atheist and proponent of 'free love', moving furtively through dark backstreets to the headquarters of a secret society – innocent-looking premises housing a printing press and a bomb factory.

A Revolutionary Catechism (1869) attributed to Bakunin and Nechaev defined the revolutionary as a man cut off from society by the renunciation of family and property, giving single-minded devotion to one cause: the overthrow of his country's government. Ideas of what was to lie beyond the revolution differed according to country and creed, but the consensus was for a socialist democracy. Nechaev parted company with Bakunin here: he called for the complete freedom of a society without government, without laws, in a state of perpetual flux, perpetual revolution – the 'nothingness' of nihilism. His followers were few.

Law-abiding socialists (urging democratic government, not perpetual revolution) inevitably suffered from the reputation laid on them by their terrorist comrades. Even in Britain, where there was minimal subversive activity among native socialists and where suffrage reform and trade unionism were the immediate objectives, socialists were scarcely respectable. In the Catholic countries of Europe, Pope Leo XIII's encyclical of 1878 denouncing socialism, anarchism and nationalism came as no surprise to those who saw the Church as an agent of political conservatism and social repression. In France and Germany, in Austria and her satellites and especially in Russia and hers, government agents and informers proliferated. The Russian Okhrana, the police force dealing with dissidents, subversives and terrorists, numbered some 50,000 by 1912, with an estimated 26,000 external agents, mainly informers.

But then, Russia was a special case . . .

Workers of Russia!
Today, March 1st, Alexander the Tyrant has been killed by us, Socialists. He was killed because he did not care for his people. He burdened them with taxes. He deprived the peasant of his lands;

he handed over the workers to plunderers and exploiters. He did not give the people freedom. He did not heed the people's tears. He cared only for the rich. He himself lived in luxury. The police maltreated the people, and he rewarded them instead of punishing them. He hanged or exiled any who stood out on behalf of the people or on behalf of justice. That is why he was killed. A tsar should be a good shepherd, ready to devote his life to his sheep. Alexander II was a ravening wolf, and a terrible death overtook him!

The words of the manifesto issued by the assassins of Alexander II, Tsar of Russia, in March 1881 show that this was not only a case of 'propaganda by deed' but one of tyrannicide. Alexander II was no figurehead ruler, and his own policies had shaped Russia for the past quarter of a century.

Even before the assassination of Alexander II caused the Russian authorities to impose the most repressive measures on the empire, Russia was a terrible place for those who opposed the regime but no less terrible for those born in serfdom. The system of serfdom blighted the lives of millions of men, women and children – 40 million people, it was estimated in 1856. They were the property of their masters, to be bought or sold, to be employed on their native manor as their master ordered or to be hired out to factories or mines (the master taking their wages), to be allowed or forbidden to marry (usually allowed, to increase the number of 'souls' the master owned) and to be punished corporally or by being sent into the army, at the master's will. Their living-conditions were of the most primitive kind. In winter, in their wood-and-clay huts, people shared living-space with their animals. Epidemics, often caused by polluted water, exacerbated by malnutrition, killed thousands every year. In the villages there was no doctor but the local 'wise woman'; many priests were as illiterate as their parishioners; it was rare for a master to allow his serfs even the most basic education. There was no one to whom ill-treated serfs could complain: their master was supreme. Rebellions did occur, frequently, but they were localised and easily dealt with by the provincial militia.

More dangerous to the Russian regime was the work of the urban intellectuals, who promulgated 'the rights of man', as encountered in western European literature. After the 1848 revolutions in the West, the importation of foreign books into Russia was forbidden and internal censorship was increased; a permit must be obtained for foreign travel, and such permits were issued to very few; school pupils and university students were strictly supervised, in an attempt to prevent dangerous doctrines' permeating among them, and their ranks were infiltrated by police spies; public meetings were banned. Those who breached the security laws were condemned to hard labour in Siberian mines.

Russians looked to one man to give freedom to the serfs and to introduce a system of government resembling those in western Europe. He was Tsar Alexander II, who came to the throne in 1855 and who was known to favour reform. In 1861 he abolished serfdom. Unfortunately, he failed to appreciate that, as the vast majority of serfs were peasants, without land-ownership they were as economically dependent on their former masters as they had ever been. Riots, murders, arson: the Russian countryside erupted in the years after 1861, and prisons became ever more full as those deemed 'troublemakers' were rounded up.

Alexander II also initiated reforms in the legal system, education, the army and local government, paving the way, it seemed, for major change in national government. Then, in 1866, Alexander had his first encounter with would-be assassins.

On 4 April 1866, the Tsar went for one of his frequent walks in St Petersburg's Summer Gardens. They were public gardens but there was no thought of any danger to him from his subjects. However, among the crowds that gazed at Alexander from a respectful distance was Dmitri Karakazov, a university student who had taken the troubles of the poor to heart. He had come to the gardens carrying a revolver, prepared to shoot the Tsar. But another man in the crowd, a hatter's apprentice named Osip Kommissarov, saw Karakazov draw his gun and aim, virtually point-blank, at the Tsar as he entered his carriage. Kommissarov hit Karakazov, and the bullet intended for Alexander struck the pavement.

Karakazov could not escape. The police had to rescue him from the howling crowd, to take him away to imprisonment, trial and, inevitably, the gallows. Kommissarov was the hero of the hour and was awarded a pension.

Despite the fact that investigation into Karakazov's background revealed that his was a solo attempt on the Tsar's life, that he was not affiliated to any secret society plotting revolution, his act so appalled Alexander that he gave orders for stricter controls in the universities, a strengthening of censorship etc. His reforms were halted, and he began to surround himself with conservatives rather than liberals in government.

In fact, the 1866 attempt was a timely warning, for others, more organised in their methods, were beginning to envisage the destruction of the Tsar. As repression increased, after 1866, their determination grew.

Although there were outposts of the main secret societies throughout Russia, the nucleus of each was in St Petersburg or Moscow; membership was confined largely to the cities' intelligentsia at this period. Chief among Russian political philosophers, Alexander Herzen, living in exile, wrote letters and articles that were smuggled into Russia. Russian liberals deplored extremist philosophy and waited for a constitution, but the émigrés living in the West saw the deficiencies of democracy, and the Russian utopia that many of them visualised was far removed from the constitutional monarchies and republics that had been the goal of the Western revolutionaries of 1831 and 1848. Some preached the gospel familiar in the twentieth century as Communism; others the destruction of all authority, of the state itself – the doctrine that the Russian novelist Turgenev called 'nihilism'. Although there were so many shades of opinion that the groups of 'revolutionists' were small-scale, disorganised and usually unco-operative with each other, there were a couple of unusually large and active societies, those named 'Death or Freedom' and 'Land and Liberty', of which the offshoot called 'The Will of the People' was dedicated to acts of violence.

The university students who secretly debated the forbidden doctrines were not mere theorists: they spent their long vacations in the countryside, teaching peasants not only to read and write but also to understand the alternatives to their political impotence. These propagandists were called 'men of the people'. Some always remained propagandists; others became insurrectionists. Unfortunately, when insurrectionists were rounded up, usually after the groups had been infiltrated by police spies, their propagandist colleagues were often implicated. The convict population of Siberia swelled.

In 1867, visiting France, Alexander II was shot at by a Polish émigré as he drove in the Bois de Boulogne with the French Emperor. In 1873 the Kiev group of 'Land and Liberty' sent a man to fire at the

Tsar; his shots went wide. In the mid 1870s, political murders became almost commonplace; there were twenty-two committed between 1878 and 1881. In 1879, a man fired at the Tsar in the garden of St Petersburg's Winter Palace. That same year 'The Will of the People' formed a 'League of Regicides' to kill Alexander II. At first they thought to blow up the imperial train, with the Tsar and his family aboard. The authorities took precautions: routes and schedules were changed not once but several times, whenever the Tsar made a journey. Still, there were five such attempts, thwarted by accident and by the terrorists' errors more than by police vigilance.

The railway plots having failed, one of the attempts on the Tsar's life was made inside the Winter Palace itself. Workmen were busy there in the early months of 1880, and it was not difficult for Stefan Khalturin to obtain employment as a carpenter and to smuggle in a supply of dynamite, to be stored two floors below the imperial dining-room. At 6.20 p.m. on 5 February 1880 there was an explosion. In the dining-room, courtiers and servants lay wounded and dead; in the guardroom on the floor below, directly above the explosion, eleven soldiers died; but the Tsar was unhurt. Unusually, he was late for his six o'clock dinner that evening and was not in the dining-room when the dynamite went off.

The case of Alexander Soloviev, the man who had tried to shoot the Tsar in 1879, gives an insight into the workings of the groups of assassins. Soloviev attempted to take a 'suicide pill' as he was being hustled away, but a sharp-eyed policeman prevented it. Soloviev said he was trying to avoid the questioning that might make him reveal the names of his associates; if he did that, he said, he would die anyway, for they would find a way to kill him, even in prison.

More is known of the Russian revolutionaries of this period than of any group of assassins, or individual assassin, in past centuries, for after the Russian Revolution in 1917 they became heroes – and heroines, for there were many women in their ranks, although feminism was not high on the revolutionaries' agenda. For example, in 1878 Vera Zasulich shot the chief of the St Petersburg police, but she was acquitted when it was discovered that he had illegally flogged a suspect in prison (one of Alexander II's reforms was thus seen to be effective). As she left the court, the police closed in to take her and her friends into custody, but amid the cheering crowd she managed to escape and subsequently to flee abroad. Sofia Perovskaia, one of the many gentlewomen who did not shrink from terrorism, became even more famous than Vera Zasulich, for she was among the conspirators who killed Alexander II in 1881.

It was customary for the Tsar to drive out in his sleigh on Sunday afternoons in winter, to go to the weekly military parade, and his route habitually took him along the Nevsky Prospect, the main thoroughfare of St Petersburg. In February 1881, the Tsar did not go to the parade for three Sundays, having given in to his family's pleas for caution. On Sunday 1 March, he was determined to go, but he agreed to avoid the Nevsky Prospect and use side roads, which could be closed to the public. At least, most of them were: the one alongside the Catherine Canal had been overlooked. It was there that some of the conspirators took up their places. Sofia Perovskaia was stationed where she could signal to them when the Tsar's sleigh approached.

A student named Rysakov threw the first grenade. It landed among the escort, killing two Cossacks (and a passing errandboy) and wounding others. The Tsar, unhurt, although his sleigh was shattered, walked through the snow to the wounded men. At that moment a Pole named Hriniewicki detonated his grenade at the Tsar's feet. Both he and Alexander were mortally wounded.

'Home to the palace to die,' the Tsar whispered to his brother, who carried him to a sleigh and held him as he lapsed into unconsciousness. Alexander II died soon after.

It was a terrible irony. That very morning the Tsar had signed a document signifying his approval of reforms that, though they were by no means favourable to democracy or a constitution, would have meant that the elected representatives of the town and country councils would have the power to advise the imperial government. That would have been a stepping-stone to a national parliament. His decree was now, of course, cancelled.

So the revolutionaries' assassination of the Tsar had happened just in time, in their view, for the extremists had no wish for slow reform, leading to democracy along Western lines. They wanted the destruction of the Russian regime, and its replacement with a system whose liberties went beyond anything known in Europe – or, for the nihilists, the advent of liberties that were boundless. As it was, even the limited reforms sanctioned by Alexander II were withheld, for his heir, now Alexander III, was no liberal, and his father's assassination only strengthened his resolve to remain the actual as well as the titular 'Autocrat of all the Russias', the most powerful man in Europe.

On 3 April 1881, the five surviving assassins were hanged, publicly, in Semenovsky Square – Sofia Perovskaia included. The crowd that watched was estimated to number some 80,000. For months afterwards, members of 'The Will of the People' were hunted down, rounded up and exiled, imprisoned or executed. Censorship was strengthened; police powers were increased; state control of universities and high schools became more rigorous; among the new restrictions on entry to higher education, those limiting women's admittance were particularly strict. But, as the nineteenth century drew to a close, it became obvious that the measures imposed to repress the revolutionaries were not effective.

Alexander III came under personal attack. In 1887 there were three attempts on his life. One of the five men hanged after the abortive attempt on the 1887 anniversary of the assassination of Alexander II was Alexander Ulyanov, a twenty-year-old student. His sixteen-year-old brother Vladimir never forgot him or ceased to honour his memory. Vladimir Ulyanov is better known by the name he later adopted: Lenin.

In 1888 the Tsar and his family were travelling on a train on the Kursk–Kharkov line when it was derailed near Borki. The tall and muscular Tsar held up the roof of his compartment, which had caved in, while members of his family and their household escaped. Twenty-eight people had been killed, more than a hundred injured. It seems that the derailment was an accident, perhaps caused by the precautionary high speed of the train, but of course 'revolutionists' were blamed.

It was nephritis, not a bomb or bullet, that killed Alexander III in 1894. His successor, Nicholas II, was a sensitive, kindly man who unfortunately felt so keenly the weight of his inheritance that to yield any part of his power seemed to him a betrayal of his ancestors. His intransigence would lead, in 1917, to the final, tragic chapter in the history of the Romanov dynasty.

CHAPTER TWELVE

THE ASSASSIN'S HEYDAY

The years 1898–1914* were the heyday of the anarchist assassin, if the term 'anarchist' may still be allowed to cover all shades of political dissidence and subversive creed and activity, as it did in those years. The assassination of monarchs and statesmen took the headlines, but they should never be allowed to obscure the far wider range of terrorist activities that struck at every level of society in that period. Nor should the scope of reprisal be forgotten: the prisons of Europe bulged with suspects as well as proven terrorists, and with men and women whose crimes were often no more heinous than breaches of censorship laws, outspokenness and 'guilt by association'.

By the last decade of the nineteenth century, the monarchs of Europe were closely guarded. The attempts on the lives of three of them in 1878 and the assassination of Tsar Alexander II in 1881 had reinforced the conviction that there must be a huge investment of men, money and effort in protecting 'crowned heads'. In Britain, free from the violent 'anarchist' dissidence common elsewhere in Europe, there was a rise in Irish nationalist activity that included violence against the public, such as the 1883 bombing of the London underground railway. As a result, Scotland Yard created its Special Branch, an elite corps of detectives, both overt and undercover, who were to undertake surveillance of those suspected of subversive activities and also to act as bodyguards to members of the British royal family and of foreign royal families visiting Britain.

Among those who worked openly, Patrick (later Sir Patrick) Quinn was the chief of Queen Victoria's bodyguards for two decades. Herbert Fitch, who wrote *Memoirs of a Royal Detective*, spoke French,

---

* This chapter covers 1898–1910. Chapter 13, which deals with Balkan history, takes the story up to 1914.

German and Russian and was often assigned to guard visiting heads of state, who rewarded him with such exotic honours as the Red Eagle of Prussia and the White Elephant of Siam. (Fitch also acted as a guide to several monarchs. The King of Bulgaria haunted the London Zoo, Fitch later reminisced; the Shah of Persia wanted to take a chorusgirl home.)

Fitch's memoirs tell how, when a foreign monarch came to Britain, his port of entry would be searched for known foreign dissidents; his train was searched too, and its London terminus. For weeks before the visit, plain-clothes men would infiltrate working men's clubs, to listen out for any word of planned violence. Fitch stressed the success of such teamwork and of attention to detail. For example, a rail route would be examined for places from which a bomb might be thrown. Along a royal visitor's carriage route to the palace, where crowds might be expected to gather, plain-clothes men were positioned to keep order by making sure that all were 'good humoured and steady' – in contrast to the Russian preventatives: mounted policemen and soldiers with sabres and guns pressing crowds back.

More dangerous plain-clothes work was undertaken by men who could pass as labourers, artisans or even foreign émigrés. For example, one detective, who posed as a cobbler, living in the slums of London's East End, used his knowledge of French, German and Yiddish to infiltrate the lives of émigré anarchists. When he had to take his turn as bodyguard to a member of the royal family, he would tell his East End friends that he had to go into hospital, and he would shave off his beard, lest anyone spot him in the royal entourage.

Members of foreign royal families must have felt safe in Britain: not one suffered an attack during a visit, despite the presence in Britain – and especially in London – of dissidents from every repressive regime on the Continent; most of them had become peaceable citizens once they were free of the tyranny in their native lands. But of course there were scares, as when a car backfired in proximity to King Alfonso XIII of Spain, visiting London in 1905. Alfonso's own Spanish detective nearly shot a suspicious-looking man standing nearby on the kerb. He turned out to be a Special Branch officer.

The most serious incident occurred in the late summer of 1909, when the Russian imperial family visited Britain. They stayed at Osborne House on the Isle of Wight, more easily defensible than any London palace. Even so, it was fortunate that the experienced John Sweeney was the Special Branch man assigned to the five-year-old Tsarevich Alexei when he and his tutor made a day trip over to Southsea: it was Sweeney who recognised two men following the party. Not leaving his charge, he signalled to two police officers shadowing them and they moved in on the suspects. They were Russians, armed with knives, though their object was apparently kidnapping, not murder. Investigation showed that they had been involved in sufficiently nefarious activities to have them deported.

Over in France, Xavier Paoli was a 'special commissary' of the Paris Sûreté who specialised in guarding distinguished visitors. His memoirs, entitled *My Royal Clients*, describe tactics similar to those employed by the British police, though the French police even went so far as to identify tenants of railside houses and to post sentries on each railway bridge on a royal route. Paoli pointed out that in Spain, Italy and Germany, when a royal visit was due to take place, hundreds of suspect people would be arrested and kept in custody until the visit was over.

However, nothing could prevent the revolutionaries' scoring some successes. In 1894 President Sadi Carnot of France was assassinated, in 1897 Prime Minister Canovas de Castillo of Spain – both by Italians. In 1898 there were attempts on the lives of Kaiser Wilhelm II of Germany and George I, King of the Hellenes, and on 10 September the Austrian Empress Elisabeth, wife of Emperor Franz Josef, was stabbed to death by an anarchist.

In her youth, Elisabeth had been called the most beautiful woman in Europe but as Empress her self-will and shirking of duty marred her life. The suicide of her only son, Crown Prince Rudolf, in 1889 was a blow from which she never wholly recovered. The Empress was not estranged from her husband, but they rarely met and for years she restlessly roamed Europe and north Africa. The French policeman Xavier Paoli, who numbered Elisabeth of Austria among his 'clients', later recorded that she had been the bane of his life, resenting the attention of the police and leaving hotels by back doors to evade her bodyguards.

In the late summer of 1898 the Empress came to Territet, near Montreux on Lac Léman. On 8 September she made an excursion across the lake to Geneva. On 10 September, planning to return to Territet on the 1.40 p.m. ferryboat, she was crossing the Quai de Mont Blanc, accompanied only by a lady-in-waiting, when Luigi Luccheni plunged a sharp file into her heart. At first bystanders thought Luccheni had tried to take the Empress's purse or watch and had merely pushed her to the ground. Raised to her feet, she went on board the ferry and then apparently fainted. It was only when her clothing was loosened that it became obvious that she had been stabbed. The boat put back to Geneva, and the Empress was carried to her hotel but she died within minutes.

Xavier Paoli arrived in Geneva on the afternoon of 10 September and heard the news at the railway station. Luccheni had been apprehended immediately, and Paoli went to inspect him in his cell, finding him 'a perfectly lucid being, boasting of his crime'. Born in Paris, of Italian ancestry, Luccheni was an unskilled labourer who read anarchist propaganda and, while employed in constructing a new post office in Lausanne, bought a file in the market, sharpened it and went out to kill the first royal visitor he encountered. He had expected to find the Duke of Orleans but Elisabeth of Austria gave him his opportunity. There was no capital punishment for murder in the canton of Geneva, and Luccheni was sentenced to life imprisonment.*

The fact that a woman had been assassinated horrified Europe, and bodyguards were assigned to even the most minor princesses, in case they became tempting 'soft targets' for further attacks. The Grand Duchess of Mecklenburg-Strelitz, born a British princess, was outraged by the dangerous insolence of anarchists. 'My plan', she wrote in August 1900, 'would be to forbid and close all meetings . . . and to muzzle the Press entirely, then take up every man or woman expressing anarchist views, have them flogged daily and, if decided murderers, have them tortured, then blown off from a Gun!'

The Grand Duchess expressed those views after an attack on the Prince of Wales (later King Edward VII) in the railway station in

---

* In October 1910 Luccheni hanged himself in his cell. In 1998 his head, preserved in formaldehyde, was discovered in a Vienna museum and buried, amid international publicity.

Brussels. The Prince and his Danish wife were *en route* to Copenhagen, on one of their rare holidays together. Usually the Prince went *en garçon* to the Côte d'Azur in the spring, but anti-British feeling in France (in fact, throughout the Continent), a revulsion against the Boer War, had caused him to change his plans that year.

In the late afternoon of 4 April 1900, the Prince and Princess of Wales and the Princess's lady-in-waiting, Charlotte Knollys, sat in the luxurious royal compartment of a train pulling out of Brussels' Gare du Nord. Before the train picked up speed, a youth jumped onto the running-board and fired several shots into the carriage. One of them lodged in the seat between the Prince and Princess; another was later found in Miss Knollys' 'bun' of hair. Having failed to do any harm (to the Prince's disgust: *he* would not have missed a target a few feet away), the young man leapt off the train and disappeared. Though he was never caught, it was later discovered that he was Jean-Baptiste Sipido, an 'anarchist' only fifteen years old, who had sought the Prince's life in revenge for the deaths of Boer prisoners of war in British concentration camps in South Africa. Obviously, Sipido did not know how absolutely powerless the Prince of Wales was, a man nearly sixty years old whose mother, Queen Victoria, allowed him no share in the constitutional duties that she had assumed at the age of eighteen.

Queen Victoria died in January 1901, having reigned for sixty-three years.

The new King Edward VII still enjoyed his annual foreign holidays, but they were no holiday for the detectives who accompanied him. When he visited Marienbad in 1903, not only did two British detectives go with him (one of them Patrick Quinn) but they were joined by six Austrians.

Elaborate precautions were taken to protect Edward VII, so when there was an explosion during a performance he attended at the Royal Court Theatre in London, there was consternation among royal detectives in the theatre and stationed outside. The auditorium was plunged into darkness, amid screams from the audience. An attendant produced a torch, which the King shone on his face to show that he was unharmed, but the cries and stampede of the panicked audience were stilled only by the announcement from the stage that there was no danger: the lighting system had failed. Then, in the darkness, the

King disappeared. Fitch, who was on duty that evening, subsequently tracked him down to a room beneath the stage, where the royal pioneer of electricity was watching the repairs in progress.

Vigilance seemed essential, in every kingdom in Europe, but no matter how many guards were assigned to a monarch or however many undercover policemen tried to ferret out plans for regicide, would-be assassins still made their attempts. Sometimes they scored a success, as when, in July 1900, another 'anarchist' took the life of Umberto I, King of Italy.

The King had escaped death in the dangerous year 1878 and had also survived an attack in 1897. On that occasion an unemployed and starving man had made a spur-of-the-moment assault on him with a dagger, as Umberto drove out of Rome to a race meeting; mounted *carabinieri* overpowered him. 'These are the risks of our profession,' Umberto wrote to Wilhelm II of Germany, when he heard of an attempt on the Kaiser's life in 1898.

There was a resurgence of republicanism in Italy in Umberto's reign. The authoritarian, militaristic King had long chafed at the restrictions placed on him by the constitution but by 1898 had managed to build a Cabinet led by generals and admirals. After the 'Beggars' Revolt' in Milan in May of that year (caused largely by the rising price of bread), he had imposed martial law on virtually half his kingdom, imprisoned leading republicans and socialists, closed universities and shut down newspapers. In November and December, at the Italian Government's international conference on combating anarchism (held *in camera*), Britain, Belgium and Switzerland came under attack for their refusal forcibly to repatriate asylum-seekers demanded by their own governments on suspicion of plotting politically motivated crimes.

Over in the United States, the large Italian immigrant population read in Italian-language newspapers of outrages in their homeland. In Paterson, New Jersey, a textile worker named Gaetano Bresci was deputed by his friends to cross to Italy and kill the King. Bresci took a cheap excursion ticket to the Paris Exposition, went on to his home town of Prato (where he privately did some target practice) and on

Sunday 29 July 1900 was at Monza, where Umberto was due to distribute prizes at a gymnastics competition. Bresci was well prepared, carrying a revolver filled with rough-edged, dirty bullets that he hoped would infect a wound even if they did not immediately kill the King.

After the competition, as King Umberto came down through cheering crowds to his carriage, Bresci fired several shots at him, wounding the King in the throat, ribs and heart. While the *carabinieri* fell on Bresci, Umberto was driven swiftly away. He died before he reached home.

Umberto's heir, now King Vittorio Emmanuele III, refused to take the repressive measures urged on him and pledged himself to liberal and constitutional rule, though this did not exempt him from an anarchist attack in 1912. Tragically for Italy, in 1922 Vittorio Emmanuele was to allow Mussolini and his *fascisti* to take power.

American newspapers avidly followed the trial of Gaetano Bresci and reported his sentencing to life imprisonment. The Polish American Leon Czolgosz collected newspaper cuttings about Bresci, and on 6 September 1901 he shot and killed William McKinley, President of the United States – the third American president to be assassinated in forty years.

There were five unsuccessful attempts on the life of Alfonso XIII, King of Spain, by Spanish anarchists, over years in which many Spaniards were killed when bombs exploded in public places. In 1905, when Alfonso was on his first official visit to France, a bomb was thrown at him as he drove through Paris with the French Prime Minister. 'I have received my baptism of fire,' said the King, 'and upon my word, it was much less exciting than I expected.' When, in 1912, a man shot at Alfonso as he rode away from a military review, the King swiftly wheeled his horse out of the line of fire. 'Polo comes in useful on these occasions,' he remarked. Were monarchs really becoming blasé about 'the risks of our profession', as the Italian King Umberto had called them, or was this a case of 'whistling in the dark'?

The best known of the Spanish assassination attempts occurred on 31 May 1906, at the wedding of Alfonso XIII and Princess

Victoria Eugénie – 'Ena' – of Battenberg, a granddaughter of Queen Victoria. It was a nightmare occasion for the Spanish police and for the bodyguards of the members of Europe's royal and imperial families who flocked to Madrid. Almost all of them had a recent story of terrorism to tell, such as the royal Belgians, whose king, Leopold II, had been fired on by an Italian anarchist as he rode home from his wife's funeral in November 1902, and the Russian-born Duchess of Edinburgh, whose father, Tsar Alexander II, had been assassinated in 1881, her brother Sergei in 1905 (see pp. 182–3 and 207). It was impossible to guarantee the safety of the wedding guests in Madrid.

In fact, there was very nearly a massacre in Madrid Cathedral during the wedding service itself. A young 'anarchist' named Mateo Morral was offered a ticket to the service by an unsuspecting American journalist who was too unwell, he thought, to attend; at the last minute the American felt better and reclaimed the ticket. Had Morral been able to throw his bomb in the crowded cathedral, his 'propaganda by deed' would have reverberated throughout Europe. As it was, he had to content himself with taking up a position on a balcony over the Calle Mayor, the narrow, ravine-like 'high street' of Madrid, along which the royal carriage would pass after the three-hour-long service.

'We'll be home in five minutes,' King Alfonso was telling his bride as Morral threw his bomb, hidden in a large bouquet. He had timed it well and would have struck the royal carriage itself had the coachman not reined in the horses at that moment, because of some delay ahead. So the bomb fell just in front of the carriage, killing one horse, wounding others, enveloping the carriage in a cloud of black smoke. As it cleared inside the carriage, the King saw Queen Ena lying back, as if dead; but she was only stunned. He helped her out into a scene of horror: the bodies of the dead, dying and wounded lay all around; the screams of the crowd and the wounded horses echoed between the tall buildings; the acrid smoke still rose and darkened the sky. By the time the King had piloted his bride into another carriage, her shoes and wedding dress were stained with blood.

'I saw a man without any legs,' Queen Ena kept repeating in dazed shock.

At the King's orders, they drove deliberately slowly to the palace, and that afternoon, after visiting the wounded in hospital, he and his wife again drove slowly through the streets of Madrid – without an armed escort.

Two days later, Morral, whom onlookers had identified, was seen at a railway station outside Madrid. When a policeman tried to arrest him, Morral shot him; then he shot himself.

'Next door' to Spain, the kingdom of Portugal was in the grip of one of the most repressive regimes in western Europe. The constitution suspended, the prime minister, João Franco, ruled with the support of King Carlos. As the year 1908 opened, Portuguese republicans attempted – but failed – to incite the country to revolution. Franco took the opportunity to send his enemies into exile.

On 1 February 1908 the royal family returned to Lisbon from their country home. They landed from the ferry at the Praço do Commercio and took their places in an open carriage, Queen Amélie carrying a bouquet she had been given. As the carriage crossed the Terreiro do Paço, a man jumped onto the back of the carriage and fired twice at the King, hitting him in the neck. The Queen tried to beat him off, striking him with her bouquet; then the police shot him down. But at the corner of the square there was another man with a gun, and he fired at the heir to the throne, Prince Luis Filipe. The Queen tried to shield her son, but he was hit in the chest and face. Again the police shot and killed the assailant. There were still two men firing from behind the pillars of a nearby building. Prince Manoel was shot in the arm.

King Carlos was dead, Prince – briefly King – Luis Filipe was dying. Before the day was out, nineteen-year-old Manoel was King of Portugal.

Prime Minister Franco resigned and left the country, and the Portuguese constitution was revived, but the Government, like the country, was split into factions, and the King was too inexperienced to manipulate them. On 3 October 1910 revolution broke out, the guns of a warship firing on the royal palace. The next day King Manoel left Portugal, never to return.

On 20 May 1910, Europe's anarchists missed the opportunity to dispatch in 'one fell swoop' eight of Europe's kings and one emperor, not to mention six queens, an empress and innumerable imperial, royal, grand ducal and serene highnesses, male and female. The funeral of the British King Edward VII had brought them from all corners of Europe, to go in procession through the streets of London behind the gun-carriage bearing the late King's coffin; after a train journey to Windsor, the coffin was carried to its resting-place in St George's Chapel.

First came the new King, George V, flanked by his first cousin the German Kaiser and their uncle the Duke of Connaught; behind them George V's two elder sons, the future Kings Edward VIII and George VI; then Frederik VIII, King of Denmark; George, King of the Hellenes; Haakon VII, King of Norway; Alfonso XIII, King of Spain; Manoel II, King of Portugal; Ferdinand, King of Bulgaria, and Albert, King of the Belgians. Among the scarcely lesser men who followed them were the Archduke Franz Ferdinand, heir to the Austro-Hungarian Empire, and the heirs to the thrones of Greece, Italy, Serbia, Romania, Bavaria, Turkey and Montenegro. Princes had come from Egypt, China and Japan, and there were several Grand Dukes, dukes and princes from all over Europe. Among the women in the carriage procession were the new British Queen and the Queen Mother, the Queens of Denmark and Norway, the Dowager Queens of Portugal and the Netherlands and the Dowager Tsarina of Russia. A grenade attack could not have failed to reap some exalted victims.

The black-and-white photographs of the time fail to do justice to the colourful array of British and foreign uniforms, the gold braid and the gleaming helmets, contrasting with the sombre clothes of the thousands lining the route. However, those photographs do show clearly the close ranks of cavalrymen, on their tall horses, standing between the crowds and the cortège, both in London and at Windsor; and the cavalry were supported by infantrymen standing to attention and by policemen free to turn their gaze on the crowds. Less noticeable is the discreet presence of men in black overcoats and top hats on the outer flanks of the cortège – officers of Special Branch, prepared for trouble.

But there was no trouble, no shot or explosion. There was no tragedy to spoil the solemn occasion.

Nevertheless, in retrospect there was potential tragedy in that scene of splendour. Three of the men who followed the coffin of Edward VII would fall to the assassin's bullet: the King of the Hellenes in 1913, Archduke Franz Ferdinand in 1914 and the then Crown Prince of Serbia – as King of Yugoslavia – in 1934. 'The assassin's heyday' had not yet passed.

CHAPTER THIRTEEN

THE BULLET THAT STARTED A WAR

By 1910, when the monarchs of Europe met at the funeral of Britain's King Edward VII, the tensions between their nations were already apparent – tensions that would snap in 1914, when they entered a war that spread from Europe to involve nations thousands of miles away. However, some of the participants at the funeral ceremonies were destined to go to war much sooner. The Bulgarian and Greek kings and the heirs to the thrones of Romania, Serbia and Turkey, present in London in that May of 1910, were already casting wary glances at each other. Two years later, the first of the twentieth century's Balkan wars erupted.

The term 'Balkan' had already entered European vocabularies to describe political systems characterised by knife-in-the-back transfers of power and by double-dealing in international relations. More properly, the Balkans were the lands between the Adriatic and Black Seas that had recently been recovered from Turkish rule – lands including Greece, Serbia, Bulgaria and Romania, which had become new kingdoms, with Austria becoming the 'protector' of Bosnia-Herzegovina and then annexing it in 1909.

The nineteenth century's Balkan wars of liberation had been inspired by one of the most potent forces in Europe: nationalism. In challenging Turkish rule, the people of the Balkans fought the alien religion and culture of Islam as well as the occupation of their lands by Turks. The Balkan insurgents found ready allies in the Great Powers, notably Russia, which saw the Slav peoples as its own natural protégés. Having gained their freedom, however, the new Balkan states were obliged to exercise the utmost diplomacy – and duplicity – to play off the rival Great Powers against each other, to benefit from their (self-interested) patronage. The man chosen to become Prince (later King, then Tsar) of Bulgaria, Ferdinand of Saxe-Coburg-Kohȧry, acquired the nickname 'Foxy Ferdy' but he was by no means the only Balkan ruler to be regarded as wily. It was an essential qualification for the career of a Balkan monarch.

Prince Ferdinand lived for years in fear of assassination, so precarious was his hold over his governments, so odious his power to many of his people. Even his wife, during a pregnancy, received letters containing death-threats: she and her unborn child were to be killed by a single thrust of a dagger, they warned. But the threats were not carried out. In fact, when Stepan Stambulov, a masterful statesman whom Bulgarians feared and hated and whom Ferdinand removed from office in 1894, was murdered in July 1895, rumours spread through Europe that Ferdinand himself had ordered the assassination.

Neighbouring Serbia was even more renowned for inflicting violent death on those who attempted to rule it.

During some five centuries of Turkish rule, the Serbs had never lost their aspirations for freedom and their sense of national identity. They had mounted countless rebellions against the Turks over the centuries, but it was not until those of 1804–13, under the native warlord Karadjordje ('Black George') Petrović, and 1813–17, under Miloš Obrenović, that they began to make headway against the Turkish forces occupying Serbia.* The two Serb leaders never united, for there was a blood feud between their families. Karadjordje had reputedly had Miloš Obrenović's half-brother poisoned. (In fact, Karadjordje was allegedly a thoroughly uncivilised character: it was said that he had killed his own mother, by clamping a hive of bees on her head.) In retaliation for the Obrenović murder, another half-brother of Miloš Obrenović killed Karadjordje in 1817; his severed head was sent to the Turkish Sultan.

In order to reimpose control over Serbia but also to shift responsibility for governing the troublesome Serbs onto another, in 1833 the Sultan created Miloš Obrenović Prince of Serbia, to rule his fellow-countrymen under Turkish overseers. Miloš, his son and grandson reigned until 1842, when the Serbs elected Karadjordje's

---

* The accented letter ć is pronounced 'ch' as in 'church'. The letter š is 'sh' as in 'shop'.

son Aleksander their prince. He lasted until 1858, when he was deposed and the Obrenović returned to power. That was not the end of the feud. When, in June 1868, the reigning Prince Mihailo Obrenović was shot dead while walking in a park near Belgrade, the Karadjordjević were inevitably blamed.

Turkey having ceded full independence in 1878, in 1882 Milan Obrenović declared Serbia a kingdom, himself its king. He had the task not only of ruling Serbia – which he did as a virtual despot – but of playing off Austria and Russia, each of which sought to make Serbia its satellite.

In April 1890 King Milan's ineptitude forced him to abdicate in favour of his thirteen-year-old son Aleksander, and only four years later Aleksander declared himself of age and took full control of his kingdom. Despite the fact that the former King Milan had left the country, his influence was still apparent in his son's government, and in 1897 he returned to become commander-in-chief of the Serbian army. When, in June 1899, a man was arrested after firing at Milan as he drove in an open carriage through Belgrade, the would-be assassin confessed that he had been hired by a Russian he had met in Bucharest and that he had been generously paid to kill the ex-king. His bullet only grazed Milan's shoulder.

Whether Russia was guilty or not (the 'confession' may well have been a fabrication designed by the Serbian Government to increase fear of Russia), Russian interest, infiltration and interference became a spectre in Serbian public affairs. Who was in Russia's pay? When the young King Aleksander married one of his own subjects, Draga Mašin, in 1900, even she was suspected as a Russian agent.

Draga Masšin had been a lady-in-waiting to Aleksander's mother, who, having separated from King Milan, had settled in Biarritz. When Queen Natalia learned that her son was courting the voluptuous widow, some decade his senior, she dismissed her – only to discover that Draga had gone to Belgrade as Aleksander's mistress. When Draga Mašin announced that she was pregnant, he married her. But the new Queen was not pregnant; she never could be, it was said, for while in France she had had an operation that made it impossible. Rumours abounded. It was said that the Queen had intended to smuggle a child into the palace, to pass off as her own. Despite all Aleksander could do to endear his wife to his people – even making her birthday a national holiday, the Queen was everywhere reviled. Whatever else her failings, the fact that she and her two brothers were known to be the chief political influence on the King was enough to damn her.

Aleksander's reign was marked by a series of political crises and by the struggle between conservatives and radicals for control of his government – a situation he resolved by taking power into his own hands. In March 1903 citizens of Belgrade demonstrated in protest, and the police were ordered to fire on them. From every side came warnings that there was a plot afoot to dethrone Aleksander, and he and Queen Draga rarely left the palace.

The main proponents of the plot were not separatists or left-wing revolutionaries but army officers. Some of the conspirators believed they were merely going to force the King to abdicate; others were intent on nothing less than murder. During the night of 10/11 June 1903, while some of their colleagues entered the guards' barracks, to prevent help being sent to the King, the main force carried explosives to blow open the palace doors. The explosion fused the electricity system, and in the darkness the conspirators roamed the palace, seeking the King and Queen and cutting down or shooting any member of the royal household who opposed them.

When Aleksander and Draga heard the explosion, they took refuge in the Queen's wardrobe closet, whose external door was papered like the walls of the bedroom, so that when the would-be killers entered, they did not notice it. For two hours the couple sheltered in their hiding-place. Then, in a lull, they emerged. The Queen looked out of a window and saw the commander of the palace guard in the courtyard below. She called to him, begging his help. The man fired at her and hurried off to tell others where they might find her.

When the conspirators confronted the King and Queen, Aleksander offered to abdicate, but it did not save his life. The couple were shot and struck with swords, then flung from a balcony. Still living, the King grasped the balcony's railing so tightly that his assailants had to cut off his fingers to make him fall to his death. The bodies of Aleksander Obrenović and Draga Mašin were hacked to pieces.

Under the influence of the regicides, the Serbs' leaders offered the crown to Petar Karadjordjević, a grandson of Black George. Only

Austria and Russia acknowledged his title at first, anxious to retain influence in Serbia; other nations initially stood aloof from a regime based on regicide. Yet Petar was a sincere liberal who, during his forty-odd years of exile, had studied political theory and closely observed political practice; he had also translated John Stuart Mill's *Essay on Liberty* into Serbian.

Under Petar, the Serbs aspired to expel the Turks from Europe. In 1912, Russia, Greece, Montenegro and Serbia went to war with Turkey – and gained a rapid victory. In the peace conference superintended by Britain in May 1913, Turkey ceded almost all its remaining European territory. Then the former allies turned on each other. Greece and Serbia allied against Bulgaria, vying for the prize of Macedonia, which was divided by their borders. Romania and Turkey joined in the fray, invading Bulgaria – though on paper both were still at war with Greece and Serbia. Faced by so many enemies, Bulgaria was defeated and in the Treaty of Bucharest of August 1913 ceded the coveted territory to the victors.

The people of Macedonia, their land chief among the spoils of the Balkan wars, were bitterly resentful that they were not accorded independence but must see the country divided up between neighbouring kingdoms. Macedonian nationalism was a potent force in Balkan politics, and it was to claim the lives of two kings, in 1913 George of Greece and in 1934 Aleksander Karadjordjević, King of Yugoslavia (see pp. 213–16).

George I, King of the Hellenes, was a former Danish prince invited to rule Greece in 1863. In March 1913, elated by Greece's recent defeat of Turkey, he paid a visit to the Macedonian city of Salonika. At lunch on 18 March (steak and onions, Danish-style), a guest begged him not to stroll through the streets of Salonika, as he did in Athens, without any guard.

Nevertheless, late that afternoon, the King and his aide-de-camp set out to walk to the harbour. As they passed a café, the Pasha Liman, a ragged man came out; returning, they saw him again, and now he shot the King in the back. The bullet entered his heart and he died.

The assassin, Alexander Skinas, was taken into custody but, before he could be brought to trial, he was found dead in the courtyard of the prison. It was said that he had committed suicide by jumping from the window of his cell. However, rumour had it that Skinas was a Macedonian nationalist and that he had been killed by his associates before he could give testimony that would point to their organisation. No evidence was ever found to confirm that story; nor did any nationalist group claim King George's death as their achievement. To Skinas, therefore, it must have seemed that fate had delivered the unprotected King to him and that he had the chance to avenge Macedonia's wrongs.

The Austrian Emperor Franz Josef had the unenviable distinction of having lost three members of his family to violent death. His brother Maximilian had been shot by a firing squad in Mexico in 1867; his son, Crown Prince Rudolf, had committed suicide in 1889; and his wife, Elisabeth of Bavaria, had been assassinated in 1898. Franz Josef himself had narrowly avoided assassination in his youth, and in 1910 another attempt was made. The Emperor was visiting Bosnia-Herzegovina, the Balkan province Austria had annexed in 1909, and in its capital, Sarajevo, a student called Bogdan Zerajić prepared to shoot the Emperor at point-blank range. However, when it came to the point, Zerajić was 'overawed by the dignity in the old man's face', as he later recorded. A fortnight later, he killed the governor of Bosnia-Herzegovina; then he turned his pistol on himself.

To the Bosnian Serbs, chafing under Austrian rule, Zerajić was a hero, though many regretted his failure to kill the Emperor. A fifteen-year-old named Gavrilo Prinćip made a vow on Zerajić's grave that he would not hesitate to kill one of the hated Habsburgs.

There was a secret society for such as Prinćip, 'Young Bosnia', which combined nationalism with revolutionary socialism. Prinćip was a member of its activist wing, 'Union or Death' – called 'The Black Hand' in sensational journalism. It was devoted to the terrorism that many believed was the only effective agent of political change and in which the use of assassination was taken for granted.

'The Black Hand' was financed by the Serbian secret service, which also supplied its members with guns. At its head (albeit unknown to all but a few members) was a man who went by the name of Apis. He was Colonel Dragutin Dmitrievič, one of the regicides of 1903 who had become chief of Serbian military intelligence. To Apis and his fellow-countrymen, Bosnia was Serb territory, to be won back at any cost. Behind Serbia lurked Russia, the vaunted champion of Pan-Slavism, which sought to unite the Slav people – under its own dominion. The 'South Slavs' of Bosnia might not wish to come under the Russian yoke, but Russia was Serbia's friend and therefore was Bosnia's too.

Many historians have sought to discover the degree of involvement of Serbia – and of Russia – in the plot that Gavrilo Prinčip hatched with his friends in 1914, but even now there are unanswered questions.

From statements (some extracted under torture) made by Prinčip and his colleagues, it seems that they first intended to assassinate General Oskar Potiorek, military governor of Sarajevo; then, in March 1914, they learned that the Archduke Franz Ferdinand, heir to the Austrian throne, was actually coming to Bosnia, to review troops in Sarajevo, in his role as commander-in-chief of the Bosnian army. Prinčip and his friend Nedelko Cabrinović went to Belgrade and there obtained guns and hand-grenades. Four other men joined them: three Bosnian Serbs, one a Muslim. On 28 June 1914 they took up their positions on the route through Sarajevo that the Archduke Franz Ferdinand would take to the town hall.

The date was significant for both the conspirators and their intended victim. On 28 June 1389 the Serbs had been defeated by the Turks at the Battle of Kosovo – a defeat that resulted in 500 years of Serbian submission to Turkish rule. In 1913 Serbia's defeat of the Turks had redressed the balance.

For the Archduke Franz Ferdinand, 28 June 1914 was the fourteenth anniversary of the day on which he had signed a document renouncing the rights of his as-yet-unborn children; he had had to do so before the Emperor would allow him to marry Countess Sophie Chotek, whose inferior birth made her ineligible to become an Austrian archduchess, let alone empress when her husband succeeded Franz Josef. Sophie Chotek was created Duchess of Hohenberg at her marriage, but the years that followed were embittered by the snubs she received from the imperial family and by the rigid Court protocol that persistently emphasised her position. By taking his wife with him to Sarajevo in June 1914, Franz Ferdinand was offering her an opportunity to play the ceremonial role of an imperial consort, a role she could not undertake in Austria under the Emperor's baleful gaze.

On the morning of 28 June 1914 the Archduke Franz Ferdinand and the Duchess of Hohenberg drove into Sarajevo in an open-topped car, accompanied by General Potiorek. As they drove along the avenue bordering the River Miljaćka's embankment, the party noticed a young man making a strange gesture with his hands. The Duchess felt something graze her neck; the Archduke brushed the object over the back of the car. It landed behind them, under the car following, containing military officers, and exploded – it was a grenade. One officer's face streamed with blood; the others leapt out of the car, and there was a scuffle with the man on the embankment; then he dived into the river. It was Nedelko Cabrinovic´, Prinćip's friend. He did not get away. In a few moments policemen were dragging him back onto the embankment, belabouring him with the flat of their swords.

The cars sped off and a few minutes later arrived at the town hall, where the mayor of Sarajevo was waiting to greet his guests. When he began his address of welcome, Franz Ferdinand interrupted him, protesting at the 'outrage' of an attempt on his life.

When the Archduke asked if there might be further danger, Potiorek, who was responsible for his protection, replied that he could not guarantee safety. Potiorek suggested cancelling the official programme, 'to punish the people of Sarajevo'. The Archduke scorned that but insisted on visiting the wounded officer, who had been taken to hospital, before continuing with his schedule.

Franz Ferdinand and Sophie returned to their car. When they set off, the Archduke's aide-de-camp, Count Harrach, was on the running-board on the side of the car on which he was seated. The car was preceded by one containing the deputy mayor and chief of police, who by some oversight had not been told the new route. When they reached the Latin Bridge, the first car turned right, and Franz Ferdinand's chauffeur began to follow it, until Potiorek gave orders to reverse and make for the hospital. At that moment a young man came out of a nearby café and, standing on the side of the car furthest from the Archduke, fired at him. At a distance of some three metres, Gavril Prinćip still managed to send only one bullet into his intended victim's body: it pierced Franz Ferdinand's chest and lodged in his spine; another bullet entered the Duchess's abdomen.

Prinćip had intended to shoot himself, but bystanders took hold of him before he could do so.

The Archduke and Duchess were still alive. 'Sophie, Sophie, don't die,' begged the Archduke. 'Live for our children.' Taken on to Potiorek's house, the couple died within minutes of each other.

Prinćip, Cabrinović and three of their colleagues were arrested; later, several young men who had known of their plans joined them in prison. Most of them were schoolboys and students. Both Prinćip and Cabrinović took prussic acid (supplied by Apis?), but it did not kill them. Prinćip was tortured but he was not hanged; nor were most of his co-conspirators, for they were under twenty-one, the legal age for capital punishment in the Austrian Empire. Only three men were hanged, the rest condemned to imprisonment. Prinćip was given a sentence of twenty years, but he died, of tuberculosis, on 28 April 1918.

It has been argued that the Archduke Franz Ferdinand died not as a figurehead, a second-best to the assassination of the Austrian Emperor, but because the extremist members of Young Bosnia feared that their plans for uniting with Serbia would be weakened if the future Emperor were to grant some measure of self-government to Bosnia-Herzegovina, as it was said he intended. Does that mean that the Serbian Government itself had prior knowledge of Prinćip's attempt on the Archduke's life? In 1917 Apis – Dragutin Dmitrievic – was executed by his own government, allegedly for having conspired with the enemy (Austria and Germany) and for having engaged in a plot to kill the Serbian Regent, Prince Aleksander. Apis was tried before a secret military tribunal, and then he was shot.

Did the Serb Government fear that Apis, as a turncoat, would reveal that they had known of – or promoted – plans to kill the heir to the Austrian throne? *En route* to his execution, Apis told one of his guards that he was to be killed 'solely because I organised the Sarajevo outrage'. In a statement written before his death, he noted that Russia had no knowledge of the assassination plans – 'on this occasion'.

Apis may have believed this to be true, but who could tell? Who can tell now? Perhaps he was being manipulated by a foreign statesman brooding over the means of setting Europe ablaze. The Conspiracy Theory, applied so often to so many events in history, has its charms.

For years before 1914, the Great Powers of Europe had been arming for war and forging international alliances in readiness for its outbreak. Each maintained a secret service, to uncover each other's secrets and illicitly to initiate events to their own advantage. Was the assassination of the Archduke Franz Ferdinand devised in some chancellery hundreds of miles from Sarajevo?

Was Germany the secret backer of the killers? If inspiration to kill Franz Ferdinand originated in Germany, a network of agents was there to carry the order down the line to surface convincingly among the Serbian dissidents.

Or did the Austrian Emperor oblige his German allies' desire for the outbreak of war and at the same time rid himself of his distasteful heir? Did his own agents infiltrate the Serbian secret societies in his own empire?

Or was there a Russian source, seeking to use international war to prevent an explosion of revolution in Russia, by turning the people's hatred against an external enemy? So expert were the agents of the Okhrana, at home and abroad, that even Apis need never have known of Russia's inspiration for 'his' plot.

Less attractively, a case might be made out against Britain, keen to ensure that the Austro-German alliance should be seen to have initiated the war, by making the first move, or France, where the ruling class feared that a French appreciation of international Socialism would displace the tradition of nationalism. (Just a month after Franz Ferdinand's death, the French Socialist leader was assassinated, three days after pleading with German Socialists not to go to war.)

Whatever the truth of the matter, the Austrians claimed to blame the Serbian Government for the assassination of the Archduke Franz Ferdinand. On 28 July 1914, Austria declared war on Serbia. The next day, Russian troops were mobilised along Russia's border with

Germany and Austria. On 1 August, Germany declared war on Russia, and on 3 August against France. On 4 August, Britain declared war on Germany. Other European countries later entered the war, and in August 1914 Japan, in April 1917 the United States, making it truly a 'world' war. Their reasons for doing so were, of course, far removed from that death in Sarajevo.

The assassination of the Austrian archduke did not cause the First World War; it merely precipitated it. Even so, there was an awesome power in that bullet that killed Franz Ferdinand of Austria, for it was used as a pretext for a war that, between 1914 and 1918, was to kill some nine million people.

CHAPTER FOURTEEN

A FEW AMONG MANY

The war to which so many men marched with patriotic fervour and militaristic zeal soon turned into a nightmare and a tragedy. In the icy waters of the North Sea, on the cliffs of Gallipoli, in the marshes of Mesopotamia, in the deserts of Arabia, but above all in the mud of the trenches of Flanders and northern France, men were killed, maimed and blinded.

Every nation was stretched to its limit to provision, clothe and arm its troops, but it soon became clear that the huge Russian Empire could not sustain the war effort: the supply of guns and ammunition, food and clothing began to fail. From headquarters to the front line, there was a chain of inefficiency born of the vastness of the campaigns and their terrain and of the great numbers of men involved, but exacerbated by the Russians' inability to co-ordinate production and consumption, whether of bullets or boots. The Russian army was riddled with revolutionaries, who lost no opportunity of pointing out the shortcomings of the generals who left their men hungry and ill-armed but still expected them to 'give their lives for the Tsar'.

Nicholas II had been in his mid-twenties when he succeeded to the Russian throne in 1894. A sensitive man, lacking self-confidence, he needed someone to lean on and chose as his prop Alix of Hesse, one of the German granddaughters of Queen Victoria, who became Tsarina Alexandra. She was always ready to strengthen his resolve when she saw him waver in the face of demands from ministers who increasingly recognised the urgency of reform.

In 1905, Russian losses in the war with Japan had brought public discontent to a head. Rioting broke out in several cities, and strikes were called; in the countryside, peasants were responsible for arson attacks on their masters' houses and farms; civil servants and policemen were shot on the streets of the cities. On a freezing cold night in January, the workers of St Petersburg marched, with their wives and children, to present a petition to the Tsar asking for an eight-hour working day and representation in a constituent assembly. Cossacks fired on them, and some five hundred were killed, thousands wounded. That was 'Bloody Sunday'.

In the following month, the Tsar's uncle Sergei Alexandrovich, governor-general of Moscow, was killed by a home-made bomb hurled by a student, a member of the Social Revolutionary party which now led the mounting insurgence.

As the summer passed, the imperial army and navy were on the very brink of mutiny. In October there was a general strike, organised in St Petersburg by members of the first workers' soviet. On 30 October 1905 Nicholas II granted Russia a constitution. For the first time, representatives elected by the people met to discuss national affairs – though not to legislate: that was the Tsar's prerogative. Inevitably, this was not nearly enough for the hardliners, and the Social Revolutionary Party split on – among many issues – the question of continued terrorist activity.

A plan to kill the Grand Duke Vladimir, commander-in-chief of the St Petersburg military district (who had given the order to fire on the crowd on Bloody Sunday), came to nothing. Explosives laid on a train standing ready to carry the Grand Duke Nicholas were found by a soldier minutes before they were due to detonate. In 1906 and 1907 plots against the life of the Tsar himself were discovered.

The Revolution of 1905, as it came to be called, had its successes, but it was followed by a period of harsh repression, as order was restored. The man blamed for the new measures was Piotr Stolypin, who became prime minister in July 1906; he was also responsible for increased persecution of the Jews.

In the late summer of 1911, the Tsar and his family visited the Ukraine, and on 1 September Nicholas II and his two elder daughters were among the audience at a performance of Rimsky-Korsakov's *Tale of Tsar Saltan* in Kiev. During the second interval, two shots were fired. The Tsar, who had left his box, returned to it and looked down into the stalls. Piotr Stolypin had been shot. He put his hat and gloves on the rail in front of him and unbuttoned his tunic. There was blood on his waistcoat. 'I am happy to die for the Tsar,' he said.

Seeing the Tsar, Stolypin made a gesture for him to stand back, for safety, but Nicholas remained there. Then Stolypin made a sign of the cross, blessing the Tsar. He was taken away to hospital and died there four days later.

The assassin was Dmitri Bogrov, a lawyer's clerk who was himself under sentence of death from fellow members of the local revolutionary cell, for embezzling their funds; he was also suspected of being a police informer. To prove his fidelity, Bogrov had agreed to kill someone – not the Tsar: Bogrov was a Jew and he feared reprisals against the Jews of Kiev. Stolypin was the obvious victim. In fact, Bogrov did have police connections and, to take suspicion off his own activities, he warned the police that an attempt was to be made on the Prime Minister's life. By the time the police realised that the plan Bogrov had outlined was a diversion, he had already killed Stolypin. But he failed to get away from the theatre. On the night of 10 September he was hanged.

Three years later, Russia was at war. As industrial production and the transport system failed increasingly to fulfil the demands made of them, and soldiers and civilians went hungry, anger mounted, and it came to be focused on the Tsar. Nicholas was completely unable to cope. He had no confidence in his Government; in fact, he had four prime ministers in the 2½ years after the outbreak of war, and he changed the heads of government departments frequently. His extended family, the vast network of Romanov uncles and cousins, despised Nicholas for his weakness, especially with regard to the vaunted influence of the mystic Grigori Rasputin, who had a strong hold on the Tsarina and through her on the Tsar. The family knew, though very few of the Tsar's subjects did, that his only son, the Tsarevich Alexei, suffered from haemophilia. Time and again the child was on the verge of death. Nicholas and Alexandra believed that Rasputin alone could save him.

Whatever Rasputin's real powers (which seem to have hinged on his ability to hypnotise), his personal life was far from that of a pious monk, but stories of his orgies were brushed aside by the Tsarina. Against her wishes, Nicholas was persuaded by his uncles to dismiss Rasputin, and he did so – until the Tsarevich's illness and Alexandra's pleading caused him to recall the 'healer'. In December 1916, one brave man, Vladimir Purishkevich, dared denounce Rasputin openly, in the Duma (the Russian parliament), and his oratory was met with thunderous applause.

Rasputin prophesied his own death. He warned the Tsar that, if he was killed by a member of the imperial family, the whole family would themselves be killed, within two years.

On the evening of 31 December 1916, Rasputin joined Prince Felix Yussupov (who had married the Tsar's niece) for supper in the Prince's flat in the Moika Palace in Petrograd (St Petersburg). The Prince plied him with poisoned food, but Rasputin showed no sign of discomfort, let alone dying. Yussupov panicked. He left Rasputin and went to consult friends, who were awaiting the outcome. They included the young Grand Duke Dmitri (a grandson of Alexander II) and Vladimir Purishkevich. Returning, Yussupov carried a revolver. When they heard a shot, his friends joined him. One of them was a doctor, and he could find no vital signs in the body. Then, suddenly, Rasputin regained consciousness. Yussupov fled, Rasputin at his heels. Purishkevich fired more shots as Rasputin made for the outside gate of the palace, and the man fell, in the snow. Yussupov hit him with a club. Then the murderers tied the body in a curtain and dropped it through a hole in the ice covering the River Neva. When the corpse was found, three days later, a post-mortem showed that Rasputin had survived all the attacks and had died of drowning.

Soon all Petrograd knew whom to thank for Rasputin's removal, and his killers were fêted. While the Tsarina wept, the Tsar dispatched the Grand Duke Dmitri to the Persian front; Yussupov was sent into internal exile; Purishkevich was immune from punishment, for fear of the Duma's displeasure. So low had the Tsar's power sunk.

Early in March 1917 (February by the Julian Calendar still in use in Russia), Petrograd was brought to a halt by riots and strikes; the troops who should have kept order refused to do so. Then events moved quickly. On 12 March the Duma named members of a provisional Government, to take charge of the country; on the 15th Nicholas II abdicated. To outsiders it might have seemed that he did so suddenly, without a fight; in fact, he had been struggling for months past to retain his hold on people and events. Since he had assumed personal command of the Russian army in September 1915, and with the failure of the Russian offensive in the summer of 1916, the Russian front had weakened, the Germans pushing eastward.

The provisional Government, made up of moderate Socialists who wished to prosecute the war more energetically, was opposed by the Bolsheviks, the extremist majority of the Social Democratic Party, now led by Vladimir Ilyich Lenin, who at sixteen had suffered the death of his elder brother in a plot to kill Tsar Alexander II. Since then he had become a Marxist, spent three years in Siberia as a political prisoner, roamed western Europe, assisted in the 1905 revolution and returned to exile. Now, in April 1917, he came back to Russia courtesy of the German Government, who sent him home in a sealed train, in expectation that he would gain power and use it to take Russia out of the war. In July Lenin failed in his attempt to overturn the provisional Government, and he fled the country. In October he returned and in November he replaced the provisional government with his Bolshevik friends. While they entrenched their regime, through workers' soviets established throughout western Russia and moving eastward, Lenin worked for an armistice with Germany, which was declared on 5 December.

There was, of course, opposition to the revolution. Moderates, who had supported the provisional Government, were easily overcome. More dangerous to the new regime were the 'Whites', who for some three years fought against the 'Red' army, from the White Sea to the Black Sea, from the Baltic to the Pacific. What they lacked was a leader: the liberation of the Tsar became a priority.

It was the news of a White army's approach that caused the captors of the imperial family to murder them, at Ekaterinburg, in July 1918.

Nicholas II, his wife Alexandra, their son Alexei, now thirteen years old, and their daughters Olga, Tatiana, Maria and Anastasia, aged between sixteen and twenty-three, had been held in varying conditions of discomfort and uncertainty for over a year. Alternating between optimism and pessimism as to their chances of being allowed to leave the country, the Tsar had seen the family's journey eastwards, through the Urals to Ekaterinburg, as potential for the longer trip to the Pacific coast and thence to freedom. He had never been a realist.

On the night of 16/17 July 1918 the imperial family were roused from sleep and told to dress quickly, as the approach of a White army meant that they must leave Ekaterinburg. They assembled downstairs, accompanied by their physician and three servants. Armed men entered the room and shot them.

Eight days later, the White army entered Ekaterinburg. There was no sign of the imperial family. It was only some six months later that searchers in the vicinity of the town found a pit containing miscellaneous bones, bearing signs of an attempt to destroy them all by acid.*

On the day after the murder of the Tsar and his immediate family, the Grand Duchess Elizabeth, widow of Grand Duke Sergei and sister of the Tsarina, and five male members of the Romanov family were thrown, alive, down a mine shaft near Alapaevsk. In case the fall had not killed them, logs and hand-grenades were thrown in after them. But still some had survived: hours later a peasant, drawn there by curiosity, heard the sound of voices singing hymns. When the White army arrived, they hauled up the corpses and found that one of the young men, who had sustained a head injury in the fall, wore a bandage made out of the Grand Duchess's handkerchief.

Back in 1905, Elizabeth of Hesse had visited the murderer of her husband in his cell and then had gone to plead with her brother-in-law for the man's life, to no avail. She had subsequently entered a convent. Her life might have been very different: she had once been courted by the future Kaiser Wilhelm II but had refused to marry him.

Other members of the Romanov dynasty shared the Tsar's fate. His younger brother Michael had been shot, at Perm, six days earlier. In January 1919 four grand dukes were shot in the fortress of Peter and Paul in Petrograd. However, Rasputin's prophecy that the entire Romanov dynasty would be wiped out was not borne out by events: many escaped from Russia to live in exile.

It was decades before the regime that displaced the Romanovs' could rid itself of the terrorism that had been intrinsic to the

---

* The bones were subsequently identified as those of the Tsar, his wife and three of their daughters and on 17 July 1998 were entombed in the Cathedral of SS Peter and Paul in St Petersburg, after a funeral service shown live on television throughout Russia. Some years later, the remains of the Tsarevich and Grand Duchess Maria were found and identified.

revolutionary movement. Rumours abound that Lenin, the idol of the masses, died of poison, probably administered to promote the career of Stalin. Stalin was certainly responsible for issuing the order for the murder of his former colleague Leon Trotsky, found with an icepick embedded in his head, in Mexico, in 1940. Thousands of other men and women were sentenced to death under Stalin, either in his 'purges' in the 1930s or in the Siberian labour camps. It was whispered that he was a reincarnation of Ivan the Terrible.

The end of the First World War, in November 1918, with the defeat of Germany and her allies, saw the demise of both the German Empire (with its constituent kingdoms, duchies and principalities) and the Austro-Hungarian Empire: they became republics. The Soviet republics that had already replaced the Russian Empire had framed their first constitution that July. Nevertheless, most of the nations of Europe were still ruled by hereditary monarchs, though legislative rights were by now the prerogative of elected representatives of their subjects.

The fact that monarchs had less power and that an individual monarch's favours, personal and political, no longer determined the complexion of governments went a long way toward minimising the number of assassination attempts on them in the years that followed. The main victims now were the presidents and prime ministers who embodied political power. In 1918, for example, both the president of Portugal and the Hungarian prime minister were assassinated, in 1921 the Spanish and Portuguese prime ministers.

Political assassination was especially rife in Bulgaria. Recently the kingdom had twice known defeat in war: in 1913, against its Balkan neighbours, and in 1918, as an ally of Germany. Bulgaria was split between the growing Communist Party, the moderate Agrarian Party and a strong right-wing element. The assassination of three moderate politicians in 1923–4 was, however, generally credited to the Macedonian Internal Revolutionary Organisation (IMRO), based in Bulgaria. Initially, at its foundation in 1895, IMRO had sought independence for Macedonia. Since Macedonia's partition between Serbia and Greece in 1913, IMRO had accepted Bulgarian patronage – a base for its terrorist activities – and from 1921 was dominated by men pledged to bring Macedonia into the kingdom of Bulgaria.

IMRO was among the suspects when, on 14 April 1925, there was an attempt on the life of Boris III, King of Bulgaria. The next day a Bulgarian general *was* shot and killed. On 16 April the King and members of his Government attended the general's funeral in Sofia Cathedral. During the service, a bomb exploded. The King and Government were unharmed, but some 130 other members of the congregation were killed.

It suited the Bulgarian Government to blame not IMRO but the Communist Party for the outrage. Its leading members were rounded up for execution and imprisonment. At the time, this attribution of the crime appeared to be so convenient to the Bulgarian Government that there were many, both inside Bulgaria and throughout Europe, who credited the attempt – of course, never designed to kill King or Government – to the Bulgarian Government itself. However, in 1948, after the Communists had taken power in Bulgaria, following the Second World War, the Bulgarian Communist Party did not claim responsibility for the bombing.

The fact that, at the time, it was difficult to believe that so obvious a culprit as the Communist Party could be responsible for the attempted assassination only shows how devious Balkan politicians were thought to be: if the Communists were the obvious suspects, the real culprits must be those who had most to gain from blaming the Communists. This was how western Europe viewed Balkan politics.

Bulgaria's western neighbour Serbia had, inevitably, taken the opposing side during the First World War, and in its aftermath of the redrawing of national boundaries had had its reward: the territory it claimed from the now defunct Austro-Hungarian Empire. Thus, on 4 December 1918, 'the Kingdom of the Serbs, Croats and Slovenes' was born, to include Bosnia-Herzegovina and Dalmatia, and later Montenegro and Istria. The kingdom was nominally ruled by the ailing King Petar, but his son Aleksander was regent. (Aleksander succeeded to the throne in 1921.) The kingdom's unity was a fiction.

In June 1928, the terrorism of disunity climaxed in a shoot-out in parliament itself in which the leader of the Peasant Party was killed. On 4 January 1929, King Aleksander dissolved parliament and took control of the kingdom. In October 1929 he changed its name to 'Yugoslavia', the land of the South Slavs, but that did not make unity any more real. Soon Yugoslavia had all the trappings of a dictatorship.

The King had enemies everywhere. Chief among them were the Croats, who wanted independence and who ranged from the respectable Peasant Party to the Croat Revolutionary Party (the Ustaše), made up largely of exiles, financed by Italy and Hungary. Even within Serbia, Aleksander's powerbase, many of his former supporters resented his withdrawal of their hard-won liberties. Communism had been outlawed as early as 1921, but there were still Communists in Yugoslavia. In the south (and over the border in Bulgaria) was IMRO, the Macedonian nationalist, terrorist organisation. An alliance forged between the Ustaše and IMRO had more substance than the improved relationship that King Aleksander worked strenuously to forge with Bulgaria.

In the autumn of 1934, the Ustaše put together a team of assassins. Some were to attempt to kill King Aleksander in Marseilles, as he began his state visit to France; others were to await the outcome and to make their move in Paris if the first attempt failed. The team's members were all Croats except one: linchpin of the Marseilles group was a Bulgarian known as 'Vlada the Chauffeur' – his real name was obscured by the aliases he had adopted as a professional killer employed by IMRO. Vlada was to shoot the King, and Mijo Kralj was then to throw a bomb as a diversion while Vlada escaped.

On the afternoon of 9 October 1934, King Aleksander and the French Foreign Minister Louis Barthou drove along the Canebière, the main street of Marseilles, in an open-topped car. Ahead of them rode a troop of cavalry.

As the car approached, Vlada leapt onto its running-board and fired, killing the King and wounding the Frenchman. He also shot a security agent in the stomach, wounded a French general and fired into the crowd, for Kralj had panicked, failed to hurl his bomb and run off. Eventually Vlada was overpowered: a policeman shot him in the head but failed to kill him, and then the crowd moved in, to hit and kick him. Vlada later died in hospital, as did four of his victims, including Barthou.

Kralj was arrested at Corbeil; the Paris standbys were stopped at the border with Switzerland. A French court found them guilty of conspiracy to murder, and they were sentenced to penal servitude for life. Others had known of, and aided, the assassination but had escaped; the two men who had carried the assassins' arms into France were sentenced to death *in absentia*.

No one profited directly from the assassination of King Aleksander of Yugoslavia. His eleven-year-old son Petar was brought home from school in Britain, to reign under the control of a three-man regency, headed by his cousin Pavle. Serbia failed to take reprisals against Croatia for the murder, so the Ustaše had no pretext for inciting the Croats to civil war, as they had planned. Hungary was censured by the League of Nations for having harboured members of the Ustaše, but Italy's contribution was ignored, for fear of harming Italy's fragile peace with Yugoslavia. In fact, over the years that followed, Italy and Yugoslavia drew closer together, and Yugoslav ties with Germany were forged.

It has been alleged that Germany – or rather Adolf Hitler – had been behind the Marseilles assassinations. It is also said that the intended victim was the staunchly anti-German French Foreign Minister, not the King of Yugoslavia. Already that year, on 30 June, Hitler had had his old friend Ernst Röhm shot, in a purge of his Stormtroopers ('Brownshirts'), and on 25 July Austrian Nazis had assassinated the Chancellor, Engelbert Dolfuss. But there is no evidence that Hitler played any role in the double assassination at Marseilles.

Yugoslavia's dependence on the two Fascist powers led to its becoming a signatory to their Tripartite Pact (with Japan) on 25 March 1941. However, on the 27th Prince Pavle, who had taken Yugoslavia into the Pact, was overthrown and the new Government refused to ratify it. Ten days later the Germans invaded Yugoslavia, and before April was out they had taken control of the country. This was the moment of the Croats' triumph. For the next four years, the Ustaše inflicted a terror regime on Yugoslavia's Jews, Communists and Serbs. Hundreds of thousands of people were 'exterminated'.

Serbia, meanwhile, was occupied by the Germans, and Bosnia-Herzegovina, with its mixed Serb and Croat population, became a battleground between the resistance movement (largely Communist) and the Croats and Germans.

To those who visited postwar Yugoslavia, reunited and peaceful, the country showed a bland face that hid festering bitterness for past wrongs mutually inflicted by Serbs and Croats. As long as President Tito lived and while there was still a threat of Russian intervention in Yugoslavia's mild Communist regime, the country held together. However, its civil wars and subsequent division into independent states in the 1990s, with a high military and civilian death toll, have confirmed that the Yugoslavs were never truly one nation. King Aleksander was by no means the only man to die to prove that point.

If Hitler or Mussolini was implicated in the assassination of King Aleksander of Yugoslavia, it was far from being the only murder with which their names were linked. When Pope Pius XI died, on 10 February 1939, he was aged 81 and was found dead in bed – nothing remarkable, one might think, except that he had recently convened a meeting of Italian bishops to deliberate on the Church's attitude to Fascism; also, a few hours before his death, the Pope had been given an injection by his physician, a man named Francesco Petucci – the father of Mussolini's mistress. Vatican opinion was divided over the cause of the Pope's death.

The same could be said of European opinion on the cause of the death of Boris III, King of Bulgaria, on 28 August 1943. That day the King was returning by plane from Germany, where he had had an interview with Hitler, when he died of a 'heart-attack'. The King was known to have had a heart condition, but the story went round that the cause of death was oxygen starvation: while he was in the air, the supply of oxygen to his mask had been cut off. Boris had taken Bulgaria into Germany's war with Britain and her allies but was adamant in his refusal to commit his country to war with Russia, the giant on his border whom Bulgaria had long feared. As it was, Russia invaded Bulgaria in 1944.

There were other royal victims of Hitler's regime. Members of the former royal family of Bavaria were outspoken opponents of Nazism and in 1937 found it wise to leave Germany for Hungary. When the German army occupied Budapest in 1944, several of their number were sent to the concentration camps at Dachau and Sachsenhausen. Among other titled prisoners were the Hohenberg brothers, sons of the Austrian Archduke Franz Ferdinand who had been assassinated in 1914. After Italy's defection from the Axis in September 1944, Hitler had the Italian Princess Mafalda and her German husband, Prince Philipp of Hesse, sent to Buchenwald, where the Princess died at the hands of the SS.

But what were the murders of a pope, a king and a princess when compared with the holocaust of Jews and political dissidents in the concentration camps? If Hitler did have Boris of Bulgaria killed, it was because the King had the power to thwart Germany's war plans: none of the other men, or the women and children, sent to the concentration camps had such power but they died in their thousands.

CHAPTER FIFTEEN

ECHOES OF BOMB AND BULLET

After the Second World War, five of Europe's monarchies disappeared. In November 1945 Yugoslavia rejected its king, in January 1946 Albania; also in 1946, Italy's monarchy was voted out by 53 percent, Bulgaria's by 92 per cent; in 1947 Romania followed suit. All but Italy became republics.

Of the remaining post-war kingdoms of Europe Great Britain, Denmark, Norway, Sweden, Belgium, the Netherlands and Greece – all but one have proved that a monarch's strictly limited power is not intolerable to the majority of modern democrats. The exception is Greece, where in 1967 a military *coup* resulted in the overthrow of King Constantine, confirmed in 1974 by a national referendum. There was no longer a monarchy in the Balkans.

In contrast, in 1975 the Spanish monarchy was restored, in the person of King Juan Carlos, grandson of the last king of Spain. Juan Carlos had been groomed by the late Generalissimo Franco to succeed him, with the intention of maintaining the repressive right-wing regime that brooked no opposition. When, soon after his accession, the King piloted Spain through free elections to a liberal constitution, yielding much of his own power in the process, it seemed to many Spaniards that he had betrayed Franco's trust.

On 23 February 1981, Spanish army officers mounted a *coup* against the Government that was foiled largely by the King himself. The following June and in October 1982, further right-wing conspiracies were thwarted. A planned assassination attempt on the King, in June 1985, did not come to light until April 1991: in view of the instability of Spanish politics in 1985, at that time it had been thought best not to reveal how close Spain had been to a virtual massacre of its leaders.

The report ran that the conspirators – again army officers – had laid explosives below a platform from which the King was due to watch a military review in the town of La CoruNa. With him would be his queen, Sofia of Greece, the Prime Minister, the Defence Minister, the Chief of the General Staff and several other high-ranking officer of the three services. That day was 1 June, Armed Forces Day; just eleven days later, Spain was due to enter the European Community.

The newspaper *El Pais* broke that story in 1991, telling how the plot had been thwarted, but it did not name any of the conspirators, nor did it give any account of their trial and punishment. Although their aim had obviously been the overthrow of government, monarchy and constitution, no details were given of their immediate plans for taking power. The 1985 conspirators were, however, apparently planning to have Spain's Basque separatist movement blamed for the massacre. In view of the record of terrorism by ETA (Euskadi ta Azkatasuna), the Basque separatists, it would be a plausible claim. The Basque threat could be used as a pretext for imposing martial law throughout Spain – including measures that could be used against dissidents of any complexion.

The most spectacular of ETA's own *coups de theatre* had occurred on 20 December 1973, when explosives laid under a Madrid street killed the Spanish Prime Minister, Admiral Carrero Blanco. At the funeral, the then Prince Juan Carlos defied the danger to himself by walking behind the hearse in its procession through the streets. The following year a plot was discovered that aimed to have the Prince kidnapped – and probably murdered – when his yacht put in to Monte Carlo; at the last minute, Franco's illness caused Juan Carlos to cancel the visit.

Among the ETA Members involved in the Monte Carlo affair was Juan José Rego Vidal. In 1978 he was arrested, having planned, that July, to launch a bomb from an inshore boat to explode on the King's car as it travelled along a coastal road on the island of Ibiza. Rego Vidal was imprisoned but later released, having been found insane. In 1979 explosives were found in a Majorcan resort in which the King was staying: Rego Vidal knew Majorca well and later allegedly became head of ETA terrorists on the island. In December of the same year, a bomb exploded in a hotel in the Spanish ski resort of BaqueiraOBeret in which Juan Carlos was staying.

In 1995 Rego Vidal reappeared in Majorca. Spanish police kept him under surveillance while he and three other men set up a sub-machine gun and a rifle with telescopic sights in a flat overlooking the Majorcan harbour in which the King's ship was due to dock. When the would-be regicides had provided enough evidence of their intention, the police moved in on them.

Although Rego Vidal's career was at an end, there were inevitably men ready to take his place, and the Spanish police remained vigilant. In the autumn of 1997, they prevented ETA's bombing the opening of the Guggenheim Museum of Art in Bilbao, in which many people would have died with the King, and in the summer of 1998 they foiled a plot to have a bomb explode on the King's route to open a new aquarium in San Sebastian.

It is not surprising that the wedding of the heir to the Spanish throne, Felipe. Prince of the Asturias, in May 2004, was treated as a hazard of the first order. Yet even while plans were being finalised for the utmost security, a new threat emerged: on 3 April members of the Islamist terrorist movement Al-Quaida attacked a Madrid commuter train, leaving some 200 people dead, hundreds were wounded.

Members of fourteen royal families had been invited to the wedding. Their gathering in Almudena Cathedral, with the entire Spanish royal family, made the wedding a one-foul-swoop target.

Madrid had never known such tight security. Not only were roads closed to traffic, but airspace over the city was closed to commercial flights; a NATO early-warning plane was drafted in; a squadron of F18 fighter aircraft patrolled a wide area around the city; the police searched for half-a-dozen hang-gliders that had recently been stolen. On the wedding day, some 10,000 police officers lined the route and patrolled nearby streets, while sharp-eyed snipers watched from rooftops as the bride and groom drove from the cathedral to the palace in a Rolls-Royce topped with a bullet-proofed glass roof.

Nothing happened – apart from a 'punch-up' on the palace steps between two Italian princes: a little 'light relief', it must have seemed, at the end of that day of high tension.

While Spain's recent history would make any attempted royal murder an unsurprising piece of news, that of Sweden – a smoothly running democracy, with a virtually powerless, popular king – is a most unlikely setting for such melodrama. But in any country one man with sufficient determination can be as dangerous as any terrorist organisation.

On the evening of 28 February 1986, the Swedish Prime Minister, Olof Palme, was shot as he walked home from the cinema with his wife; he was dead on arrival at hospital. A small-time burglar named Christer Petersson was convicted of the killing but in 1989 acquitted, for lack of evidence. Then in March 1997 reports of the 'deathbed confession' of one Lars Tingstrom re-alleged Petersson's guilt. Tingstrom had died in prison in 1993, serving a sentence of life imprisonment for terrorism. He had asked his lawyer not to release news of his confession until after the tenth anniversary of Palme's death.

Tingstrom claimed that, while in prison, he had originated the plot to kill not only the Prime Minister but also Sweden's king, Carl XVI Gustaf, and that Petersson had agreed to 'do the deed'. According to Tingstrom, the King should have been the first victim, but by chance Petersson had spotted Palme in the street and seized the opportunity to kill him.

Petersson denied Tingstrom's allegation. Nor could the police 'make it stick', for there was no proof. Tingstrom said that Petersson had thrown the murder weapon into one of the canals between Stockholm's islands, but that was impossible, for they were covered in thick ice in February 1986. But even if a gun were found, by dredging, it could never be proved that Petersson had fired at Palme. He died in 2004.

Although Juan Carlos, King of Spain, resigned much of the power that Franco had bequeathed him when he swore loyalty to Spain's new constitution, he has been more influential – both overtly and discreetly – in his kingdom's affairs that any other monarch of modern Europe. For that reason he still has enemies among the separatists. Elsewhere in Europe, the role of the constitutional monarch is so strictly limited that a monarch is likely to become an assassin's target more as a figurehead than as a participant in government.

But why should anyone wish to kill the 'pretender' to the throne of a defunct kingdom?

In 1989 a Scottish court heard allegations of a plot against the life of Alexander Karadjordjević, the exiled Crown Prince of Yugoslavia.* With the country's Communist regime crumbling at that time, it seemed possible that Yugoslavia would become a kingdom again and Alexander be called upon to reign. What limited enthusiasm there was for the restoration of the Yugoslav monarchy came from Serbia, which sought to hold Yugoslavia together. In Croatia, Slovenia and much of Bosnia, there were already plans for the dismemberment of Yugoslavia, in favour of separate republics. Restoration of the monarchy, bulwarking Yugoslav unity, was anathema to such separatists. Thus the targeting of Crown Prince Alexander seemed plausible.

In Scotland, a Croat standing trial for the attempted murder of an émigré fellow-countryman claimed that the alleged victim had tried to blackmail him into killing Alexander. Both the accused, Vinko Sindićić, and the victim, Nikola Stedul, had for years been members of the Croat Movement for Statehood, an apparently non-violent organisation. However, Sindićić had been a suspect in more than one political murder abroad, and Stedul had settled in Scotland for fear of the Yugoslav authorities. On 20 October 1988 Stedul was shot several times outside his home in Kirkaldy and, having survived the attack, named Sindićić as his assailant. In a trial featuring spying, treachery and blackmail, it was alleged that Stedul had threatened to tell the British authorities that Sindićić was in the country on an illegal passport – unless Sindićić would agree to assassinate Prince Alexander.

In the kingdoms beyond Europe, notably those of the Middle and Far East, monarchs still wield real power. That accounts for the assassination of King Abdullah of Jordan in 1951 in the al-Aqsa mosque in Jerusalem. The King's fifteen-year-old grandson Hussein was at his side when he died and himself became King of Jordan in 1952. Six years later his cousin King Faisal of Iraq was assassinated at the age of nineteen. Hussein survived eleven attempts on his life, to die (of cancer) in 1999. King Hassan of Morocco, who died in the

---

* Never having reigned in Yugoslavia (he was born after his father King Petar's deposition), Alexander Karadjordjević chose to retain the title of Crown Prince after his father's death.

same year, was also familiar with danger: attacks on him included an attempted assassination when 1,400 army cadets surrounded and entered his palace during his birthday party in1971. Shooting haphazardly, they killed over a hundred people and wounded some 200. In 1972 the Moroccan Minister of Defence, General Oufkir, sent fighter planes to attack an aircraft in which King Hassan was a passenger. The King himself landed the plane, only to be fired on again by Oufkir's. Again Hassan survived. Oufkir was subsequently reported as having committed suicide.

The assassination of John Kennedy, President of the United States, on 22 November 1963, was – apparently though not certainly – the work of a 'lone gunman'. On the other hand, the seventeen attempts on the life of Charles de Gaulle, President of France, between 1961 and 1965 have allegedly been traced back to various political sources, notably the Secret Army Organisation (OAS), which opposed de Gaulle's concession of independence to Algeria.

In 1973 the Spanish prime minister, Admiral Carrero Blanco, was assassinated, in 1978 the Italian prime minister, Aldo Moro, in 1986 the Swedish prime minister, Olof Palme. The first was a victim of the Basque terrorist organisation ETA, the second of the extreme left-wing Red Brigades, the third – allegedly (see pp. 233–4) – of a man defying the social structure for which his victim stood.

Apart from the assassin alienated from society, whose grudges are personal and various, modern assassins of heads of state have had three main motives, sometimes overlapping: nationalism, religion and politics.

Under 'politics' come the motives of the right-wing officers of Spain who sought to kill King Juan Carlos and with him exterminate the liberal constitution. At the opposite end of the spectrum are the extremist groups such as the Red Brigades and the Red Army Faction, whose guerrilla tactics intruded on Europe's peace in the 1970s and 1980s. They did not, however, include royal murder in their repertoire of terrorism.

Nationalism and with it the separatist impulse feature, in varying degrees, in many European countries' troubles. In France the Bretons, in Spain the Basques, in Italy the former Austrian population of the Alto Adige, in Belgium the Walloons: these and other minorities demand, work for and sometimes kill for the right of self-determination or secession from a nation. In Britain,

Scottish and Welsh nationalism have none of the force, bitterness and desperation that have characterised the 'freedom fighters' of Northern Ireland. For the separatist cause, only ETA in Spain and the IRA in Britain have made monarchs and their families targets for assassination.

However, Europe's record of the assassination of heads of state and politicians cannot now be divorced from that of the rest of the world, as it could with validity for past centuries. By the end of the twentieth century, the world had 'become smaller' through the increased speed of global communication, and events taking place on the other side of the world had repercussions on finance, politics and social life in Europe. So it seems essential to remark here that President Sadat of Egypt was assassinated in 1981, in 1984 Indira Gandhi, Prime Minister of India, in 1991 her son, Prime Minister Rajiv Gandhi, and in 1995 Yitzhak Rabin, Prime Minister of Israel.

In that context, assassinations on the global scale appear to promote others. In the ten months from September 1980, not only was President Sadat of Egypt assassinated but there were attempts on the lives of Pope John Paul II and President Reagan of the United States.

And three times between May and December 1981 the life of Elizabeth II, the British queen, was threatened by her subjects, in Britain, Australia and New Zealand – real threats to kill her, though the most fearsome, the fourth, was in fact a false alarm (see p. 232).

Yet, still 'crowned heads' were targets. In the small east African kingdom of Rwanda, in 1994 seven members of the royal family were hacked to death, among the half-million Rwandans killed in the three months of genocide inflicted on the Tutsi people by the Hutu government. In 2003, discovery of a plot to assassinate King Mohammed VI of Morocco and members of his family resulted in the imprisonment of two fourteen-year-old girls, twin sisters, who were volunteer suicide bombers. Also in 2003, Saudi Arabia alleged there had been a Libyan plan to assassinate Crown Prince Abdullah, Saudi Arabia's virtual ruler since his half-brother King Fahd's health failed in the mid-1990s.

Two thousand miles east of the Arabian desert, the mountain kingdom of Nepal boasted the oldest surviving monarchy in Asia

– more than 200 years old – when Birendra of the House of Shah ascended the throne in 1972. He reigned as absolute monarch over one of the poorest nations in the world. In 1990 national unrest induced the King to grant a democratic constitution, but the new regime was bedevilled by faction-ridden, unstable governments and, from 1996, with Maoist insurgency. However, as in Europe in centuries past, no insurgent terrorist or foreign enemy is as dangerous as a close relation.

On a June evening in 2001 Crown Prince Dipendra of Nepal sat at dinner with his parents and several other members of the royal family. He was drinking heavily and his misbehaviour caused his father, King Birendra, to order him out of the room. Half an hour later, Dipendra returned, now carrying three guns, including an automatic assault rifle, with which he opened fire on his family. First the King fell, then others – Queen Aiswarya, Dipendra's younger brother and sister and four other members of the family, their bodies strewn across the palace garden, which had provided no refuge when they fled. At the end of this 'spree' Dipendra shot himself with his 9mm pistol. He died in hospital two days later, apparently unaware that he had been declared king.

The motive? Dipendra had dared to choose his own wife, to the displeasure of his mother (generally thought to be 'the power behind the throne', with undue influence on matters far more important than her son's marriage). The Prince had been brought up to believe in his dynasty's right to absolute power – and that his father was the reincarnation of the god Vishnu; he had seen his father accept the role of constitutional monarch and had himself failed, as Colonel-in Chief of the Nepalese army, to put down the Maoist rebels. Humiliated, power-hungry, angry with his parents – and drunk, the Prince had just lost control.

Kathmandu offered other explanations of the royal massacre. In the days that followed, while royalists mourned their king-god Birendra and there was sporadic rioting, doubt was thrown on 'King' Dipendra's alleged guilt: his successor, his uncle Gyanendra, had not been present at the dinner party, and rumours abounded that he (and his son, who had been there) had masterminded the murders. It was also said that Dipendra had been shot in the back.

King Gyanendra never won the respect accorded to King Birendra for his adherence to his limited powers after 1990. At odds with his governments, aware that the Maoists were gaining ground, in 2005 the King reclaimed absolute power – but only briefly. In 2006 the mainstream political parties joined with the Maoists to form a government. In April 2008 a general election (Nepal's first since 1999) led to the Maoists' becoming the largest party in parliament – and, in June, to the end of the monarchy in Nepal.

CHAPTER SIXTEEN

BEYOND BELIEF

Elizabeth II has faced more personal danger than any European monarch in modern times. From the 1960s, the main threat came from the Irish Republican Army (the IRA), the terrorist wing of the Northern Ireland separatists, who had pressed for the unification of Ireland, as a republic, since its division in 1921. In both Northern Ireland and mainland Britain, hundreds of lives were lost to IRA bomb and bullet; yet more were claimed in Loyalist retaliation.

However, it was Canadian, not Irish, separatists who were seen as the threat to the Queen when she visited Canada in 1964, only months after President Kennedy had been assassinated in the United States. She arrived in Quebec to find that precautions had been taken to protect her from the French-speaking separatists who had threatened to kill her. During the royal visit there were riots, and on 'le jour de la matraque' – 'the day of the truncheon' – many people were injured when police confronted the protesters.

Two years later, an Irish separatist hurled a block of concrete at the Queen's car on her visit to Belfast – one of the earliest demonstrations of the terrorism that was to blight life in Northern Ireland in the years that followed.

Welsh nationalism was also a matter of concern when, in 1969, the heir to the throne was invested as Prince of Wales in Caernarvon Castle. Welsh nationalists threatened to bomb the castle during the ceremony, but the threat was not fulfilled. Nevertheless, then and during later royal visits to Wales there have been demonstrations by Welsh nationalists, and security precautions are always strictly observed.

The Prince of Wales was only twenty-one years old when he faced the danger at Caernarvon. His sister, Princess Anne, was twenty-three when she suffered an attack that might well have cost her her life.

On the evening of 20 March 1974, the Princess and her husband, Captain Mark Phillips, were being driven by their chauffeur down the Mall towards Buckingham Palace; they were accompanied by the Princess's policeman bodyguard, Jim Beaton, and her lady-in-waiting. Suddenly, a car pulled over in front of them, bringing them to a standstill. From the other car, a man approached, firing a gun. A shot smashed one of the windows of the Princess's car. Beaton made to tackle the gunman and was shot in the chest. Then the car door was pulled open, Princess Anne's arm seized. 'Get away! Get away!' the Princess shouted. Her husband took tight hold of her and tried to drag her back; that and the Princess's own resistance enabled her to break free and they slammed the door shut.

The worst moment came when the attacker threatened to fire again if the car door was not opened. Jim Beaton, despite the pain of his injury, put his hand over the muzzle of the gun. Still, the gunman fired again and again, wounding him in the hand and shoulder. As the shots flew, the chauffeur, a police officer who had joined the fray and a journalist who had leaped from a passing taxi were all wounded too. At last a police car bore down on them, and at the sight of it the attacker sought to escape into St James's Park, but a policeman went in pursuit, and he crashed the gunman to the ground in a rugby tackle.

Ian Ball had not intended to murder Princess Anne, though any of his wild shots might have killed her or her companions. His plan was to kidnap the Princess and hold her to ransom for £3 million. He could only plead guilty at his trial, but examination showed that he had long been insane, and he was committed to a psychiatric hospital.

The Queen honoured those who had protected her daughter by awards of the Royal Victorian Order, which is in her gift. Beaton received the George Cross, Britain's highest award for civilian courage.

The attack on Princess Anne demonstrated the vulnerability of members of the royal family 'off duty'. An attack on a member of the royal family on a public occasion might be a triumph for its perpetrators' propaganda but there were many obstacles to such an achievement: more success could be gained by concentrating on a so-called soft target. This was the opinion of members of the IRA when, in 1979, they set out to kill Lord Mountbatten.

Louis Mountbatten, created Earl Mountbatten of Burma after distinguished service in the Far East in the Second World War, was a great-grandson of Queen Victoria, in the female line, and thus a distant cousin of Elizabeth II. His forefathers were German princes, but in the previous generation the family had become British subjects. Mountbatten was always close to his sister's son, Prince Philip of Greece, who became Duke of Edinburgh on his marriage to Princess – later Queen – Elizabeth in 1947. He was also regarded as an 'honorary grandfather' by the Prince of Wales.

Lord Mountbatten was selected as an IRA victim not for his own power to do – or refuse to do – anything for the cause of Irish republicanism, for he had no such power. His was a 'symbolic assassination', in that he represented the British royal family.

The Earl was in the habit of spending a few weeks each summer at Classiebawn Castle, overlooking the harbour of Mullaghmore in County Sligo. On 27 August 1979 he, his daughter and son-in-law, Lord and Lady Brabourne, Lord Brabourne's mother, their two sons and a friend, Paul Maxwell, went out in the family's boat. They were some 400 metres from shore when there was an explosion on board. Lord Mountbatten, his fourteen-year-old grandson Nicholas Knatchbull and fifteen-year-old Paul Maxwell were killed. The other members of the family were badly injured, and the elder Lady Brabourne died soon after.

At the memorial service, the Prince of Wales spoke bitterly of the 'mindless cruelty' of the 'subhuman extremists' who had killed Lord Mountbatten. Three days after his death, the IRA had described the assassination as 'a discriminate act to bring to the attention of the English [sic] people the continuing occupation of our country. . . . For this we will tear out their sentimental imperialist hearts.' On the same day, Thomas McMahon was arrested for the murders, having been suspected during a routine police check. On his clothes were traces of explosives and of green paint matching that on the boat. Three months later, a Dublin criminal court sentenced him to life imprisonment. A second defendant was acquitted, for lack of conclusive forensic evidence.

It is often forgotten, by those who write of this most recent British royal murder, that on the day on which Mountbatten was assassinated eighteen British soldiers and a civilian were killed by bomb and bullet in Northern Ireland.

And so to the year 1981, in which the British Queen faced more danger than ever before.

In May the IRA planted a bomb at the Sullom Voe oil terminal, in the Shetland Islands, where the Queen was due to turn on the flow of a new pipeline. The bomb detonated some distance from the Queen, and no one was harmed. But how could such a breach of security have gone undetected at such a vulnerable site?

More impressively, in the same month two workers at a London postal sorting-office spotted a letter-bomb addressed to the Prince of Wales. No one claimed responsibility for it, but it was thought significant that it came the day after the death of an IRA hunger-striker in prison. The postal department at Buckingham Palace is also vigilant for letter-bombs.

On Saturday 13 June the Queen rode out from Buckingham Palace bound for the Whitehall parade ground on which the ceremony of Trooping the Colour takes place annually. Millions of television viewers watched as she rode side-saddle on her nineteen-year-old black mare Burmese, followed by her husband and eldest son, also mounted, and by the Sovereign's Escort of Household Cavalry. As she turned out of the Mall onto Horseguards Parade, the Queen saw a man in the crowd, less than three metres from her, raise a gun and take aim. He fired six times.

The Queen was unhurt, but her horse shied at the noise – or, as the Queen claimed, defending Burmese's courage, it may have been the quick movement of her husband and son to her side that frightened Burmese. Before they reached the Queen, she already had the horse under control. She rode on and went through the long ceremony outwardly calm.

Back on the roadside, the crowd had turned on the young man who had apparently tried to kill the Queen, but a guardsman and policeman quickly intervened, and moments later armed police took him away. They seemed to have come from nowhere; only the uniformed police, lining the route, had been in evidence before. Now the crowd also became aware of armed men on the roof of the nearby Admiralty building.

It transpired that seventeen-year-old Marcus Serjeant's pistol had fired blanks. He was no terrorist, only a fame-seeker. In fact, he had sent a warning, by post, to Buckingham Palace, which read: 'Your Majesty, don't go to the Trooping the Colour ceremony because there is an assassin set to kill you, waiting just outside the palace.' What could be done? Was the Queen to cancel her appearance that day because of a threat that might not be fulfilled? But if she did ride out, even with the utmost vigilance on the part of the police, she would be at risk. That was nothing new to her, and the Queen did not hesitate to face the danger. When she saw Serjeant point his gun, at such close range, she must have believed that he would kill her.

Marcus Serjeant was tried on a charge of treason, under section two of the 1842 Treason Act (one of several Acts of Parliament that had amended that of 1352). The charge against him was one of 'wilfully discharging at the person of Her Majesty the Queen a blank cartridge pistol with intent to alarm her'. Had the pistol been loaded with live ammunition, had Serjeant intended to kill the Queen and had he been over eighteen, he would have been liable to the death penalty, since treason remains a capital offence.

Serjeant had spent three months in the Royal Marines and then he had applied to join both the police and the fire brigade – unsuccessfully. He was the archetypal 'loner', fascinated by the royal family and latterly obsessed with assassinating the Queen. Although police psychiatrists found him sane 'within the meaning of the Health Act' and he was sentenced to serve five years in prison, he was sent to Grendon Underwood, a prison specialising in treating psychiatric disorders.

Riding high above the crowd, at low speed, the Queen had presented a virtual sitting target to Serjeant – and to any IRA gunman who might have been sent to kill her.

At the time, newspapers recalled that on 16 July 1936 Britain's uncrowned king, Edward VIII, was riding in a procession on Constitution Hill when a man aimed a loaded revolver at him. A policeman saw the gun and knocked it out of his hand; it skidded across the road, falling under the hooves of the King's horse. The would-be assassin was George Andrew Campbell McMahon, alias Jerome Fannigan, aged thirty-four, who later claimed that a 'foreign power' had paid him £150 to kill the King; that was never proved. Like Serjeant, he was convicted under the 1842 Act, and he was sentenced to a year's imprisonment with hard labour.*

* A government file released in January 2005 offers evidence that the foreign power was Nazi Germany.

The Trooping the Colour scare of 1981 came six weeks before the wedding of the Prince of Wales, who was due to ride home from St Paul's Cathedral in an open carriage with his bride. In an attempt to prevent a 'copycat' crime, hundreds of extra police were drafted to line the route, and the scarlet-and-gold-clad man who rode on the carriage box next to the driver was in fact a sharpshooter policeman with a concealed pistol-holster. Plain-clothes police mingled with the crowd, and once again there were armed men on the rooftops.

The danger did not recede. In November, on a visit to Australia, the Queen learned that police had uncovered an IRA plot to kill her there. The following month, in Dunedin, New Zealand, a man discharged a rifle near – but not at – her. After recent events, the sound of that shot must have unnerved the Queen, but again she did not allow it to lessen her smiles or curtail her itinerary.

Other threats to the Queen's peace of mind – if not her life – came closer to home in the following year. On 17 June 1982, a man wielding a knife threatened the policeman guarding the North Centre Gate of Buckingham Palace. When he entered the forecourt, a policeman ran after him, but it was a guardsman who turned him back, at bayonet-point. The man was found to be 'mentally disturbed' and was placed on a year's probation.

Ten days earlier, Michael Fagan, an unemployed thirty-five-year-old 'of no fixed abode', had managed to gain entry to Buckingham Palace at night. He drank half a bottle of wine, then he left, still unobserved.

On 9 July he returned. In the early morning a policeman spotted him climbing the palace railings and raised the alarm. When the police made a search of the grounds, there was no sign of him – because he was already inside the palace. Having entered through an unlocked window on the ground floor and found himself in the room housing the royal stamp collection, Fagan was thwarted by a locked door. He left the building, climbed a drainpipe and entered by another unlocked window. This time he found his way to the Queen's private apartments.

Fagan's mind was more on his own problems than on his whereabouts. Despairing of his future, alienated from his family, he broke a glass ashtray (accidentally cutting his hand), intending to use the shards to cut his wrists.

At 7.18 a.m. Fagan entered the Queen's bedroom and drew the curtains. As she awoke, he sat down on the end of the bed, his cut hand bleeding on the counterpane.

The Queen pressed the bedside alarm bell, but it brought no aid, nor did the bell in the corridor, for the police sergeant on night duty had left, as usual, at six, and the footman had taken the royal corgis out for exercise. The Queen lifted the bedside telephone and asked the palace operator to alert the police. Six minutes later, when they had not arrived, she repeated the call. (The operator's excuse, given later, was that the Queen's voice had been so calm there seemed no urgency in her request.)

By now, Fagan was pouring out his sad story, the Queen answering him sympathetically while her mind raced, planning escape. Her chance came when Fagan asked for a cigarette. The Queen said she would fetch some, and she left the room. In the corridor she encountered a housemaid, and then the footman returned. While the Queen held the corgis in check, the footman and maid accosted Fagan and pushed him into a nearby pantry.

The police arrived some eight minutes after the Queen's first call.

But what was Fagan's crime? There is no law against trespass. This time he had not stolen anything. He had not even 'broken and entered', for he had not needed to force a window. Certainly he had not intended to harm the Queen, nor had he meant to alarm her. The Director of Public Prosecutions could find no charge to bring against Fagan relating to the events of 9 July, and when he stood trial at the Old Bailey, for his theft of the wine (worth £3), he was acquitted. Committed to a mental hospital, he was released the following January.

At his trial, Fagan claimed, 'I've done the Queen a favour. I've proved that her security system is no good.' He was right. If he had been a member of the IRA, armed with a gun . . .

Soon it was being rumoured that the Queen had agreed to having the SAS (Special Air Service) test palace security and that they had managed five times to enter the palace and gain the private apartments without police intervention. They were not the only intruders: just ten days after Fagan's second entry, three German tourists scaled the garden wall and looked around the palace grounds – thinking they were in Hyde Park, they later claimed.

Their escapade underlined the ease with which an assassin might still enter.

An official Home Office report, published on 22 July 1982, pointed out the inefficiency of the palace police and their lax deployment of the closed-circuit cameras surveying the grounds. A rapid review of royal security was set in motion. The recommendations of security experts called for a wide range of measures, largely adopted. The royal train is now 'a tank on wheels', so heavy is its frame, to withstand mortar attacks. Its windows are bullet-proof; it carries an emergency oxygen supply, for use if there is a gas attack; a radio in each compartment is linked to the headquarters of the Royal Protection Squad. Royal cars are similarly reinforced and now always followed by a back-up car (carrying blood plasma of the appropriate group) and accompanied by outriders on motorcycles. When any member of the royal family travels by car, it is fitted with a homing device by which its route can be tracked.

Before a royal visit to any part of Britain, members of the Royal Protection Squad reconnoitre both the route and the destination, looking for danger points. During a royal visit, officers of the Special Branch supplement the regular bodyguards by doing plain-clothes duty. For example, it was Special Branch Officers who spotted a man carrying a pistol (in fact, only a starting-pistol) near Princess Anne as she opened a shopping-centre at Bracknell in Berkshire in September 1984. However, the Queen still insists on the freedom to walk among her subjects and meet them. Royal 'walkabouts' have for so long been a popular feature of her visits, at home and abroad, that she would allow nothing to interfere with them, even though they remain a source of danger to her.

After the 1982 review, the number of the Queen's bodyguards, and the intensity of their training, increased. Now every member of the team is trained in unarmed combat and in the use of several weapons, largely by attending courses run by the SAS. But, like the top-hatted men at Edward VII's funeral, they must 'blend in' at ceremonial and social functions: at Ascot, they appear in tailcoats and top hats. A policeman in the Prince of Wales's team was trained to ski, in order to follow him down mountainsides.

Even so, the Prince's vulnerability was proved when on 26 January 1994 a man fired shots at him, in Australia. The Prince was standing on a dais, at Barling Harbour, waiting to distribute prizes to schoolchildren on Australia Day. As a man emerged from the crowd of onlookers, firing, the Prince's bodyguard, Colin Trimming, barged into the Prince and shielded him. The man tripped on the dais, and a policeman seized him. The weapon was only a starting-pistol, firing blanks, and David Kang, an Australian student of Cambodian parentage, had intended merely to draw attention to the sore plight of the 'boat people'. The only feasible charge against him was one of 'threatening behaviour' and, as so often happens, he was recommended to psychiatric treatment.

Inevitably, in view of 1982's events, the security of Buckingham Palace and its grounds was a pivotal issue in the security review. The outer walls were to be topped by a spiked rail and razor wire and provided with surveillance cameras. Alarm-controlled tripwires and other electronic devices were to be installed throughout the grounds. Inside the palace, the control room of the technological protection system must be manned twenty-four hours a day.

And yet there were still breaches of that security. In July 1992, an unemployed man gained entry to the palace and was arrested in the presence of the Queen. A few days later, in broad daylight, a German tourist was caught climbing the palace walls, near Hyde Park Corner. A year later, anti-nuclear protesters managed to scale the walls and to make their message clearly heard in the palace. In February 1994, an American paraglider – naked – touched down on the roof of the palace. In January 1995 a man rammed the police gates with his car.

Buckingham Palace is not the only royal residence to have supposedly impenetrable security: Windsor Castle, Balmoral and Sandringham were also reinforced after the 1982 review. At the same time, the residences of other members of the royal family had their security measures upgraded. And yet in April 1993 a frenzied drug addict reached the doorstep of Princess Margaret's house in the Kensington Palace apartments that are home to several members of the royal family. In February 1994 the Prince of Wales's rooms in St James's Palace were burgled.

In the spring of 1995, an IRA man travelling on a London bus accidentally detonated the bomb he was carrying. He died in the explosion. When police searched his South London lodgings, they found groundplans of both Buckingham Palace and St James's Palace.

On 29 April 1997 the news broke that in the early hours of the 28th another man had managed to enter the grounds of Buckingham Palace – and to leave through the palace gates unchallenged.

Later that day, a taxi-driver listened in amazement as his passenger boasted of having toured the palace gardens. When the man left the cab, the driver alerted the police, and they moved quickly to arrest him. The intruder was a patient at an 'open' mental hospital in Sussex and was said to be 'anti-authority'. If it were not enough that the man had been able to enter the palace grounds and spend some four hours there, he recounted how he had left by the main gates – where the police on guard wished him 'Good morning' as he passed them.

The apparently harmless episode shows how easily Buckingham Palace could have been penetrated by a 'hit squad' of the IRA. In the weeks before the General Election (due on 1 May 1997), the IRA had already planted bombs and issued false-alarm warnings, which between them had paralysed the Midlands road system, halted trains between London, Liverpool and Manchester, gridlocked London's traffic and caused the running of the Grand National to be postponed at the last moment. Surely the police must have been alert for any sign of an intruder in the grounds of Buckingham Palace? Yet a man had been able to enter, loiter and leave without hindrance.

In 1998, Thomas McMahon, who had been sentenced to life imprisonment for the murder of Lord Mountbatten (see p. 229), was freed, as a result of the Good Friday Agreement, which promised peace in Northern Ireland. Since then there has been no Irish attempt on royal lives. That is not to say that there have been no alarms, from other quarters.

The year 2004 was a particularly bad one – for the royal security police as well as for the royal family. In April a bodyguard discharged his automatic handgun just a few feet from Prince Andrew, Duke of York, who sensibly 'dived for cover' as the bullet hit a wall. In June a notorious hoaxer, Aaron Barschak, gatecrashed Prince William's 21st birthday party at Windsor Castle. He had gained entry by scaling a wall and climbing a tree overhanging the inner precincts of the castle.

Questioned by police, he had claimed to be a party entertainer and was allowed to go in. The Prince was making a speech; Barschak took over the microphone, using a 'comedy routine', then he kissed Prince William on both cheeks.

Barschak was dressed as Osama bin Laden. As he later said himself: 'If I had been a real terrorist, the entire royal family would have been wiped out.

That September, a seventeen-year-old Scottish schoolboy was found guilty of sending forty-four letters, some containing the poison ricin, others the deadly germ anthrax, to politicians and other notables, including Prince William of Wales. The young man had been recruited, on the internet, by an (unnamed in court) anti-English (sic) terrorist organisation and supplied with the means to spread fear – his letters did, however, give warning of their deadly contents and no one was harmed. Prince William's letter was not sent to Buckingham Palace, where staff are prepared for postal hazards, but to a department at the Prince's Scottish university.

The ultimate warning-signal for royal security police came in November 2003, when a palace footman, Ryan Parry, 'broke cover' to reveal himself as a *Daily Mirror* reporter. He had worked for two months at Buckingham Palace, with access to the royal family's private rooms and observing their off-duty life. The *Daily Mirror* claimed that Parry had been 'acting entirely in the public interest' in showing how easy it would be for a terrorist to gain employment in the palace. He had been given the job on the basis of one forged reference and on of virtually no substance.

On 20 November, the day of the *Daily Mirror*'s revelations, President Bush was the Queen's guest, staying at Buckingham Palace. Like Barschak, Parry emphasised the danger: 'Had I been a terrorist intent on assassinating the Queen or American president George Bush, I could have done so with absolute ease.' He said he had never been searched while working at the palace.

In response to the events of 2003, an independent commission under the ægis of the Cabinet Office, reviewed the parlous state of royal security. It offered recommendations resembling those it had issued at its previous reviews, in 1986, 1995 and 2000.

Whether because of the success of the commission's injunctions or for other reasons, there is nothing further to report. Those 'other reasons could be that since 2004 there really has been no recent attempt (beyond a couple of innocuous abseilers on the palace's façade); that respect for the Queen's age (she was eighty in 2006) stays the hands of her enemies; that the IRA are now pacified, or that it has become a rule of royal security, with the media's compliance, not to make public any threat to or attempt on the life of any member of the royal family. In view of the now ever-present danger of terrorist attacks anywhere, against anyone, it seems probable that royal security is now impeccably efficient.

On Sunday 31 August 1997 Britain awoke to the news that Diana, Princess of Wales, ex-wife of the heir to the throne, had been killed overnight in a car crash in Paris.

The known facts are these. On the evening of Saturday 30 August 1997, Diana, Princess of Wales, he lover, Dodi al Fayed, and her bodyguard left the Ritz hotel in Paris and entered a chauffeur-driven car that set off for al Fayed's house. Reporters and photographers – the 'paparazzi' – gave chase, on motorcycles. The car entered an underpass at high speed. It crashed. Dodi al Fayed and the chauffeur were killed outright; the Princess died of her injuries at about 3a.m.; the bodyguard was seriously injured.

In the first few days after the news broke, the crash was attributed to the party's attempt to escape the paparazzi. It was alleged that the chauffeur had been drunk, unable to control the car at high speed. But even from the first, not one but many voices had whispered, spoken, shouted, 'Murder!' The British media walked wearily through the minefield of libel; the foreign media were more forthright. The British 'Establishment', they said, would not stand for the Princess, mother of a future British king, marrying a Muslim, as she had apparently intended. 'The Palace', the British security services MI5 and MI6 or the American CIA – even the Freemasons or the Israelis: all were accredited motives for killing the Princess. The means to the alleged murder was supposedly a car seen – by some, not all of the witnesses – to have sped away from the crash.

A French investigation of the three deaths began immediately; it was very thorough: over 300 people were interviewed and a 6,000-page file of evidence was compiled. The final ruling stated simply that the chauffeur had drunk enough to make him incapable of controlling the car when the paparazzi gave chase, causing the fatal crash. Although that ruling was given in September 1999, it was 2004 before French legal processes were completed and a coroner opened the British inquest. In the months that followed, the London Metropolitan Commissioner Sir John (later lord) Stevens headed an enquiry that reported to the coroner but which also fuelled the media's – and the nation's – appetite for stories about the late Princess's life, as well as her death. Her name was rarely out of the news.

Nor was that of Dodi Fayed's father, Mohammed al-Fayed, the Egyptian millionaire owner of the London department store Harrods. Mr al-Fayed was convinced that his son and the Princess had been murdered. Chief among his suspects was Prince Philip, Duke of Edinburgh, the Princess's former father-in-law. It was, al-Fayed claimed, the Duke who had sent MI6 agents to Paris to kill the Princess before she could disgrace the royal family by marrying Dodi Fayed.

Had the Princess intended to marry Dodi Fayed? His father said so, citing the ring the couple had bought together only hours before their death – and Mohammed al-Fayed claimed, the Princess had been pregnant by his son. He insisted that her body had been embalmed before it left France lest a British examination reveal the pregnancy. Mr al-Fayed had further ideas, more suspects, and he chafed at the delays that prevented the exposure of the 'killers'. He pressed for an inquest with a jury (rare in British procedure) but it was not until 2007 that jurors were marshalled.

Press coverage of that last phase of the inquest introduced several intriguing characters. The Princess's father was already well-known: he had been her close confidant, he assured the avid public, giving an intimate picture of her home life, tribulations and sorrows. In addition, there was a masseuse, a complementary therapist-cum-spiritual healer, an acupuncturist and a voice coach, to all of whom the Princess had 'poured out her heart'. However, the largest headlines came not from their words but from the Princess's own – written evidence that she believed she would be murdered: she would die in a car crash, she had predicted. The butler claimed that the Queen herself had warned him of 'powers at work' – he had assumed she was referring to the security agencies. The Princess had apparently been certain that one of her earlier loves, a police bodyguard, had been murdered; he had died in a road accident.

Of all the theories flying, one was never mentioned at the inquest: the one that had the Princess still alive, far away. The car crash had been faked; many people, French as well as British, had been complicit in a plan, to give Diana, Princess of Wales, her freedom. It was beyond belief –'conspiracy theory gone mad' – yet it had its adherents.

The Princess's friends dispelled other myths: she had not intended to marry Dodi Fayed – 'I need marriage like a rash on my face' she had said; she was not pregnant.

In April 2008, the coroner called upon the jury to give their verdict. With a majority of nine to two, they announced 'unlawful killing': the chauffeur's drunken driving exacerbated by the pressure of the pursuing paparazzi. The inquest and the police investigation had cost the tax-payer over £12 million and had added nothing to the French ruling of 1999. Even Mohammed al-Fayed agreed to accept this verdict – or at least not to continue his quest for a different one.

It seems unlikely that anything factual will now be added to the evidence on the cause of the death of Diana, Princess of Wales, to challenge the 2008 verdict. Yet it also seems unlikely that the suspicion of murder will ever be forgotten.

The stories of the Princess's death, its context and investigation, and that of members of the Nepalese royal family some four years later provide a modern climax to a history of royal murder. Yet their melodrama obscured the prosaic, everyday courage of monarchs – and their families – who must be always prepared for violent death. Their vulnerability is all too obvious. They know they could be attacked and killed at any time, even in the supposed safety of their homes. A lone 'madman's' bullets are just as lethal as a terrorist group's bomb. One day a palace intruder may be armed or a bullet fired in a public place may find its mark. As long as there are monarchs, the risk of royal murder will remain.

SOURCES AND FURTHER READING

'Are you going to read *all* those books?', someone asked as I carried ten home from the London Library one day. 'Yes,' I replied, adding that there would be ten more a week or fortnight later. But then I realised that I should have said that I would use those books rather than read them. In fact, I used over 500 books. Some I did read, of course – and re-read, with close attention; many more I merely dipped into; the majority furnished some information without the need to read the whole.

To cite every one of those books would be as uninteresting to the reader as it would be tedious for me. This is by no means an academic history of royal murders, and few of its readers who care to do any 'further reading' will have access to either the British Library or the London Library which furnished the many books I used. I reckon that all but about half a dozen are out of print; only 30 per cent, at most, have been written in the past half-century.

The list that follows is thus not representative of the number or type of books I have used, nor are the books cited necessarily the best on their subject, because often the best would be too difficult to obtain to make naming them worthwhile. (Sometimes there is no modern source at all: for example, there were English-language biographies of Giovanna I, Queen of Naples, published in 1893 and 1910, but none since; there is no twentieth-century English-language biography of Gustav III, King of Sweden.) Where I have cited a book written twenty or thirty years ago, it is because I have seen a reprint of that book or copies in more than one public library, or if I have noticed that it can be found in several secondhand bookshops.

The fact that I have to offer these excuses reflects my regret that I am unable to pay tribute to the hundreds of writers, in past centuries as well as the present, who have provided the information garnered for this book.

Many of the books named here have their own 'further reading' lists. There you will find the names of earlier books that also have bibliographies, and so on. That is how I came to trace some of the more obscure books that I have not named here.

Three books have been of special interest and I have gone back to them time and again. They led me to delve more deeply into the political and religious philosophy of some of the murderers/ assassins/killers than was strictly necessary for researching this book, but it was a fascinating sidetracking. If I have used contentions found in any of those works, it is because the writers have pinpointed the essence of some philosophy, not because I have blindly copied. If my own interpretations, analyses and conclusions are naïve, superficial or ill-conceived, it is not the fault of those erudite writers:

E. Hyams, *Killing No Murder* (Nelson, 1969)
F.L. Ford, *Political Murder* (Harvard University Press, 1985)
B. Bailey, *The Assassination File* (W.H. Allen, 1991)

1. SWORD AND ARROW

As background and a solid foundation for a study of medieval Europe, there are the eight volumes of the Cambridge Medieval History of Europe (Cambridge University Press, 1924–36), matched by the Oxford History of England (Oxford University Press, 1943–61), in fourteen volumes.

For the death of William II, King of England, I looked at several medieval chronicles, as named in the text, and chose nineteenth-century translations when I quoted from them. B. Smalley's *Historians of the Middle Ages* (Thames & Hudson, 1974) is an interesting introduction to the chroniclers, with illustrations and a bibliography. For a modern assessment of the evidence, see D. Grinnell Milne's *The Killing of William Rufus* (David & Charles, 1968).

W.L. Warren's *Henry II* (Eyre Methuen, 1974) and *King John* (Eyre & Spottiswoode, 1962) are useful, as is F. Barlow's *Becket* (Weidenfeld & Nicolson, 1986).

C. Wilson, *The Order of Assassins* (R. Hart-Davies, 1972) and B. Lewis, *The Assassins* (Weidenfeld & Nicolson, 1967) are interesting studies of the Middle Eastern sect.

2. A WOMAN'S WEAPONS

A sparse collection here, as so few biographies of medieval women have been written. An exception is Eleanor of Aquitaine, and a notable English-language biography of her is by Desmond Seward (David & Charles, 1978). The career of Isabelle of France can be traced in H.F. Hutchinson's *Edward II: The Pliant King* (Eyre & Spottiswoode, 1971).

Agnes Strickland's eight-volume *Lives of the Queens of England* (1857–60) was matched in usefulness by such works as A. George, *Memoirs of the Queens of Spain* (1853). I name them only for interest's sake. I used many other such books, published in an age more appreciative of and remunerative to non-academic historical biographers.

3. A FAMILY AFFAIR

Again the Cambridge Medieval History of Europe and Oxford History of England are invaluable, covering plain fact and underlying philosophies. The 'flavour' of European life at this period is richly tasted in B.W. Tuchman's *A Distant Mirror* (Macmillan, 1979).

For the Burgundy–Orleans feud, see R. Vaughan, *John the Fearless* (Longman, 1966) and *Valois Burgundy* (Allen Lane, 1975).

In *The Wars of the Roses* (Thames & Hudson, 1976) C. Ross presents a complex subject very clearly, with illustrations.

For England's royal murders of the fifteenth century:

A. Steel, *Richard II* (Cambridge University Press, 1962)

N. Saul, *Richard II* (Yale University Press, 1997)

C. Ross, *Edward IV* (Eyre Methuen, 1974)

–– *Richard III* (Methuen, 1990)

P. Murray Kendall, *Richard III* (George Allen & Unwin, 1955)

E. Jenkins, *The Princes in the Tower* (Hamish Hamilton, 1978)

For the story of Philip II, King of Spain, and Don Carlos: C. Petrie, *Philip II of Spain* (Eyre & Spottiswoode, 1963) and G. Parker, *Philip II* (Hutchinson, 1971).

4. SCOTLAND

Though not the latest published works on the subject, the following are 'solid reads' still to be found on public library shelves:

W.C. Dickinson, *Scotland from the Earliest Times to 1603* (Nelson, 1961)

J.H. Glover, *The Story of Scotland* (Faber & Faber, 1960)

R. Mitchison, *A History of Scotland* (Methuen, 1970)

G. Donaldson, *Scottish Kings* (Batsford, 1967)

E. Linklater, *The Royal House of Scotland* (Macmillan, 1970)

D.H. Willson, *James VI and I* (Jonathan Cape, 1967)

G. Donaldson's *Mary, Queen of Scots* (Blackwell, 1988) reads well in conjunction with G.J.M. Thomson, *The Crime of Mary Stuart* (Hutchinson, 1967) and with C. Bingham's *Darnley* (Constable, 1995).

The Ruthven quotation on p. 64 comes from his narrative of Rizzio's murder, published in the appendix to the three-volume *History of the Affairs of Church and State in Scotland down to 1567* (1844–50) by R. Keith.

5. MURDER BY MAGIC

There have been so many interesting books on witchcraft published in recent years that it is possible to pick one up at any public library and to pursue the subject through that book's bibliography.

Of all England's alleged royal witches, only one, Anne Boleyn, has been the subject of recent biographies, of which that by H.W. Chapman (Jonathan Cape, 1974) may be recommended.

James VI and I's interest in witchcraft is well covered in the bibliography named for chapter 4.

Among the biographies of Louis XIV, King of France, *The Sun King* by Nancy Mitford (Hamish Hamilton, 1966) is a delightful introduction; see also G. Mossiker, *The Affair of the Poisons* (Victor Gollancz, 1970)

The sources of the two direct quotations in this chapter are as follows: that on p. 79 concerning the playing card is taken from A. Strickland's *Lives of the Queens of England* (1856), iv, p. 778; the extract on p. 81 from James VI and I's letter to his son the Prince of Wales comes from *The Letters of the Kings of England* (1846), edited by J.O. Halliwell, II, p. 102.

6. FOR GOD'S SAKE

A palatable and digestible history of the European Church at this period is O. Chadwick's *The Reformation* (Penguin, 1964).

The best English-language biography of William the Silent, Prince of Orange, is still that by C.V. Wedgwood (Jonathan Cape, 1948).

For the murdered – and murderous – French kings, see D. Seward, *The First Bourbon* and *The Bourbon Kings of France* (both Constable, 1971 and 1976 respectively), which also cover the murder of Henri III, and H. Mousnier, translated by J. Spencer, *The Assassination of Henry IV* (Faber & Faber, 1973). H.R. Williamson's *Catherine de' Medici* (Michael Joseph, 1975) demonstrates the Queen's role in murder and massacre.

Of the many books on the Gunpowder Plot of 1605, that by M. Nicholls, *Investigating Gunpowder Plot* (Manchester University Press, 1991) is one of the most recent.

For the lives of the later Stuart kings of England and Scotland see the biographies of Charles II and James VII and II by M. Ashley (J.M. Dent, 1966 and 1974 respectively) and of William III by N. Robb (Heinemann, 1966).

7. KILLING NO MURDER

This chapter owes much to *Regicide and Revolution* (Cambridge University Press, 1974), edited by M. Walzer, the most thought-provoking of the books on this subject.

In addition to the books on Mary, Queen of Scots, named in chapter 4, see A. Plowden, *Two Queens in One Isle* (Harvester Press, 1984) and A. Somerset, *Elizabeth I* (Weidenfeld & Nicolson, 1991).

J. Bowle's *Charles I* (Weidenfeld & Nicolson, 1975) offers a balanced view of the King's life and reign.

Everyone who reads about the French Revolution swears by one particular book or another. For me, it is C. Hibbert, *The French Revolution* (Allen Lane, 1980). B. Faÿ, translated by F. O'Brian, *Louis XVI or The End of a World* (W.H. Allen, 1968) sets the King's life in the context of the early part of the revolution.

The quotation on p. 112 concerning the projected murder of Mary, Queen of Scots, in prison comes from H. Nicholas's *Life of Davison* (1823), appendix. The quotation on p. 115 about the execution of Charles I is taken from *The Diaries and Letters of Philip Henry, 1631–96*, edited by M.H. Lee (1882), p. 12.

8. RUSSIA

Another subject for rival preferences in books. B. Pares, *A History of Russia* (Jonathan Cape, 1947, frequently reprinted) is not as long as N.V. Riasanovsky's work of the same title (Oxford University Press, 1963) but both need a strong arm to hold them, a strong mind to persevere with reading them and a strong stomach to digest them.

F. Carr, *Ivan the Terrible* (David & Charles, 1981) is one of the best of the English-language biographies of the Tsar. For the history of the Romanov tsars, see E.M. Almedingen, *The Romanovs* (Bodley Head, 1966) and J.D. Bergamini, *The Tragic Dynasty* (Constable, 1970). See also R.K. Massie, *Peter the Great* (Gollancz, 1981) and V. Cronin, *Catherine, Empress of All the Russias* (Collins, 1978). E.M. Almedingen's *So Dark a Stream* (Hutchinson, 1959) is a biography of Paul I and is followed by her *Alexander I* (Bodley Head, 1964); he is also the subject of a biography by J.M. Hartley (Longman, 1994).

9. MARKSMEN, MADMEN AND THE INFERNAL MACHINE

It might be well to begin a study of Napoleon with a straightforward biography such as V. Cronin's (Collins, 1971) and the illustrated book by D. Chandler (Weidenfeld & Nicolson, 1993), but there are so many books on Napoleon that one could start practically anywhere.

Lacking a twentieth-century English-language biography of the Swedish king Gustav III, see the context of his death in I. Anderson's *History of Sweden* (Weidenfeld & Nicolson, 1958) translated by C. Hannay.

Of the many books on George III and Queen Victoria, I recommend those by I. Brooke (Constable, 1972) and C. Woodham Smith (Hamish Hamilton, 1972; on 1819–61) respectively, and E. Longford, *Victoria, R.I.* (Weidenfeld & Nicolson, 1964), and on Louis-Philippe, King of the French, T.E.B. Howarth, *Citizen King* (Eyre & Spottiswoode, 1961).

The quotation from the letter from Queen Victoria to her eldest daughter, Victoria, Crown Princess of Prussia, of 8 July 1868, derives from *Your Dear Letter*, ed. R. Fulford (Evans Bros, 1971), p. 200.

10. CROWNED KILLERS

The Damnable Duke of Cumberland (Barrie & Rockliff, 1966) by A. Bird is a biography of Queen Victoria's 'wicked uncle'.

The Dream King (Hamish Hamilton, 1970) by W. Blunt is a lavishly illustrated short account of Ludwig II of Bavaria's life.

L. Cassels, *Clash of Generations* (John Murray, 1973) offers a brief survey of the Mayerling affair, amplified in J.H. Listowel, *Habsburg Tragedy: Rudolph of Austria* (Ascent Books, 1978).

11. PROPAGANDA BY DEED

T.A.B. Conley's *Democratic Despot* (Barrie & Rockliff, 1961) sets in context the attempt on Napoleon III's life that is described in *The Bombs of Orsini* (Secker & Warburg, 1957) by M. St J. Packe.

E.M. Almedingen's *Emperor Alexander II* (Bodley Head, 1962) fits into the larger picture provided by R. Seth, *The Russian Terrorists* (Barrie & Rockliff, 1966), V. Cowles, *The Russian Dagger* (Collins, 1969) and W. Laqueur, *The Age of Terrorism* (Weidenfeld & Nicolson, 1987).

The quotation on p. 151 is taken from D. Footman's *Red Prelude* (Cresset Press, 1954; permission sought).

12. THE ASSASSIN'S HEYDAY

The three books that deal with Victorian police bodyguards are long since out of print but are cited here as they would be treasures to seek in a secondhand bookshop:

X. Paoli, *My Royal Clients* (Hodder & Stoughton, 1911)

H.T. Fitch, *Memoirs of a Royal Detective* (Hurst & Blackett, 1936)

E.T. Woodhall, *Guardians of the Great* (Blandford, 1934)

J. Finestone's *The Last Courts of Europe* (Dent, 1981) is a lavishly illustrated survey of the ruling Houses of Europe at this period.

The books named in chapter 11 on the Russian revolutionary movement and its influence in Europe are also appropriate here.

Some biographies of individual monarchs and general histories that put their lives in context:

P. Magnus, *Edward VII* (John Murray, 1964)

R. Katz, *The Fall of the House of Savoy* (George Allen & Unwin, 1972)

J. Haslip, *The Lonely Empress* (Weidenfeld & Nicolson, 1965)

C. Petrie, *King Alfonso XIII and His Age* (Chapman & Hall, 1963)

G. Noel, *Ena: Spain's English Queen* (Constable, 1984)

H.V. Livermore, *A History of Spain* (George Allen & Unwin, 1958)

— *A New History of Portugal* (Cambridge University Press, 1976)

The quotation from the letter from the Grand Duchess of Mecklenburg-Strelitz to the future Queen Mary, of 3 August 1900, quoted on p. 187, derives from J. Pope-Hennessy, *Queen Mary* (George Allen & Unwin, 1959), p. 238.

13. THE BULLET THAT STARTED A WAR

There have been many books studying the causes of the First World War since L. Albertini's *The Origins of the War of 1914* (Oxford University Press, 1953) but that 'heavyweight' sets the assassination of the Archduke Franz Ferdinand in a convincing perspective of long-term international tension.

There are also many books on the Archduke's assassination. I recommend H. Pauli, *The Secret of Sarajevo* (Collins, 1966), a lively narrative to counter-balance Albertini, and L. Cassels, *The Archduke and the Assassin* (Frederick Muller, 1984).

14. A FEW AMONG MANY

For the causes and course of the Russian Revolution, see the general histories cited for chapters 8 and 11 or enjoy C. Pipes, *A Concise History of the Russian Revolution* (Harvill Press, 1995). For the Romanov story, see M. Ferro, *Nicholas II*

(Viking, 1991) and V. Cowles, *The Last Tsar and Tsarina* (Weidenfeld & Nicolson, 1977), beautifully illustrated.

The effect of the First World War on Europe's monarchies is the subject of T. Aronson, *Crowns in Conflict* (John Murray, 1986).

For the 1934 assassination of King Aleksander of Yugoslavia, the only specialist work I have seen is E. Graham's *Alexander of Yugoslavia* (Cassel, 1938). Maybe an interested reader might like to try to track down T. Eckhardt's *Regicide at Marseilles* (American-Hungarian Library and Historical Society, New York, 1964). More accessible is the often-reprinted *Black Lamb and Grey Falcon* (Macmillan, 1942) by Rebecca West.

15. Echoes of Bomb and Bullet and 16. Beyond Belief

For several years I have collected newspaper cuttings about royal assassination attempts, with this book in mind. For both British and foreign news stories, I owe a large debt to *The Guardian*. However, it was *The Scotsman* (24 April–5 May 1989) that provided details of the Sindićić case, even though it proved something of a damp squib as far as royal murders are concerned. If any big news breaks, *Majesty* magazine will cover it well.

INDEX